## **Praise for *Leonar***

"Leonard Cohen and Philo
*a connection: not only thro*
*medievalist Québécois Catholicism*
*Zen Buddhism, but also via his tutoring in the "School of Hard Knocks" that is the pop-rock balladeer scene, from coffeehouse to sports arena, from album liner-notes to concert reviews. Editor Jason Holt, himself a fine absurdist experimental poet and a professor of philosophy, draws us into examining the kōan of Cohen, so to speak, by postulating the first immediate paradox of the artist: an essential, post-modern poet, respected by ye Literature professors, and a bluesy cantor / singer, whose smoky vocals coax matrons and teens alike to toss their panties on stage. Is Cohen really both pop star and poet, and, if so, might one add the label, 'philosopher,' too? Holt assembles twenty scholars to ponder the ideational links between Cohen as writer / songwriter and a cosmopolitan who's who of philosophers: Adorno, Beauvoir, Camus, Derrida, etc. Reading these superb assessments of Cohen's (sung) words bids us read and / or hear the bard ever more intensively, to recognize in him the extension of a troubadour tradition, ex the Holy Land and Provence, marrying Judeo-Christian and 'Pagan' deathless notions of love, sex, ritual, and romance, blending David and Dante, Peter and Petrarch, the Song of Songs and Sade."*

—George Elliott Clarke, William Lyon Mackenzie King Professor of Canadian Studies, Harvard University (2013-14) & Poet Laureate of Toronto (2012-15)

*"Cohen famously said that there is a crack in everything, that's how the light gets in. This book takes the brilliant light of Cohen's words and shines it into Plato's cave with such strength the prisoners are not only free but see the sun."*

—Kimberly Baltzer-Jaray, author of *Doorway to the World of Essences*

"Leonard Cohen and Philosophy *deals with a wide range of issues, including the metaphysical world created in 'Suzanne,' . . . the poetics of relationships , . . . and the phenomenology of time. . . . This volume presents perspectives not to be found elsewhere and offers readers a fuller resonance with Cohen's work."*

—DrHGuy on Heck Of A Guy: The Other Leonard Cohen Site

*"Anyone interested in Leonard Cohen—whether a newcomer to his work or a longtime fan—will find much to reflect upon and savor here. Exploring Cohen's songs, albums, poems, and novels through the prism of philosophical and religious ideas, this volume covers diverse ground—from Hellenistic philosophy to existentialism, from Stoicism to phenomenology, from literary theory to gender studies, from Judeo-Christian concepts such as* katechon *to Buddhist concepts such as nirvana. In the process, certain themes receive special focus, such as romantic love, authenticity, irony, perceptions of time, embodied consciousness, the Holocaust and the banality of evil, and the process of redemption. As these essays make manifestly clear, Cohen's work brings light to many philosophical and religious concepts, even as those concepts in turn help to illuminate and complement the depth of thought and feeling in Cohen's rich and varied lyrical, poetical work."*

—KATHLEEN LEAGUE, author of *Adorno, Radical Negativity, and Cultural Critique*

*"It is rare for a promising young literary figure to become an influential pop music star, but that is exactly what Leonard Cohen has accomplished. The various works of the Canadian singer-songwriter-poet-novelist frequently bridge such issues as personal identity, skepticism, inter-personal relationships, and inter-cultural spiritual influences. The chapters in this book run the gamut from classical and modern philosophical contexts to Cohen's varied masculinities and prophetic tone to his unusual singing voice and concepts of beauty, authenticity, irony, love, evil, and transcendence."*

—DURRELL BOWMAN, author of *Experiencing Rush: A Listener's Companion* and co-editor of *Rush and Philosophy: Heart and Mind United*

*"Leonard Cohen, a Canadian literary and music icon, has provoked excitement, disgust, bewilderment and uncertainty among his fans and critics alike.* Leonard Cohen and Philosophy *wonderfully captures and examines all of those sentiments and more. It provides a delightful and engrossing philosophical journey through the life and art of Leonard Cohen. Jason Holt and his roster of engaging contributors make you want to travel with them—and you'll be glad you did."*

—SHAUN P. YOUNG, editor of *Jeopardy and Philosophy*

# Leonard Cohen and Philosophy

# Popular Culture and Philosophy® Series Editor: George A. Reisch

**Volume 1** *Seinfeld and Philosophy: A Book about Everything and Nothing* (2000)

**Volume 2** *The Simpsons and Philosophy: The D'oh! of Homer* (2001)

**Volume 3** *The Matrix and Philosophy: Welcome to the Desert of the Real* (2002)

**Volume 4** *Buffy the Vampire Slayer and Philosophy: Fear and Trembling in Sunnydale* (2003)

**Volume 5** *The Lord of the Rings and Philosophy: One Book to Rule Them All* (2003)

**Volume 9** *Harry Potter and Philosophy: If Aristotle Ran Hogwarts* (2004)

**Volume 12** *Star Wars and Philosophy: More Powerful than You Can Possibly Imagine* (2005)

**Volume 13** *Superheroes and Philosophy: Truth, Justice, and the Socratic Way* (2005)

**Volume 19** *Monty Python and Philosophy: Nudge Nudge, Think Think!* (2006)

**Volume 25** *The Beatles and Philosophy: Nothing You Can Think that Can't Be Thunk* (2006)

**Volume 26** *South Park and Philosophy: Bigger, Longer, and More Penetrating* (2007)

**Volume 30** *Pink Floyd and Philosophy: Careful with that Axiom, Eugene!* (2007)

**Volume 33** *Battlestar Galactica and Philosophy: Mission Accomplished or Mission Frakked Up?* (2008)

**Volume 35** *Star Trek and Philosophy: The Wrath of Kant* (2008)

**Volume 36** *The Legend of Zelda and Philosophy: I Link Therefore I Am* (2008)

**Volume 37** *The Wizard of Oz and Philosophy: Wicked Wisdom of the West* (2008)

**Volume 38** *Radiohead and Philosophy: Fitter Happier More Deductive* (2009)

**Volume 39** *Jimmy Buffett and Philosophy: The Porpoise Driven Life* (2009) Edited by Erin McKenna and Scott L. Pratt

**Volume 41** *Stephen Colbert and Philosophy: I Am Philosophy (And So Can You!)* (2009) Edited by Aaron Allen Schiller

**Volume 42** *Supervillains and Philosophy: Sometimes, Evil Is Its Own Reward* (2009) Edited by Ben Dyer

**Volume 43** *The Golden Compass and Philosophy: God Bites the Dust* (2009) Edited by Richard Greene and Rachel Robison

**Volume 44** *Led Zeppelin and Philosophy: All Will Be Revealed* (2009) Edited by Scott Calef

**Volume 45** *World of Warcraft and Philosophy: Wrath of the Philosopher King* (2009) Edited by Luke Cuddy and John Nordlinger

**Volume 46** *Mr. Monk and Philosophy: The Curious Case of the Defective Detective* (2010) Edited by D.E. Wittkower

**Volume 47** *Anime and Philosophy: Wide Eyed Wonder* (2010) Edited by Josef Steiff and Tristan D. Tamplin

**Volume 48** *The Red Sox and Philosophy: Green Monster Meditations* (2010) Edited by Michael Macomber

**Volume 49** *Zombies, Vampires, and Philosophy: New Life for the Undead* (2010) Edited by Richard Greene and K. Silem Mohammad

**Volume 50** *Facebook and Philosophy: What's on Your Mind?* (2010) Edited by D.E. Wittkower

**Volume 51** *Soccer and Philosophy: Beautiful Thoughts on the Beautiful Game* (2010) Edited by Ted Richards

**Volume 52** *Manga and Philosophy: Fullmetal Metaphysician* (2010) Edited by Josef Steiff and Adam Barkman

**Volume 53** *Martial Arts and Philosophy: Beating and Nothingness* (2010) Edited by Graham Priest and Damon Young

**Volume 54** *The Onion and Philosophy: Fake News Story True, Alleges Indignant Area Professor* (2010) Edited by Sharon M. Kaye

**Volume 55** *Doctor Who and Philosophy: Bigger on the Inside* (2010) Edited by Courtland Lewis and Paula Smithka

**Volume 56** *Dune and Philosophy: Weirding Way of the Mentat* (2011) Edited by Jeffery Nicholas

**Volume 57** *Rush and Philosophy: Heart and Mind United* (2011) Edited by Jim Berti and Durrell Bowman

**Volume 58** *Dexter and Philosophy: Mind over Spatter* (2011) Edited by Richard Greene, George A. Reisch, and Rachel Robison-Greene

**Volume 59** *Halo and Philosophy: Intellect Evolved* (2011) Edited by Luke Cuddy

**Volume 60** *SpongeBob SquarePants and Philosophy: Soaking Up Secrets Under the Sea!* (2011) Edited by Joseph J. Foy

**Volume 61** *Sherlock Holmes and Philosophy: The Footprints of a Gigantic Mind* (2011) Edited by Josef Steiff

**Volume 62** *Inception and Philosophy: Ideas to Die For* (2011) Edited by Thorsten Botz-Bornstein

**Volume 63** *Philip K. Dick and Philosophy: Do Androids Have Kindred Spirits?* (2011) Edited by D.E. Wittkower

**Volume 64** *The Rolling Stones and Philosophy: It's Just a Thought Away* (2012) Edited by Luke Dick and George A. Reisch

**Volume 65** *Chuck Klosterman and Philosophy: The Real and the Cereal* (2012) Edited by Seth Vannatta

**Volume 66** *Neil Gaiman and Philosophy: Gods Gone Wild!* (2012) Edited by Tracy L. Bealer, Rachel Luria, and Wayne Yuen

**Volume 67** *Breaking Bad and Philosophy: Badder Living through Chemistry* (2012) Edited by David R. Koepsell and Robert Arp

**Volume 68** *The Walking Dead and Philosophy: Zombie Apocalypse Now* (2012) Edited by Wayne Yuen

**Volume 69** *Curb Your Enthusiasm and Philosophy: Awaken the Social Assassin Within* (2012) Edited by Mark Ralkowski

**Volume 70** *Dungeons and Dragons and Philosophy: Raiding the Temple of Wisdom* (2012) Edited by Jon Cogburn and Mark Silcox

**Volume 71** *The Catcher in the Rye and Philosophy: A Book for Bastards, Morons, and Madmen* (2012) Edited by Keith Dromm and Heather Salter

**Volume 72** *Jeopardy! and Philosophy: What Is Knowledge in the Form of a Question?* (2012) Edited by Shaun P. Young

**Volume 73** *The Wire and Philosophy: This America, Man* (2013) Edited by David Bzdak, Joanna Crosby, and Seth Vannatta

**Volume 74** *Planet of the Apes and Philosophy: Great Apes Think Alike* (2013) Edited by John Huss

**Volume 75** *Psych and Philosophy: Some Dark Juju-Magumbo* (2013) Edited by Robert Arp

**Volume 76** *The Good Wife and Philosophy: Temptations of Saint Alicia* (2013) Edited by Kimberly Baltzer-Jaray and Robert Arp

**Volume 77** *Boardwalk Empire and Philosophy: Bootleg This Book* (2013) Edited by Richard Greene and Rachel Robison-Greene

**Volume 78** *Futurama and Philosophy: Bite My Shiny Metal Axiom* (2013) Edited by Courtland Lewis and Shaun P. Young

**Volume 79** *Frankenstein and Philosophy: The Shocking Truth* (2013) Edited by Nicolas Michaud

**Volume 80** *Ender's Game and Philosophy: Genocide Is Child's Play* (2013) Edited by D.E. Wittkower and Lucinda Rush

**Volume 81** *How I Met Your Mother and Philosophy: Being and Awesomeness* (2014) Edited by Lorenzo von Matterhorn

**Volume 82** *Jurassic Park and Philosophy: The Truth Is Terrifying* (2014) Edited by Nicolas Michaud and Jessica Watkins

**Volume 83** *The Devil and Philosophy: The Nature of His Game* (2014) Edited by Robert Arp

**Volume 84** *Leonard Cohen and Philosophy: Various Positions* (2014) Edited by Jason Holt

**In Preparation:**

*Homeland and Philosophy* (2014) Edited by Robert Arp

*Adventure Time and Philosophy* (2014) Edited by Nicolas Michaud

*Girls and Philosophy* (2014) Edited by Richard Greene and Rachel Robison-Greene

*Justified and Philosophy* (2014) Edited by Rod Carveth and Robert Arp

For full details of all Popular Culture and Philosophy® books, visit www.opencourtbooks.com.

Popular Culture and Philosophy®

# Leonard Cohen and Philosophy

*Various Positions*

Edited by

JASON HOLT

OPEN COURT
Chicago, Illinois

*Volume 84 in the series, Popular Culture and Philosophy*®, edited by George A. Reisch

**This book has not been prepared, authorized, or endorsed by Leonard Cohen.**

**To order books from Open Court, call toll-free 1-800-815-2280, or visit our website at www.opencourtbooks.com.**

Open Court Publishing Company is a division of Carus Publishing Company, dba Cricket Media.



First printing 2014



Printed and bound in the United States of America.

**Library of Congress Cataloging-in-Publication Data**

Leonard Cohen and philosophy / edited by Jason Holt.
pages cm. — (Popular culture and philosophy ; Volume 84)
Includes biographical references and index.
ISBN 978-0-8126-9856-5 (trade paper : alk. paper) 1. Cohen, Leonard, 1934—Criticism and interpretation. I. Holt, Jason, 1971-.
ML.410.C734L46 2014
782.42164092—dc23

2014016534

# Contents

# Acknowledgments

Thanks to Series Editor George Reisch, David Ramsay Steele, Kerri Mommer, and everyone at Open Court for their encouragement and support.

"The Unified Heart" and "The Blessing to End Disunity" symbols by Leonard Cohen. Copyright © 1984, 2007 Leonard Cohen. Used by permission.

Excerpts from "The First Murder," "My Old Layton," "How It Happened in the Middle of the Day," "A Migrating Dialogue," "Folk," and "Another Night with Telescope" from *Flowers for Hitler* by Leonard Cohen. Copyright © 1964 Leonard Cohen. Reprinted by permission of McClelland & Stewart, a division of Random House of Canada Limited, a Penguin Random House Company.

Excerpts from "Psalm 25," "Psalm 29," and "Psalm 40" from *Book of Mercy* by Leonard Cohen. Copyright © 1984 Leonard Cohen. Reprinted by permission of McClelland & Stewart, a division of Random House of Canada Limited, a Penguin Random House Company.

Excerpts from "Beneath My Hands," "The Music Crept by Us," "You Do Not Have to Love Me," "You Have Sweetened Your Word," "Israel," and "All My Life" from *Stranger Music: Selected Poems and Songs* by Leonard Cohen. Copyright © 1993 Leonard Cohen. Reprinted by permission of McClelland & Stewart, a division of Random House of Canada Limited, a Penguin Random House Company.

Brief excerpts from "To a Young Nun" (p. 228), "The Luckiest Man in the World" (p. 228), "Moving into a Period" (p. 222), "All My News" (p. 223), and "Robert Appears Again" (p. 288), from *Book of Longing* by Leonard Cohen. Copyright © 2006 Leonard Cohen. Reprinted by permission of McClelland & Stewart, a division of Random House of Canada Limited, a Penguin Random House Company.

Brief excerpts from "To a Young Nun" (p. 228), "The Luckiest Man in the World" (p. 228), "Moving into a Period" (p. 222), "All My News" (p. 223), and "Robert Appears Again" (p. 288) from *Book of Longing* by Leonard Cohen. Copyright © 2006 Leonard Cohen. Reprinted by permission of HarperCollins Publishers (US).

Brief excerpts from "To a Young Nun" (p. 228), "The Luckiest Man in the World" (p. 228), "Moving into a Period" (p. 222), "All My News" (p. 223), and "Robert Appears Again" (p. 288) from *Book of Longing* by Leonard Cohen. Copyright © 2006 Leonard Cohen. Reprinted by permission of Penguin Books Ltd. (UK).

A SINGER MUST DIE
Written by Leonard Cohen
© 1974 Sony/ATV Songs LLC
All rights administered by Sony/ATV Music Publishing LLC., 424 Church Street, Nashville, TN 37219. All rights reserved. Used by permission.
Excerpts also from *Stranger Music: Selected Poems and Songs* by Leonard Cohen. Copyright © 1993 Leonard Cohen. Reprinted by permission of McClelland & Stewart, a division of Random House of Canada Limited, a Penguin Random House Company.

A THOUSAND KISSES DEEP
Written by Leonard Cohen & Sharon Robinson
© 2001 Sony/ATV Songs LLC & Publisher(s) Unknown
All rights on behalf of Sony/ATV Songs LLC administered by Sony/ATV Music Publishing LLC., 424 Church Street, Nashville, TN 37219. All rights reserved. Used by permission.

ANTHEM
Written by Leonard Cohen
© 1992 Sony/ATV Songs LLC
All rights administered by Sony/ATV Music Publishing LLC., 424 Church Street, Nashville, TN 37219. All rights reserved. Used by permission.

BALLAD OF THE ABSENT MARE
Written by Leonard Cohen
© 1979 Sony/ATV Songs LLC
All rights administered by Sony/ATV Music Publishing LLC., 424 Church Street, Nashville, TN 37219. All rights reserved. Used by permission.

BIRD ON THE WIRE
Written by Leonard Cohen
© 1969 Sony/ATV Songs LLC
All rights administered by Sony/ATV Music Publishing LLC., 424 Church Street, Nashville, TN 37219. All rights reserved. Used by permission.
Excerpts also from *Stranger Music: Selected Poems and Songs* by Leonard Cohen. Copyright © 1993 Leonard Cohen. Reprinted by permission of McClelland & Stewart, a division of Random House of Canada Limited, a Penguin Random House Company.

CLOSING TIME
Written by Leonard Cohen
© 1992 Sony/ATV Songs LLC
All rights administered by Sony/ATV Music Publishing LLC., 424 Church Street, Nashville, TN 37219. All rights reserved. Used by permission.

COME HEALING
Written by Leonard Cohen & Patrick Leonard
© 2012 Old Ideas LLC & Publisher(s) Unknown
All rights on behalf of Old Ideas LLC administered by Sony/ATV Music Publishing LLC., 424 Church Street, Nashville, TN 37219. All rights reserved. Used by permission.

DEMOCRACY
Written by Leonard Cohen
© 1992 Sony/ATV Songs LLC
All rights administered by Sony/ATV Music Publishing LLC., 424 Church Street, Nashville, TN 37219. All rights reserved. Used by permission.

EVERYBODY KNOWS
Written by Leonard Cohen & Sharon Robinson
© 1988 Sony/ATV Songs LLC & Publisher(s) Unknown
All rights on behalf of Sony/ATV Songs LLC administered by Sony/ATV Music Publishing LLC., 424 Church Street, Nashville, TN 37219. All rights reserved. Used by permission.

FAMOUS BLUE RAINCOAT
Written by Leonard Cohen
© 1971 Sony/ATV Songs LLC
All rights administered by Sony/ATV Music Publishing LLC., 424 Church Street, Nashville, TN 37219. All rights reserved. Used by permission.
Excerpts also from *Stranger Music: Selected Poems and Songs* by Leonard Cohen. Copyright © 1993 Leonard Cohen. Reprinted by permission of McClelland & Stewart, a division of Random House of Canada Limited, a Penguin Random House Company.

FIRST WE TAKE MANHATTAN
Written by Leonard Cohen
© 1988 Sony/ATV Songs LLC
All rights administered by Sony/ATV Music Publishing LLC., 424 Church Street, Nashville, TN 37219. All rights reserved. Used by permission.

HALLELUJAH
Written by Leonard Cohen
© 1984 Sony/ATV Songs LLC
All rights administered by Sony/ATV Music Publishing LLC., 424 Church Street, Nashville, TN 37219. All rights reserved. Used by permission.

HEY THAT'S NO WAY TO SAY GOODBYE
Written by Leonard Cohen
© 1967 Sony/ATV Songs LLC
All rights administered by Sony/ATV Music Publishing LLC., 424 Church Street, Nashville, TN 37219. All rights reserved. Used by permission.
Excerpts also *from Stranger Music: Selected Poems and Songs* by Leonard Cohen. Copyright © 1993 Leonard Cohen. Reprinted by permission of McClelland & Stewart, a division of Random House of Canada Limited, a Penguin Random House Company.

IF IT BE YOUR WILL
Written by Leonard Cohen
© 1984 Sony/ATV Songs LLC
All rights administered by Sony/ATV Music Publishing LLC., 424 Church Street, Nashville, TN 37219. All rights reserved. Used by permission.

# Acknowledgments

I'M YOUR MAN
Written by Leonard Cohen
© 1988 Sony/ATV Songs LLC
All rights administered by Sony/ATV Music Publishing LLC., 424 Church Street, Nashville, TN 37219. All rights reserved. Used by permission.

IN MY SECRET LIFE
Written by Leonard Cohen & Sharon Robinson
© 2001 Sony/ATV Songs LLC & Publisher(s) Unknown
All rights on behalf of Sony/ATV Songs LLC administered by Sony/ATV Music Publishing LLC., 424 Church Street, Nashville, TN 37219. All rights reserved. Used by permission.

IS THIS WHAT YOU WANTED
Written by Leonard Cohen
© 1974 Sony/ATV Songs LLC
All rights administered by Sony/ATV Music Publishing LLC., 424 Church Street, Nashville, TN 37219. All rights reserved. Used by permission.
Excerpts also from *Stranger Music: Selected Poems and Songs* by Leonard Cohen. Copyright © 1993 Leonard Cohen. Reprinted by permission of McClelland & Stewart, a division of Random House of Canada Limited, a Penguin Random House Company.

LOVE ITSELF
Written by Leonard Cohen & Sharon Robinson
© 2001 Sony/ATV Songs LLC & Publisher(s) Unknown
All rights on behalf of Sony/ATV Songs LLC administered by Sony/ATV Music Publishing LLC., 424 Church Street, Nashville, TN 37219. All rights reserved. Used by permission.

LOVER LOVER LOVER
Written by Leonard Cohen
© 1974 Sony/ATV Songs LLC
All rights administered by Sony/ATV Music Publishing LLC., 424 Church Street, Nashville, TN 37219. All rights reserved. Used by permission.

MEMORIES
Written by Leonard Cohen & Phil Spector
© 1977 Sony/ATV Songs LLC, Abkco Music Inc., & Mother Bertha Music Inc.
All rights administered by Sony/ATV Music Publishing LLC., 424 Church Street, Nashville, TN 37219. All rights reserved. Used by permission.

NIGHT COMES ON
Written by Leonard Cohen
© 1984 Sony/ATV Songs LLC
All rights administered by Sony/ATV Music Publishing LLC., 424 Church Street, Nashville, TN 37219. All rights reserved. Used by permission.

NIGHTINGALE
Written by Leonard Cohen & Anjani Thomas
© 2004 Old Ideas LLC & Little Fountain Music
All rights administered by Sony/ATV Music Publishing LLC., 424 Church Street, Nashville, TN 37219. All rights reserved. Used by permission.

SHOW ME THE PLACE
Written by Leonard Cohen & Patrick Leonard
© 2012 Old Ideas LLC & Publisher(s) Unknown
All rights on behalf of Old Ideas LLC administered by Sony/ATV Music Publishing LLC., 424 Church Street, Nashville, TN 37219. All rights reserved. Used by permission.

SO LONG MARIANNE
Written by Leonard Cohen
© 1967 Sony/ATV Songs LLC
All rights administered by Sony/ATV Music Publishing LLC., 424 Church Street, Nashville, TN 37219. All rights reserved. Used by permission.
Excerpts also from *Stranger Music: Selected Poems and Songs* by Leonard Cohen. Copyright © 1993 Leonard Cohen. Reprinted by permission of McClelland & Stewart, a division of Random House of Canada Limited, a Penguin Random House Company.

STORY OF ISAAC
Written by Leonard Cohen
© 1969 Sony/ATV Songs LLC
All rights administered by Sony/ATV Music Publishing LLC., 424 Church Street, Nashville, TN 37219. All rights reserved. Used by permission.
Excerpts also from *Stranger Music: Selected Poems and* Songs by Leonard Cohen. Copyright © 1993 Leonard Cohen. Reprinted by permission of McClelland & Stewart, a division of Random House of Canada Limited, a Penguin Random House Company.

SUZANNE
Written by Leonard Cohen
© 1967 Sony/ATV Songs LLC
All rights administered by Sony/ATV Music Publishing LLC., 424 Church Street, Nashville, TN 37219. All rights reserved. Used by permission.

TAKE THIS LONGING
Written by Leonard Cohen
© 1974 Sony/ATV Songs LLC
All rights administered by Sony/ATV Music Publishing LLC., 424 Church Street, Nashville, TN 37219. All rights reserved. Used by permission.
Excerpts also from *Stranger Music: Selected Poems and Songs* by Leonard Cohen. Copyright © 1993 Leonard Cohen. Reprinted by permission of McClelland & Stewart, a division of Random House of Canada Limited, a Penguin Random House Company.

TENNESSEE WALTZ
Written by Pee Wee King & Redd Stewart, Additional verse by Leonard Cohen
© 1948 Sony/ATV Acuff Rose Music
All rights administered by Sony/ATV Music Publishing LLC., 424 Church Street, Nashville, TN 37219. All rights reserved. Used by permission.

THE FAITH
Written by Leonard Cohen
© 2004 Old Ideas LLC
All rights administered by Sony/ATV Music Publishing LLC., 424 Church Street, Nashville, TN 37219. All rights reserved. Used by permission.

THE FUTURE
Written by Leonard Cohen
© 1992 Sony/ATV Songs LLC
All rights administered by Sony/ATV Music Publishing LLC., 424 Church Street, Nashville, TN 37219. All rights reserved. Used by permission.

THE GUESTS
Written by Leonard Cohen
© 1979 Sony/ATV Songs LLC
All rights administered by Sony/ATV Music Publishing LLC., 424 Church Street, Nashville, TN 37219. All rights reserved. Used by permission.

THE LAND OF PLENTY
Written by Leonard Cohen & Sharon Robinson
© 2001 Sony/ATV Songs LLC & Publisher(s) Unknown
All rights on behalf of Sony/ATV Songs LLC administered by Sony/ATV Music Publishing LLC., 424 Church Street, Nashville, TN 37219. All rights reserved. Used by permission.

THE STRANGER SONG
Written by Leonard Cohen
© 1967 Sony/ATV Songs LLC
All rights administered by Sony/ATV Music Publishing LLC., 424 Church Street, Nashville, TN 37219. All rights reserved. Used by permission.

THE WINDOW
Written by Leonard Cohen
© 1979 Sony/ATV Songs LLC
All rights administered by Sony/ATV Music Publishing LLC., 424 Church Street, Nashville, TN 37219. All rights reserved. Used by permission.

THERE FOR YOU
Written by Leonard Cohen & Sharon Robinson
© 2004 Old Ideas LLC & Publisher(s) Unknown
All rights on behalf of Old Ideas LLC administered by Sony/ATV Music Publishing LLC., 424 Church Street, Nashville, TN 37219. All rights reserved. Used by permission.

THERE IS A WAR
Written by Leonard Cohen
© 1974 Sony/ATV Songs LLC
All rights administered by Sony/ATV Music Publishing LLC., 424 Church Street, Nashville, TN 37219. All rights reserved. Used by permission.
Excerpts also from *Stranger Music: Selected Poems and Songs* by Leonard Cohen. Copyright © 1993 Leonard Cohen. Reprinted by permission of McClelland & Stewart, a division of Random House of Canada Limited, a Penguin Random House Company.

TOWER OF SONG
Written by Leonard Cohen
© 1988 Sony/ATV Songs LLC
All rights administered by Sony/ATV Music Publishing LLC., 424 Church Street, Nashville, TN 37219. All rights reserved. Used by permission.

VILLANELLE FOR OUR TIME
Written by Leonard Cohen & Frank Scott
© 2004 Old Ideas LLC & Publisher(s) Unknown
All rights on behalf of Old Ideas LLC administered by Sony/ATV Music Publishing LLC., 424 Church Street, Nashville, TN 37219. All rights reserved. Used by permission.

WAITING FOR THE MIRACLE
Written by Leonard Cohen & Sharon Robinson
© 1992 Sony/ATV Songs LLC & Publisher(s) Unknown
All rights on behalf of Sony/ATV Songs LLC administered by Sony/ATV Music Publishing LLC., 424 Church Street, Nashville, TN 37219. All rights reserved. Used by permission.

WHO BY FIRE
Written by Leonard Cohen
© 1974 Sony/ATV Songs LLC
All rights administered by Sony/ATV Music Publishing LLC., 424 Church Street, Nashville, TN 37219. All rights reserved. Used by permission.
Excerpts also from *Stranger Music: Selected Poems and Songs* by Leonard Cohen. Copyright © 1993 Leonard Cohen. Reprinted by permission of McClelland & Stewart, a division of Random House of Canada Limited, a Penguin Random House Company.

YOU KNOW WHO I AM
Written by Leonard Cohen
© 1969 Sony/ATV Songs LLC
All rights administered by Sony/ATV Music Publishing LLC., 424 Church Street, Nashville, TN 37219. All rights reserved. Used by permission.
Excerpts also from *Stranger Music: Selected Poems and Songs* by Leonard Cohen. Copyright © 1993 Leonard Cohen. Reprinted by permission of McClelland & Stewart, a division of Random House of Canada Limited, a Penguin Random House Company.

# The Pop Star–Poet Paradox

JASON HOLT

There seems to be a contradiction between Leonard Cohen the pop star and Leonard Cohen the poet. The pop star was inducted into the Rock and Roll Hall of Fame; the poet refused Canada's prestigious Governor General's Literary Award. On some level, these two facets don't seem to go together, as if Cohen has a split artistic personality. Think of his portrait on the *Recent Songs* album cover (1979): the two bilateral halves, put together, do look like him, although the face is noticeably asymmetrical. No stranger to tension and duality, "the stranger" appears particularly tailor-suited to such visual representation.

There's nothing altogether unusual about starting out in one line and shifting later to another. From a certain point of view, that's in fact what Cohen did. He started out as a poet, a worker in literature, and then became primarily a worker in song. Nor is there anything strange about a musician publishing poetry. Plenty of popular musicians have done so: Jim Morrison, Joni Mitchell, Bob Dylan, Lou Reed, Tom Waits, Jewel, Tupac Shakur. Others, like Patti Smith and Jim Carroll, have achieved a notable presence as poets and even some critical cachet. It is, though, clear enough, if not entirely uncontroversial, that Leonard Cohen ranks supreme as the quintessential pop star–poet. We can leave aside the related issue of the poetics of popular song lyrics—

the metrical appeal of Chuck Berry, for instance—or including spoken word pieces on albums à la Ani DiFranco.

Preeminence as a pop star–poet is only one of many things that make Leonard Cohen a paradoxical figure, one of the most enigmatic, mysterious, and compelling in all of pop music. He's a *Canadian*, of all things, but with international appeal. Cohen is utterly depressing, but wickedly funny. He's deadly serious, but somehow above it all, lighthearted; nostalgic and yet hopeful; hopeful but resigned; unremittingly cruel, yet undeniably gentle; unblinkingly realistic, yet almost blindly romantic; a Jew but seemingly Christian; Judeo-Christian but Buddhist. He speaks eloquently of silence, and his silence speaks volumes, illuminating darkness even as it swallows up the light. He shouldn't be—but somehow is—so much fun.

These tensions, these dualities are paradoxes only in a mild sense. A more strict sense limits paradoxes to apparently inescapable, genuine contradictions—where it seems logically impossible to have both things at once, and yet it seems we do have them. To take a common example, if I write "This sentence is false," that's paradoxical because assuming it's true (the world is as the sentence says), then it's false, and if it's false (the world isn't so), then it's true. It's not just in the mild sense that Leonard Cohen is paradoxical. He's also paradoxical in the stricter sense. The pop star–poet paradox isn't that Cohen writes poetry and popular music, but rather that his songs count *both* as poetry *and* as popular music.

Why is this a paradox? There's a presumed hard distinction between so-called high and popular art. Where poetry is a high art, folk or pop music is deemed a popular art, lower if not lowbrow. Actually, any art form will have highbrow and popular varieties. Music, for instance, has both highbrow varieties (classical, opera), and less "refined" popular types (country, rock). Poetry, too, may be seen as having comparatively popular varieties like rap alongside its more rarefied, and to popular tastes often less engaging, traditional examples: Drake and Blake. It's not just philosophers, but most of us, who consider the distinction absolute in that any artwork will count *either* as high art *or* as popular entertainment—*but never both*.

We can now see the potential paradox in the music of Leonard Cohen. It's not simply a matter of setting poetry to music, although that sometimes was the process, but the fact that the songs themselves count both as traditional poetry (high art) and folk or pop music (popular art). From a poetic perspective, Cohen's songs are unquestionably a cut above—too good, in a way, for popular music. Still, folk and pop, Cohen's musical genres, are *decidedly* popular. Cohen's songs appear to transcend and yet still remain within the genres they inhabit.

Film theorists sometimes appeal to something called "auteur theory" to explain how in some cases movies, a typically popular art form, can be transformed into high art when a great filmmaker expresses a singular vision. In the films of Alfred Hitchcock, for instance, we have popular movie genres—the thriller, the horror, the film noir—elevated beyond the confines of more generic examples. Similar to a literary author (*auteur*), the creative control and exacting standards of the genius filmmaker allow them to make high art out of what, in ordinary hands, would be merely popular art. In such cases, the label "popular art," however popular the work itself may be, is effectively inapplicable.

We might think of resolving the pop star–poet paradox for Cohen by thinking that he's also an auteur—and not just because he's literally an author—that he transcends the limits of folk and pop music to create high art out of popular material (see Boucher's book, *Dylan and Cohen,* pp. 75–77), just as Hitchcock does with the thriller. That's one possibility. Here's another: though the poetry of Cohen's songs makes them high art, the musical profiles of these songs don't allow them any supra-popular transubstantiation. They're folk, or pop, glorious but not transcendent. Perhaps this is unlike Hitchcock, though perhaps here too the paradox that auteur theory seems to help resolve remains intact.

Either way, in Leonard Cohen's music we find a challenge to the distinction between high and popular art. Witness the fact that, on this distinction, the undeniable high art of the lyrics as poetry gets somehow "degraded" by *adding* to it aesthetically pleasing melody: a paradox of literary lyrics. We'd hardly agree with Louis Dudek, an early literary mentor of Cohen, who thought that his taking up the guitar was somehow throwing away his talent, a betrayal of poetry. The two are perfect complements, as everybody knows.

# I

# Songs of Existence

# 1
# Leonard Cohen as a Guide to Life

BRENDAN SHEA

> To study philosophy is nothing but to prepare one's self to die.
>
> —CICERO

When asked to describe what separates Leonard Cohen's songs from those of other singer-songwriters, many of his fans might be tempted to say "he's more philosophical." And this is surely right—after all, this is a book on Leonard Cohen and philosophy!

Cohen's songs resonate with so many of us because they focus on profoundly important human themes such as the nature of love, sex, death, and what makes for a meaningful life. An influential group of ancient Greek philosophers who lived during the period from 300 BCE to 200 CE sought to answer questions related to these same themes. The three major "schools" of Greek philosophy during this period, known as *Hellenistic* philosophy, included the Stoics, the Skeptics, and the Epicureans. The philosophers in these different schools don't always agree with each other (or with Cohen) on the nature of the problems or their solutions.

## A Philosopher Must Die

> For if you kill me you will not easily find a successor to me, who, if I may use such a ludicrous figure of speech, am a sort of gadfly,

> given to the state by God; and the state is a great and noble steed who is tardy in his motions owing to his very size, and requires to be stirred into life. I am that gadfly which God has attached to the state, and all day long and in all places am always fastening upon you, arousing and persuading and reproaching you.
>
> —SOCRATES (*Apology*, section 30e)

In "A Singer Must Die," Cohen writes from the perspective of a singer who has been accused of betraying with "the lie in his voice." The singer offers a sarcastic apology, thanking his accusers for doing their duty as "keepers of truth" and "guardians of beauty." He goes on to consider his own complex motivations for writing his songs, which are tightly tied up with his human desire for sex and love. He concludes with a more direct attack on the motives and methods of the government, which often tries to suppress this sort of art with a "knee in your balls" and "fist in your face."

The conflict between the democratic state and the individual seeker of truth has a long history, and one of its earliest victims, Socrates, served as something like a secular "saint" to Hellenistic philosophers. Socrates (469 to 399 BCE) was a citizen of Athens, the birthplace of modern democracy. Most of what we know about Socrates is due to his equally famous student, the philosopher Plato (427 to 347 BCE). Socrates was by all accounts a loyal citizen, who served bravely in the military and devoted his life to determining how one could live a virtuous, happy life. He most commonly did this by approaching important Athenians and asking them to describe and defend their answers to "big questions" about subjects such as justice, religion, and love. Like Cohen's character in "Chelsea Hotel #2," Socrates was at once known as a sex object (the young men of Athens often made unsuccessful passes at him) and as a somewhat ugly man (Plato's dialogues contain frequent jokes about the shape of Socrates's nose).

Socrates's habit of acting like a "gadfly" who annoyed the rich and powerful earned him enemies, however, and he soon found himself in the same situation as Cohen's singer. Socrates was accused of corrupting the youth and denying the gods of the state. His (often sarcastic) defense was in many ways similar to the one described by Cohen. He argued that he was driven to seek the truth (though he claimed to never have found it) by an inner "daemon" he could not and would not control, and said that his accusers ought to thank him for his service to the city. Socrates argued that it would be better to die than to do what he thought wrong, since only the latter harms the soul. In a famous miscarriage of justice, the jury voted to convict Socrates and sentenced him to death.

In his final statement to the members of the jury, Socrates offered a warning that echoes Cohen's threat of first taking Manhattan, then Berlin, and told the jurors that their problems would only be made worse by killing him. His death would, he predicted, increase both the number of future critics and their radicalism. If democracy is to survive, he suggested, citizens must learn how to deal rationally with their problems, and to deal productively with the criticisms raised by poets and philosophers. If not, democracy can easily turn into tyranny, as both the fearful majority and the increasingly desperate minority seek to protect their own places in society.

Like Cohen, Socrates was a person who combined considerable empathy for individual human beings with a realistic and somewhat cynical view about the horrible ways that they usually behaved. Similarly, while he was fiercely loyal to Athens, and even risked death by defying a group of tyrants who briefly overthrew the democracy, he was deeply pessimistic about the ability of the majority to craft a just, rational society. Cohen songs such as "Everybody Knows" and "Democracy" exhibit something close to a Socratic attitude toward modern society. In the former song, Cohen emphasizes that people will behave in predictably bad ways; in the latter, he identifies both the shortcomings and the potential of American democracy.

**Brendan Shea**

## Hey, That's the Way Stoics Say Goodbye

> Never say about anything "I have lost it" but say "I have restored it." Is your child dead? It has been restored. Is your wife dead? She has been restored. . . . So long as he may allow you, take care of it as a thing which belongs to another, as travelers do with their inn.
>
> —EPICTETUS (section 11)

Immediately after Socrates's death, philosophy in Athens was dominated first by Plato and then by Aristotle (384 to 322 BCE), who helped launch research into areas such as physics, biology, logic, metaphysics, and political science. The Hellenistic period of philosophy officially "starts" with the death of Alexander the Great and the subsequent exile of Aristotle from Athens in 323 BCE. Like their hero Socrates, the Hellenistic philosophers were less concerned with the "academic" pursuits of Plato and Aristotle than with what they saw as a more fundamental question: "How should I live?"

The Stoic school of philosophy was founded in Athens by Zeno of Citium (334 to 264 BCE), and included thinkers such as Epictetus (55 to 135 CE) and the Roman Emperor Marcus Aurelius (121 to 180 CE ).The Stoics were especially worried about how we can learn to live with tragedy, suffering, or loss. This same problem is addressed in many of Cohen's songs, including "Hallelujah," which (at least in parts) celebrates a painful relationship, and "If It Be Your Will," a prayer-like song that emphasizes the essential powerlessness of humans to control the world around us. Stoic themes are especially prominent in Cohen's parting words to a lover in "Hey, That's No Way to Say Goodbye." Like Cohen, the Stoics emphasize the importance of appropriately valuing the relationship that you are currently in, while giving up on future-oriented talk of "love or chains and things we can't untie." The Stoics would agree with Cohen's focus on the present, shown both by his refusal to think of new lovers and calm acceptance that his current relationship was ending. They would also concur with his plea to avoid the sort of extreme sadness that often marks the end of relationships. While the Stoics were not "anti-emotion" (as the modern word "stoic" sometimes suggests) they did consider the extremes of sadness, anger, and lust among the biggest obstacles to leading a good life. These sorts of self-centered emotions make it more difficult for us to be happy and to treat others (such as romantic partners) the way they deserve.

While the Stoics did not believe in an afterlife, they did believe in a benevolent, eternally existing universe (the Stoic "God") in which everything occurred as it was "fated to." Many of them also believed that time was cyclical, and that each event we experience has happened (and will happen) an infinite number of times. For the Stoics, this might have served a therapeutic purpose, much like the song's reminder that "many loved before us" and "we are not new." The idea that we are *not* unique can, somewhat surprisingly, take some of the pressure off of us to "not screw things up" or to "fight against the inevitable." Instead, we realize that we (just like everyone else) must learn to accept that there are many things that are beyond our control, and that it is useless to fight against them. This change of perspective reminds us of our relatively small, but nevertheless essential, place in the larger universe. From this perspective, we can see the foolishness of assuming that our present concerns are the "center of the universe"; however, it also reminds us that these concerns are *real*, and that we ought to respond to them appropriately.

The Stoics recommend that we focus on the present, and adopt an attitude of "resigned acceptance" toward whatever the future holds. This is not always easy, of course, as "Hey, That's No Way to Say Goodbye" beautifully illustrates. As humans, we all want to "hold on" to things even after we realize that we cannot do so. The Stoics, and Cohen, remind us that our lives will be better if we learn to let go.

## A Skeptical Story about Leonard's Raincoat

> For he who is of the opinion that anything is either good or bad by nature is always troubled, and when he does not possess those things that seem to him good he thinks that he is tortured by the things which are by nature bad, and pursues those that he thinks to be good. Having acquired them, however, he falls into greater perturbation, because he is excited beyond reason and without measure from fear of a change, and he does everything in his power to retain the things that seem to him good.
>
> —Sextus Empiricus (book 1, section 12)

In "Famous Blue Raincoat" the narrator (apparently Cohen himself, if we are to believe the song's final line) is writing a letter to a man who had an affair with the narrator's wife Jane and then disappeared. Somewhat surprisingly, the narrator shows considerable compassion for the mysterious man, calling him his "brother," and noting concern for the man's apparent isolation. At the end of the song, the narrator says that "I guess that I miss you" and "I guess I forgive you" and thanks him for standing in his way. More specifically, the narrator suggests that having the affair helped Jane in ways that he himself couldn't have done (apparently because he believed falsely that the "trouble in her eyes" could not be helped, and so he hadn't tried to do anything).

One unifying theme of the song concerns the characters' seeming *ignorance* of what the effects of their actions are, and what actions they could take to make their lives better. Most obviously, the narrator has slowly come to realize that the affair has, oddly, turned out for the best, at least in some respects. The letter's recipient, by contrast, at one time believed that he needed to "go clear," and change his life in some way, but it seems likely he has given up on this now, and perhaps wonders if he has done something unforgivable. We get the suggestion that Jane too is worried about questions that have no easy answers. Unlike ordinary ignorance, the sort of deep uncertainty experienced by these characters cannot be cured simply by reading a book, asking an expert, or doing an experiment. Instead, it concerns some of the deepest, most fundamental questions: What is it to love someone? How can I live an ethical, authentic life?

The Skeptical school of philosophy, apparently founded by the Greek philosopher Pyrrho (360 to 270 BCE) and later defended by the Roman physician Sextus Empiricus (160 to 210 CE), argued that achieving this state of complete, unresolvable ignorance was in fact the *goal* of philosophy. While this may seem strange, "Famous Blue Raincoat" provides a good starting point for understanding the Skeptics' fundamental insight. Sextus Empiricus argues that people become skeptics by accident. They begin by seeking the answer to some particular "philosophical" question, perhaps in the hope that finding out the answer will give them "closure" or allow them to move forward with their lives. So, perhaps the narrator began with the question, "How did my wife's affair change our relationship?" As the blossoming skeptic begins trying to answer the question, he notices that there is evidence in favor of multiple, mutually contradictory answers ("It has destroyed the relationship" versus "It has made us stronger"). He is left in a state of indecision, and is unable to decide what to believe.

This is where the skeptic comes in, and asks the person "How does this state of indecision make you feel?" According to Sextus Empiricus, the typical answer will be "calm" or "tranquil." After all, the person has now gotten rid of the unfounded belief that certain things (like being cheated on) are inherently bad, while other things (being the one your spouse loves "best") are inherently good. The skeptic does not conclude "Well, there is no right answer, so I might as well just give up on this whole philosophy thing" (after all, the claim that *there is no right answer* is far too dogmatic for a good skeptic). Instead they resolve to continue a calm, thorough, skeptical investigation into the philosophical questions at issue. The song illustrates this process, as well. The narrator continues to try and reach out to the letter's recipient, and to think carefully about what has happened to him.

While Sextus Empiricus emphasizes that a good skeptic will likely reject any "philosophical" claim about religion, love, death, or the like, he also warns against letting philosophical reflection dominate one's life. In many areas of life, including drinking with friends, enjoying a nice meal, or flirting with someone, Sextus Empiricus thinks that philosophical beliefs can be (and ought to be) largely ignored. Instead, we should simply act as our emotions and habits direct us to. This conclusion also resonates with many of Cohen's songs. In "Famous Blue Raincoat," for example, the skeptic would say that it is good that the narrator has taken a moment to reflect on the past, although it would be a mistake to allow this sort of reflection to consume too much of his day-to-day life.

## The End of All Winning Streaks

> Therefore death to us / Is nothing, nor concerns us in the least, / Since nature of mind is mortal evermore . . . / When comes that sundering of our body and soul . . . / Verily naught to us, us then no more / Can come to pass, naught move our senses then. . . .
>
> —LUCRETIUS (book 3, lines 835–840)

In "A Thousand Kisses Deep," the narrator reflects on youth, old age, and the slow approach of death. His younger years would be counted by many people as very successful ones, filled with beautiful women and beating the odds to achieve various successes. The narrator knows, however, that this "little winning streak" will eventually end and that the coming defeat is "invincible." Through a variety of metaphors, he emphasizes both the "unreality" of the pleasures of youth, and of the ultimate need to come to grips to with what will ultimately happen.

Determining the proper attitude toward death is a difficult philosophical problem, and it was addressed in different ways by many of the Hellenistic thinkers. This problem held a special significance, however, for the Atomist and Epicurean philosophers, a group which included the Greek thinkers Democritus (460 to 370 BCE) and Epicurus (341 to 270 BCE) and the Roman thinker Lucretius (99 to 55 BCE). This school was distinguished by, among other things, the argument that reality consists of nothing but "atoms in the void" and by their contention that the only truly good thing in life is pleasure and the only truly bad thing pain. On the Epicurean view, humans came into existence by chance collisions of atoms, lived for a brief time, and then dissolved back into their constituent atoms.

The Epicurean solution to the problem of death closely resembles the stance taken in "A Thousand Kisses Deep." The first step involves recognizing, as the song's narrator does, that not all desires are equally "real" or "worthwhile." Some desires, such as those for adequate food and sleep, as well as for companionship, are both *natural* and *necessary,* and it makes perfect sense for us to pursue these. Others, such as sexual desire or the desire for gourmet food and drink, are perfectly *natural,* but are unnecessary. Epicureans held that it was okay to enjoy these things when they were obtained from a pursuit of natural, necessary desires, but it would be a mistake to devote our lives to their pursuit, as they can never *truly* be satisfied, and chasing them can easily be a recipe for misery. This seems to have been one of the mistakes made by the narrator in "A Thousand Kisses Deep" in his youth.

Along with the two categories of natural desires, the Epicureans also recognized a category of *unnatural* or *empty* desires, which they argued had no place whatsoever in a happy human life. These include things like greed, reflected by things like betting on ponies, and the desire for immortality, reflected by a willingness to "ditch it all to stay alive." These desires are dangerous precisely because they are *impossible* to satisfy—there is no amount of money that will satisfy the gambler, and there is no way of escaping death.

So, how can we learn to accept death, in the way that both the Epicureans and "A Thousand Kisses Deep" would counsel? Lucretius argues that the secret is to recognize that death is *nothing;* once we are dead, we have ceased to exist, and thus, nothing bad can come to pass. So while it makes sense for us to fear *painful* experiences such as being injured in a war, or having our hearts broken (since we can imagine what these things will feel like), it *doesn't* make sense for us to fear not existing. As Lucretius points out, we don't regret the experiences we missed out on *by not being born sooner* (that happened before we were born). He contends that it makes equally little sense for us to regret the things we will miss out on by *dying sooner than we wanted to.*

## Hypatia and Joan of Arc

> Hypatia . . . who made such attainments in literature and science, as to far surpass all the philosophers of her own time . . . fell a victim to the political jealousy which at that time prevailed. Some . . . therefore, hurried away by a fierce and bigoted zeal . . . waylaid her returning home . . . completely stripped her, and then murdered her with tiles. After tearing her body in pieces, they took her mangled limbs to a place called Cinaron, and there burnt them.
>
> —Socrates of Constantinople

As we've seen, the Hellenistic philosophers believed strongly that practicing philosophy was a key element in a happy, meaningful life. However, doing philosophy could also be dangerous, as Socrates (among others) painfully discovered. Cohen's song "Joan of Arc" illustrates a similar point: while many of us long for the clarity of "love and light," a life dedicated to the pursuit of such lofty goals can, at times, be both lonely and painful.

While there is no universally accepted "end point" of Hellenistic philosophy, the ideas of Greek philosophy were slowly supplanted by the emergence of Christianity as the dominant ideology in the late Roman Empire. One of the last remaining strongholds of Hellenistic thought was Alexandria, Egypt, which for hundreds of years was home to the largest library in the Western world, and which had been founded at the very beginning of the Hellenistic period. As the Hellenists' valuing of literature, science, and philosophy fell out of favor, the library was left to decay. Finally, in 391 CE, what remained of the library was destroyed by the order of the Christian bishops. Thousands of books, including many by notable Hellenistic philosophers, were lost forever—say goodbye to Alexandria lost.

In an ending that would seem to fit in a Leonard Cohen song, the Hellenistic era ended as it began: with a philosopher dying for unpopular beliefs. In this case, the victim was Hypatia of Alexandria, a famous mathematician, astronomer, and teacher of Hellenistic philosophy. All of her writings have been lost, and it seems that she fell victim to both political intrigue and religious persecution. In an event whose exact causes are still debated, she was brutally killed by a mob of local Christians in 405 CE, who may (or may not) have been acting with the complicity of the local bishops.

Her story bears close similarities to Catherine of Alexandria, the Catholic "patron saint of philosophy," who Joan of Arc would later claim to see in visions, and it is at least possible that Catherine was in fact simply a fictionalized version of Hypatia herself. In any case, Cohen's description of the celibate, fiercely committed Joan of Arc resonates with what we know of Hypatia. For her, as for the Hellenistic philosophers that preceded her, philosophy was not simply a collection of theories and arguments learned in the classroom, or a hobby that could be picked up briefly and then forgotten. It was instead an all-consuming passion that demanded total commitment, and which in turn promised the reward of a meaningful, fulfilling life.

It is this basic idea—that leading a meaningful, examined life requires both reflection and effort—that links Cohen's songs so closely with the ideas of the philosophers discussed in this chapter. For many Cohen fans, this is among the many aspects of his music that make it worthwhile for us to return to it again and again. It illustrates beautifully both how *difficult* the examined life can be, and why it is so worthwhile to continue to strive after it.

# 2
# The Existential Cohen

AGUST MAGNUSSON

They call him the "High Priest of Pathos," "Grand Master of Melancholia," and the amazingly awesome "Spin Doctor for the Apocalypse." The stereotypical image of Leonard Cohen is that of a man primarily concerned with the darker aspects of the human condition. The enormous (and hilarious) array of aliases given to him by the press mostly label him as an artist whose stock-in-trade seemingly consists of little else than making people feel miserable.

This popular conception of Cohen as a peddler of doom has always bothered his devotees, and rightly so, for what is immediately apparent to anyone with ears to truly hear Cohen's music and poetry is that there's an immense amount of grace, beauty, and joy to be found in his songs. In fact, one might say that the darkness in his works (and there is, indeed, a great deal of darkness) throws into sharp relief the light that permeates human existence. This may be why it's so common to hear people speak of Cohen's music as a source of healing and comfort in times of suffering and despair, which is the exact opposite of the Cohen cliché perpetuated in popular culture which mostly evokes images of unhappy and angst-ridden depressives wallowing in their pain.

Even though Cohen has been famously hesitant to admit to any cohesive philosophy behind his artistic output he has, on more than one occasion, alluded to this fundamental element of finding the light in the darkness as a kind of spiritual signpost for a great deal of his work. This philosophy is perhaps most explicitly articulated in the chorus of the beautiful song "Anthem" which appears on Cohen's 1992 masterpiece *The Future*: "There is a crack in everything / That's how the light gets in." In an interview given shortly after the album's release Cohen said that these lines are "The closest thing I can describe to a credo. That idea is one of the foundations, one of the fundamental positions behind a lot of the songs" ("Sincerely, L. Cohen").

This notion of the light coming in through the cracks in many ways goes against the prevailing philosophy of our age which tells us that we are to fill up the cracks as best we can, no matter the cost. Cohen's insistence in "Anthem" that we must forget our "perfect offering" stands in stark contrast to a culture where one's value as a human being is measured by material success and the extent to which we have attained a perfection (physical and otherwise) which is, ultimately, unattainable. Many people fall prey to depression, drug addiction, and sometimes even suicide in their attempt to fit into predefined societal norms which have little or nothing to do with who they truly are, reminding us that no sacrifice is too great on the altar of perfection.

Cohen's artistic output is, in many ways, a rebellious cry against this point of view, a celebration of the beautiful losers (as his second novel was so aptly titled), those who resign themselves to the brokenness and suffering of the human condition and in doing so find great reserves of compassion, goodness, grace, and joy.

This notion of finding compassion through suffering, life through death, is a central philosophical tenet in almost all of the great spiritual traditions. Zen Buddhism, Judaism, and Christianity all contain a great deal of wisdom on the insight so beautifully conveyed by Cohen in "Anthem," and all three of these traditions have been deep sources of inspiration and guidance for Cohen's art and life. I will not be focusing on these religious sources of inspiration for Cohen (some of which are covered elsewhere in this book) but would instead like to use the next few pages to examine a different parallel to Cohen's thought on this subject, one which is found in the philosophical tradition of existentialism, one of the most important philosophical movements of the past two centuries.

## Waiting for the Miracle: Cohen and Camus on the Absurd

What is existentialism? French philosopher Jean-Paul Sartre in his work *Existentialism Is a Humanism* claimed that all the philosophers under this peculiar heading share the belief that "existence comes before essence—or, if you will, that we must begin from the subjective" (p. 348). What this means is that philosophy, and our thinking about human existence, must be grounded in the lived experience of the individual human person and not in some abstract theory or system. This is not to say that existentialism opposes all attempts at systematically understanding the world (through natural science, for example) but rather that such methods of understanding reality are never complete and that they indeed often fail to address the most pressing concerns of human beings.

Though existentialism dates back to the nineteenth century it rose to prominence during and after World War II. This period represents one of the great spiritual crises of human civilization, an era where the promise and hope of technology, science, and civilization were shattered in the unspeakable brutality and horror of genocide and war. Traditional ways of thinking about good and evil, man and God, were no longer possible following Auschwitz and Hiroshima. The old systems had failed.

It's in this dark period of history that Albert Camus wrote his famous essay *The Myth of Sisyphus*, first published in 1942. Camus, much like Sartre, wanted to develop a philosophy that could address the terror that so many people were feeling in their lives. He centered his essay on the Greek myth of Sisyphus, which tells the story of a man who defies the gods and frees human beings from the domain of death. This was to commit the greatest of all sins in Greek culture, that of *hubris*, of trying to be like the gods, so the deities of Mount Olympus devised a particularly horrendous punishment for Sisyphus which was to last all eternity: He was to roll an enormous boulder up a hill and just as he was about to reach the top, after much pain and sweat, the boulder would roll back to the bottom, forcing Sisyphus to descend the mountain and begin all over again.

The reason why this punishment is so horrifying to us is because the gods effectively rob Sisyphus's life of all meaning. His life becomes absurd, a bad joke, filled with strife and suffering from which there seems no escape. Camus, living through the horrors of the war, saw Sisyphus's predicament as mirroring human existence. Human life, he wrote, is fundamentally absurd (pp. 5–6). All of our efforts throughout history to overcome this absurdity and to infuse our life with meaning by appealing to some transcendent, absolute Truth—whether through art, love, religion, philosophy, or science—have ultimately failed. The horrors of World War II represented for Camus the chilling realization that underneath the surface of human invention, advancement, and progress lay the unavoidable reality of the absurd, waiting to break forth in the form of suffering, alienation, and despair.

Leonard Cohen's "Waiting for the Miracle" from the album *The Future* is an ironic echo of Camus's insight that if we base our life on the hope of some transcendent reality, some higher power, system, or science that will somehow make sense of everything, we're simply out of luck. It's obvious that the narrator of "Waiting for the Miracle" might as well be waiting for Godot. There is no miracle, so you might as well stop waiting and get on with your life.

Cohen is reminding us in this song of a real danger, the danger of missing the beauty and grace right in front of our noses because we have our heads in the clouds, worshipping idols of our own creation and thereby losing sight of the divine. If you obsess about perfection everything becomes ugly;

the maestro will sound like bubblegum and the beautiful woman (or man) in front of you who tells you that she loves you will be lost to the sands of time, unnoticed because she didn't fit some ideal notion of what a woman is supposed to be like.

Like Moses with his hammer, shattering Aaron's idol, Cohen brings us down to earth, because that's where the difficult but astoundingly beautiful business of being alive has to take place. As Cohen's teacher Roshi used to say: Heaven sounds like a great place but it doesn't have any restaurants or toilets.

Camus's philosophy is, to say the least, not exactly the most cheerful view of human existence (if Cohen is the High Priest of Pathos then Camus is the Pope of Doom). Yet he, just like Cohen, ultimately espouses a very life-affirming philosophy. Not content with diagnosing human suffering, Camus also suggests a way to overcome it. He claims that the more we run away from despair, the more we pretend that the absurd isn't there, the worse off we become. The absurd is, for Camus, like a quicksand, where the more you struggle and fight the more you are engulfed. The only answer is to let go, to stop fighting, and to stand still in the predicament.

The most traditional way by which we run away from the absurd is by trying to devise some belief system intended to make all of our fears and anxieties go away. This could include science, philosophy, entertainment, religion, art, or politics; whatever it is that makes us think we've got it all figured out, that we've found The Answer to life's great questions. Camus was deeply frightened by people who claim to have The Answer, given the fact that he had experienced Nazi occupation, and insistently claimed that there is no such thing, that our happiness, in fact, is dependent upon our resigning ourselves to the absurdity of life and to embrace its essential mystery.

When Cohen's narrator at the end of "Waiting for the Miracle" finally breaks, accepts love, and suggests marriage, it's not a breakdown at all but rather a building up. He (she?)

says to hell with perfection and accepts that the messy reality we live in is what is truly beautiful and that the idealized beauty he sought is actually monstrously ugly, as all idols ultimately are. This acceptance, as Camus and other existentialists tell us, is ultimately self-acceptance, *choosing* to be who we truly are instead of obsessing over some ridiculous, idealized notion of who we should be.

Camus, in the famous closing lines of *The Myth of Sisyphus*, says that we must imagine Sisyphus to be happy. If Sisyphus realizes the absurdity of his condition and embraces it, instead of gnashing his teeth or trying to escape the situation, he will be free. Make no mistake; he's still forced to roll the rock up the hill over and over again. There is, after all, no way to put an end to human strife or suffering in this life. Yet he is free to make of this situation whatever he wants. There is no absolute meaning behind what Sisyphus is doing so he himself must make it meaningful. Instead of feeling sorry for himself Sisyphus can light a cigarette, tighten up his gut, flip the gods off (sanctimonious bastards that they are), and roll that rock up the hill with a spring in his step and a smile on his face.

## Democracy Is Coming

Yet this is not to say that any of this is easy. Resignation is serious business, something that we strive for throughout our lives. We inevitably have ambiguous feelings about giving up on the old absolutes, the beliefs that have anchored us and given guidance throughout the ages. Cohen's song "The Future" is both a hilarious and a frightening reminder of this dilemma. Either we cling to ideologies that often result in (spiritual and physical) war and destruction or we fall into the dark seas of relativism where there are no absolutes and anything goes. The narrator of "The Future" is sickened by this modern age, plaintively crying out for Christ or Hiroshima, Stalin or Saint Paul, true good and evil, right and wrong, anything but this age of mediocrity and in-betweens.

This specter of relativism is among the most common objections to existentialist philosophy. Both Camus and Sartre blackened many a page attempting to exorcize it, arguing that existentialism is a kind of humanism, a belief that goodness is not dependent on the old gods but rather the solicitude of human beings. "'Everything is permitted' does not mean nothing is forbidden" (p. 67) Camus says, hoping to put to rest the fear so profoundly expressed by Dostoyevsky in *The Brothers Karamazov* that a world without God is a world without meaning; *any* meaning, human or otherwise.

Cohen's album *The Future* is a profound discussion of this issue, a dialectic, a back and forth where the horrifying chaos of "The Future" (where things become so unhinged that even white men start dancing) finds its resolution in the hopefulness of "Democracy." There is sorrow in the streets indeed, and some people (the homeless and the gay, to name a few) are ostracized and forgotten, a fact that runs like an ugly scar over the sickening smile of the American dream. Yet from this chaos, rising out of its ashes like a Phoenix, comes hope for truth and community, which is what this mythical concept "democracy" symbolizes for us. We may not understand the Sermon on the Mount, and we shouldn't even pretend to, because it's an invitation to a mystery, an invitation to a resignation where we let go of our prejudices and fears and abandon the entrenched beliefs that create inequality and hate. To embrace the absurd is to be neither left nor right. It is to recognize that the true greatness of a nation comes not from the might of its military or its political power but rather from a society that is open to all and where people embrace each other in their suffering.

Even though there are many existentialist themes in "Democracy," the song also points to a problematic element found in many of the existentialist writers, Camus included, namely that they often seem to be advocating a kind of individualism where we must seek meaning and truth apart from our fellow human beings, lone, tortured, Sisyphean heroes that we are. Even though Camus admirably went to great lengths to give an account of the social nature of the absurd hero, he never quite overcame this irritatingly macho tendency towards glorifying the lone wolf, the man apart (and I mean *man*).

Cohen, in songs such as "Democracy" and "Anthem" and especially in his famous "Hallelujah," seems to be hinting at a communion which extends beyond the cocky meaning-making grittiness of Camus. If love is "the only engine of survival," as Cohen says ("The Future"), then Kierkegaard, with his dark honesty and profound meditation on love, will help illustrate why Cohen's poetry and song are uplifting even in their sadness.

## The Hallelujah of Resignation

Søren Kierkegaard wrote his dark ruminations on God and human despair a good century before Camus faced the absurd. This melancholy Dane is generally considered the founding father of existentialism and his primary philosophical motivation was to critique what he saw as the spiritless and mechanical nature of the modern world, especially what he saw as the modern obsession with systematic thinking, of trying to devise some economic system, philosophy, or science that provides The Answer. Kierkegaard believed that the messy business of being human was much too complex to be contained within any system and thus suggested that we start our philosophizing with the subjective lived experience of the "poor existing individuals." Even though fancy systems can be pretty great they really aren't that much help on Boogie Street.

In one of his most famous works, *Fear and Trembling*, written under the pseudonym "Johannes de Silentio," Kierkegaard touches on many of the same issues we previously discussed from Camus's essay on Sisyphus. Yet Kierkegaard's absurd hero is not a figure from Greek mythology but rather the Old Testament figure Abraham, the father of faith, who was asked by God to sacrifice his only son Isaac on Mount Moriah. (Cohen's "Story of Isaac" explores the familiar story in an uncharacteristic way, from the son's perspective.) As Bob Dylan pointed out in his song "Highway

61," Abraham's initial answer to god was probably: "Man, you must be putting me on." But after that, being the *mensch* that he was, Abraham said "Yes" to God's command, proving his absolute faith and dedication.

Now, this decision obviously seems absolutely nuts, especially if the story is taken literally (which tends to be a terrible way of reading religious mythology in general). Some people have read Kierkegaard to be advocating for some kind of "divine command ethics," which basically means that whatever God says is good truly *is* good, no matter how evil it may seem. Kierkegaard actually makes a great deal of fun of this view in *Fear and Trembling*, meaning that such a literal interpretation is probably more than a little off base.

The story of Abraham is ultimately a symbolic one, and what it symbolizes is faith as love. Abraham doesn't have any rational knowledge of God's purpose, but he does know something about *who* God is. God had promised Abraham that he would bear a son and that this son would become the father of the nations. Abraham has absolute trust in God because he knows that his God is a God of love. His trust is so absolute that he believes that even if he were to sacrifice Isaac, God would not break his promise.

Which, of course, doesn't seem to make a whole lot of sense. But that's exactly the point, says Kierkegaard, the lover of the absurd. When Abraham says "yes" to God he moves beyond what Kierkegaard calls "the ethical" realm into "the religious." The ethical realm represents what can be rationally understood, our duties and responsibilities as determined by our position in life and our commitments. The religious, on the other hand, represents that which lies beyond the realm of the reasonable. It is to believe in the impossible, to sail beyond the harbors of what is normal and safe and to enter into the uncharted waters of risk and possibility. To live a "religious" life does not primarily mean going to certain kinds of services or saying certain kinds of prayers (Kierkegaard is one of the great critics of superficial religiousness). It means, rather, to be a certain kind of person, to say to hell with what is safe and comfortable. When someone says "I love you" we can't ask for some kind of scientific proof or philosophical theory that will prove their love to us. All we can do is take the plunge.

So resignation for Kierkegaard is not just about letting go of The Answer but also about letting go of yourself, which is what Cohen's beautiful "Hallelujah" encapsulates so well. The version made famous by John Cale and the late Jeff Buckley emphasizes the bitter in this bittersweet song, ending as it does with the notion that all our Hallelujahs are as cold as they are broken. In Cohen's original version from *Various Positions* the cynical view of these later versions, that love is only a game of one-upmanship, a matter of who shoots first, is overcome in a moment of faith where the ego is transcended and we realize that it really doesn't matter if our Hallelujahs are holy or broken, sacred or profane, as long as we sing them with all our might, for then every word will be ablaze with light and love. Even if it does all go wrong, if all our best-laid plans come to nothing, it's still worth risking it all, to take the leap into the unknown, to live a life that's not obsessed with safety or comfort but rather with generosity and love. If we live in this way we can stand, broken but proud, naked but unashamed, before the Lord of Song.

The human self is a constant work in process, Kierkegaard wrote in *The Sickness unto Death* (pp. 13–22). The path towards overcoming despair has not so much to do with gritting our teeth like Sisyphus and making our peace with the absurd but rather with constantly transcending ourselves, with letting go of our obsessions and our ego, and with committing ourselves to other people and to God (whatever we mean by that beautiful, mysterious word). In *Book of Mercy* Cohen writes: "Let me raise the brokenness to you, to the world where the breaking is for love" (psalm 49). We may never be perfect but that is exactly why we're capable of such great love, a love as great as God's. Suffering begets compassion, and compassion begets love. But this is only true as long as we resign ourselves to our brokenness and embrace it as the thread that binds us to our fellow human beings who also suffer. We're all citizens of Boogie Street.

Without that resignation we can neither offer love nor accept it. As Cohen puts it again in *Book of Mercy*: "Why do you welcome me? asks the bitter heart. Why do you comfort me? asks the heart that is not broken enough" (psalm 40).

The term "joyful sorrow," which originated in ancient Christian mysticism, perfectly encapsulates the beauty of Cohen's art. There is, indeed, a great deal of darkness in the broken night. Yet Cohen reminds us that in that darkness there is light, in the sorrow there is joy. Cohen's songs are uplifting *because* they are dark, unlike the cornucopia of sugary pop songs that assail us from the airwaves and which do nothing but exacerbate our despair with their forced "happiness" (if anyone is the grand master of melancholia it's Justin Bieber, God bless him). The existentialism in Cohen's art is the hopeful reassurance that our sadness is an essential part of what makes us human and that it is deeply intertwined with our joy. The fact that we're not perfect, that we are shy and anxious and confused and suffering, is what makes us capable of love, which, as the poet W.H. Auden pointed out, is what being happy truly means. Or, as Leonard Cohen put it, "that's how the light gets in."

# 3
# Why Cohen's Our Man

WIELAND SCHWANEBECK

Over the course of his career as a singer and songwriter (not to mention poet, philosopher, ladies' man, and bearer of the gift of a golden voice), not only has Leonard Cohen been on a quest to spread wisdom and precious melancholia to the sounds of his guitar, and (lately) to outperform Bob Dylan as the most diligent touring artist in the world, but also he seems to have embarked on a personal mission to dedicate a song to every female first name there is. Yet don't let all those Heathers, Suzannes, Mariannes, and Nancys fool you: the number of women he name-checks is no match for the variety of masculinities in his work, even though men are not as frequently evoked in name or shape. Already in 1970, Cohen's fellow countryman Michael Ondaatje (in *Leonard Cohen*) was one of the first to draw attention to the abundance of different masculinities in Cohen—better known as a poet than a singer back then—including "the magician, the wit, the aesthete, the wounded man"; Cohen's women, on the other hand, tended to be "dangerously similar" (p. 13). This observation holds just as true for the impressive song catalogue Cohen has assembled over the decades, in which femininity always appears in similar embodiments: angels of compassion, sisters of mercy, and ladies of solitude.

By looking at the masculinities evoked in Cohen's songs (and his very own versatile performance as a singer and songwriter), we can better assess the quality of his writing and his insight into human nature, for Leonard Cohen has a lot to say about gender relations and the dubious nature of traditional gender images. So let's apply some Johnny Walker wisdom and find out just how many different masculinities Cohen's songs and stage performances offer, why there is no contradiction between his stable image as a wise and witty singer-songwriter and the idea of embodying different masculinities, and how he continues to inspire both men and women to "become naked in their different ways" for him ("Because Of")—okay, so we may not really get to the bottom of the last one. There is only so much that philosophy can do.

What I will talk about is not Cohen the man but rather the "lyrical self," a concept that literary scholars use in order to avoid confusion between the historical person who wrote the poem (the author) and the voice that is speaking in the poem. The lyrical self is a handy tool to use to avoid upsetting Mrs. Shakespeare, for instance, because otherwise we'd be speculating about how many of her husband's 154 sonnets were dedicated to others he may have had a crush on. It is linked to the concept of the persona in the performing arts, a term originally applied to ancient Greek theater masks which—through their exaggerated features (a sad face, a laughing face)—helped the audience members distinguish between characters. In the modern age, we sometimes talk about a persona adopted by an actor who is nothing like the characters he plays on stage or on screen, but who tends to play similar roles, resulting in his audience's inability to distinguish between the real person and the type of character he plays. The same thing can happen to tenants in the Tower of Song, of course.

So for the time being, let's just assume that the following remarks don't directly concern Leonard Cohen himself, but rather the fictitious man who comes alive in the music and lyrics that are written and performed by the actual Leonard Cohen. The former makes frequent appearances in the latter's verse—not only in spirit but also in name, be it as

"L. Cohen," the signer of the dreariest holiday card ever ("Famous Blue Raincoat") or as "Leonard," the self-deprecating, lazy bastard that lives in his suit ("Going Home").

## He's Our Man, and Then Some

In one of his most enduring anthems (and one which he continues to perform in his concerts to this very day), Leonard Cohen tells his audience, "I'm your man." Having performed the song over the course of nearly three decades, Cohen still pulls off a remarkable feat that is part of the crooner's handbook: making each audience member believe that she or he alone is the sole addressee of this promise. But the statement can also be read in a slightly different way, for unlike other languages, English does not distinguish between the second person singular and plural: not only does it remain ambiguous who exactly "you" is, but also how many people are meant ("you" the individual, or "you" the crowd). If Leonard is different people's man, then this would mean that he can be different people's *idea* of a man, and oh boy (or should that be, "oh man"?), can these ideas differ!

Maybe you've heard: there's "a war between the man and the woman" ("There Is a War"). It's been going on for some time, but turned into a full-on academic battle of the sexes (and genders) in the twentieth century, as feminism became far more prominent in the Western world, especially throughout the 1960s and 1970s, even though some people slept through those wild years in a room in the Chelsea Hotel. Feminists challenged much of traditional Western philosophy and thought, fighting against social injustice and for political participation, killing one or another ladies' man in the process. It took some time, however, before men, rather than being merely attacked for the injustices they had wreaked, became studied and theorized *as men*. It wasn't until a few years later—around the same time Leonard Cohen wrote said song, which you can find on the album of the same name—that men and masculinities were examined in a variety of fields, which even resulted in the founding of a new academic discipline: first known as Men's Studies, later as Masculinity Studies.

Up until then, men had played a surprisingly small role in the field of Gender Studies, which was more or less synonymous with the study of women. Yet by focusing mostly on women, much of the story remains untold, for we can only hope to improve society gender-wise if we acknowledge that part of the reason women (or members of the LGBT community) often get treated so unfairly is that so many dominant notions of masculinity are just never questioned. Though it is their task to put received wisdom in doubt and to question what we take for granted, many philosophers have contributed to this state of things. Many of them (including Aristotle, Friedrich Nietzsche, and Arthur Schopenhauer) not only took the dominance of men for granted, but also assumed that women have limited intellectual capacities.

At the same time, it's not exactly like the majority of men were crying out to subject themselves to the critical eye of sociologists or psychoanalysts. On the contrary, when feminists called out for the boys to sing another song (as the previous one had grown old and bitter), most of them turned a deaf ear. It took some time for middle-class white men to understand, as Michael Kimmel put it, "that race, class, and gender didn't refer only to other people, who were marginalized by race, class, or gender privilege," and that they had been pretending their masculinity was invisible, as if "gender applied only to women" *(The Gendered Society,* pp. 6–7).

Since putting the category of masculinity on the map, scholars in Masculinity Studies have dedicated a lot to coming to terms with several ideas that seem mutually exclusive at first sight: that masculinity is, on the one hand, privileged yet somehow also, on the other, troubled by contrasting demands; that in a patriarchal society, men are generally considered the more powerful group, yet this pressure can simultaneously lead to expectations nobody can really fulfill; and—maybe the weirdest paradox of them all—that masculinity is perceived as something that is steadfast and reliable, but also in flux all the time—in other words, "a man is still a man," even though he's constantly "passing through."

Leonard Cohen's songs reflect this strange predicament. A large part of his work's appeal can be traced back to it, for he seems able to deliver any kind of masculinity his audience could possibly want. Sometimes we need him naked, sometimes we need him wild, and Leonard-the-singer is extremely versatile as he adopts a variety of male disguises, all of which come with their very own history of manhood and involve not just *old* ideas, but really *ancient* ones. Like the lovers he sings about in "Hey, That's No Way to Say Goodbye," Cohen's men are not new and many have been there before them, but the gallery he assembles is still impressive. There is the suave, fearless "Field Commander Cohen," the super-spy who crashes diplomatic cocktail parties and nearly drives Castro out of Cuba (not even 007 succeeded on this front). There are countless soldiers, some of them fighting in the army of Joan of Arc, some of them fighting for children of snow ("Winter Lady"). And there are all kinds of religious men: rabbis, Biblical shepherds, saints, and pilgrims (many of which symbols have certainly been inspired by Leonard's own spiritual guide, the legendary Roshi).

It is very tempting to see Leonard Cohen not just as someone whose songs are brimming with archaic male images (even the knight in "Bird on the Wire" is borrowed from "some old-fashioned book"), but also as someone wholeheartedly in favor of this kind of manhood: the enigmatic stranger who will leave you in the morning, the deserting soldier, the eternal pilgrim—all of whom struggle with companionship and prefer to remain alone, renting rooms in the Tower of Song or browsing through their very own Book of Longing. Hollywood film producers evidently went with this first association, the enigmatic stranger, and have employed Cohen's music accordingly (in addition to casting Cohen himself as the mysterious François Zolan in a 1986 episode of *Miami Vice*). If you want to learn his songs exclusively through film soundtracks, then brace yourself for a rough ride through the most male-centered movie genres you can think of: the Western (Robert Altman's *McCabe & Mrs. Miller*, 1970), the action movie (John Badham's *Bird on a Wire*, 1990), the serial-killer film (Oliver Stone's *Natural Born Killers*, 1994), or the superhero tale (Zack Snyder's *Watchmen*, 2009). But there is more to it, for the masculinities advertised in Cohen's lyrics are not as simple and straightforward as they appear at first glance. This is philosophy, after all—the only field where you can tell people about a mysterious stranger or about Superman and they will think Albert Camus (not Clint Eastwood) and Friedrich Nietzsche (not the last survivor of Krypton).

## Working for Our Smile

You didn't think it was that easy, did you? Just when we thought we had him categorized as the favorite balladeer of cowboys, sportsmen, and shepherds, a more careful glance reveals Cohen's masculinities to be a lot more elusive than that. He is not one of your typical guys to hang out with, even though one of his most famous songs has him brag about sexual favors received from a then-unidentified if later revealed fellow celebrity ("Chelsea Hotel #2")—a rare kiss-and-tell, but maybe it doesn't count if you sing it. We owe Leonard Cohen a thorough reading of his lyrics, if only in order to find out that masculinity is a little more complicated and that we have to acknowledge various positions, not just one.

One major factor that puts a twist on Cohen's masculinities is his well-known association with Jewish faith and tradition, which can be grasped in many of his songs. Historically, Jewish men were frequently subjected to mockery and discrimination, especially since the Jewish people have so often suffered persecution and injustice. Following centuries of marginalization and violence against Jews, this anti-Semitic heritage prevails in the form of stereotypes that are everywhere in popular culture. The classic comedy *Airplane!* (1980), for example, features a scene where one of the passengers asks the flight attendant for a bit of light reading, and is handed a suspiciously slim pamphlet about "Famous Jewish Sports Legends."

The alleged lack of athletic skill is just one of the stereotypes about Jewish men that can overshadow other, more important achievements: Woody Allen keeps telling interviewers that he was neither a bookworm nor a troubled existentialist in his youth but a gifted athlete, but somehow, it hasn't really affected his persona. According to other, equally dominant stereotypes, Jewish men are associated with virtues such as wisdom and religious scholarship, which results in their being depicted in cartoons throughout history as hunched over books and wearing glasses. Thus, as Harry Brod says in "Jewish Men," oppositions such as "mind over body, or brains over brawn," are very important "in the lives of Jewish men, resulting in the life of the mind becoming valued and overvalued as a source of Jewish male identity" ( p. 442). All this amounts to a denigration of male Jews as somewhat incomplete men—"real men" don't read but lead, and when they get into a dispute, they prefer to rely on their fists instead of well-crafted arguments.

Cohen himself often acknowledges these stereotypes and addresses them in his songs, sometimes with cynicism and anger (like when he identifies with the money lender or "the very reverend Freud" in "Is This What You Wanted"), but usually with irony and self-deprecating wit. He frequently reminds us of an inconvenient truth that anti-Semites will find hard to stomach: it is the Jewish tradition which is at the heart of Christian culture, and not just because it was a "little Jew who wrote the Bible" ("The Future"). One strategy which Cohen often resorts to in order to put a spin on stereotypes is to seemingly embrace and affirm them, before turning them all the more strikingly on their head—which means we have to add Socrates and his elaborate use of irony to the list of Cohen's spiritual ancestors. Cohen's pilgrims and saints, for instance, are not quite as pure and abstinent as you might think: On one occasion, Leonard practices on his sainthood, giving generously to everyone, before we're informed that all he's interested in is building a reputation for himself as virtuous so as to impress a woman ("Came So Far for Beauty"). Master-pupil relationships are similarly infused with sexual undertones ("Master Song").

Similarly, we may have said that archaic images of respected kinds of manhood prevail in Cohen's songs, but that doesn't stop him from mocking them wherever he can. The Old Testament world that his characters inhabit offers plenty of occasions for this, with its sheer endless story about the most dysfunctional family you can think of, where "murder, theft, deception, and other crimes too numerous to mention" are the rule rather than the exception ("Jewish Men," p. 441). The Old Testament may teach us to obey our parents and instruct wives to remain under the authority of their husbands, but what a world dominated by these stern patriarchal views would look like is frequently illustrated in Cohen's songs—and it is hardly the Garden of Eden which the listener will be reminded of. Cohen adapts the well-known "Story of Isaac" to show where father can lead son, and that it is a truly terrible world in which fathers are willing to sacrifice their children because they believe themselves to be on a divine mission. For the sons, inheriting the world and its rulebook from their fathers carries all kinds of burdens and obstacles, and you'll often find them rejecting the legacy, or begging their fathers to change their names which are "covered up / with fear and filth and cowardice and shame" ("Lover Lover Lover"). And troubled manhood doesn't end here.

Even if you are part of the pantheon of male role models, you can still fall short of the ideal. Sure, Cohen's lyrical self often claims to be a soldier or a proud captain—but what good are these ranks if you are not part of the winning army in a battle, but a partisan whose side has already lost and who is now at the mercy of old women ("The Partisan")? A cowboy who is neither patrolling the frontier nor protecting a town from bandits but one whose horse has run away ("Ballad of the Absent Mare")? A captain whose ship is either leaking ("Everybody Knows") or has not even been built ("Heart with No Companion"), or whose crew has left him

("The Captain")? All these examples show that the uniforms and badges which allegedly make a man are easy to mock—and, more troublingly for the men in question, they are even easier to mimic. Anybody, as Cohen himself will tell you, can pin an iron cross to his lapel, walk up to "the tallest and the blondest girl," and ask her to remove her clothes ("Memories"), and the idea that much-admired men, whom young boys are supposed to look up to in order to learn about the importance of duty and ethics, might be frauds and impostors can be difficult to handle.

Some men (biological essentialists) thus take the view that a "real man" should not be defined by the medals he has won or the ideas he has created, but mainly by his alleged genetic "nature": what they mean usually amounts to a dangerous cocktail of chromosomes, testosterone, and primary sexual characteristics. Is Cohen one of those guys because of the jokes he heaps on military men and sailors? Absolutely not. If anything, his humor turns even darker when he considers the kind of man who likes to eat meat, or who feels some kind of primordial beast awakening in him. Some of them are gently reminded that a mighty erection might not be the best of advisors ("Don't Go Home with Your Hard-on"), some of them are lampooned for howling with the wolves ("I'm Your Man"). And don't forget the artwork of that particular record: *I'm Your Man* comes with a photo of Cohen, the most enigmatic singer-songwriter, holding a peeled banana. The raw and uncivilized idea of a man comes dangerously close to an ape—not really a creature you'd want to model your gender identity on.

## Giving Us All He's Got

His rejection of a biological approach to gender and masculinity brings us to Cohen-the-performer, one (and, since the launch of his monumental world tour in 2008, maybe the most popular) of Leonard Cohen's various fields of activity as an artist. Within Gender Studies, the concept of performance and performativity is linked to one of the most influential and radical theories of the recent past. Few thinkers are as strongly opposed to defining relationships between men and women solely on the basis of their biological makeup as Judith Butler. In her groundbreaking book, *Gender Trouble* (1990), Butler introduces the idea that the classic distinction between sex (as biological) and gender (as cultural) does not hold up, that the very idea of sex is culturally produced as well, and that gender must be thought of as something that is *performed* (rather than embodied) by individuals. Masculinity, for instance, is something that has to be fought for, defended, proven, and put into practice time and again: when talking to friends, when building a career, when competing out on the sports field.

According to Butler, although traditional accounts of gender are based on the idea of original gender ideals, the latter are just a myth: it is only in the act of performing femininity and masculinity that the idea of the gender ideals comes about in the first place: "an expectation that ends up producing the very phenomenon that it anticipates" (p. xv). This theory of gender identities seems to fit contemporary culture, especially the music business, where most people want to experience their favorite artists, whether pop sensations or renowned singer-songwriters, live on stage, as opposed to merely listening to their records. Legendary artists like Bob Dylan or Leonard Cohen, who have played thousands of concerts in the course of their careers, have always relied on direct interaction with their audience to build their reputation.

Leonard Cohen's masculinity is much more than the sum of his lyrics. If there is one thing that the audience members who have attended one of Cohen's more than 300 concerts since he started touring again in 2008 can agree on, it is that Cohen, much like the wine that is flowing in his songs ("The Guests"), has aged remarkably well. Being in your seventies appears to liberate you from what current fashion dictates, for once you have been around long enough to witness styles blossom, wither, and perish before getting repackaged as nostalgia, you have pretty much earned the privilege of creating your own style. His trademark suit and fedora might make

Cohen resemble last century's man rather than "Last Year's Man," but here is a man so comfortable in his skin that he won't mind appearing out of date to some people—he is timeless to others.

Cohen's suave performance onstage is unlikely to be pigeonholed as modern-day dandyism, for not only is he generous with smiles and frequently bows to the audience and his fellow musicians, he also adopts different masculinities throughout the performance, being neither averse to clowning and self-mockery (listen to the recording of his 2008 London concert and his hilarious monologue on the various anti-depressants he has been on) nor to sprinkling the concert with little moments of ambiguity, which add to his performance even more layers of significance. Occasionally, Cohen will kneel during a song, which can carry wildly different meanings depending on the context—he may be taking time for a little prayer (a pilgrim who has seen the angels, "the sublime Webb Sisters"), he may be serenading an absent mistress or his "shepherd of strings," Javier Mas, like a devoted fan or even a gay lover. Either way, Cohen's masculine performance is powerful enough to be taken seriously while still remaining in flux and ironical, driving home Butler's point that true gender identity is a fiction, always "an imitation without an origin" (p. 188).

In this way, Cohen's songs ultimately answer the question "What is a real man?" by putting this very idea into doubt. If there were such a thing, of course, he'd "know that kind of man" ("The Stranger Song"). He knows them all.

# 4
# The End of the World and Other Times in *The Future*

GARY SHAPIRO

In an interview with his biographer Sylvie Simmons, Leonard Cohen identifies the main interests in his work as "women, song, religion" (p. 280). These are not merely personal concerns for Cohen, they are dimensions of the world that he tries to understand as a poet, singer, and thinker.

Now it's something of a cliché to see the modern romantic or post-romantic singer or poet in terms of personal struggles, failures, triumphs, and reversals. Poets sometimes respond by adopting elusive, ironic, enigmatic, or parodic voices: think, in their different ways, of Bob Dylan and Anne Carson. Yet Cohen has always worn his heart on his sleeve or some less clothed part of his body: he let us know, for example, that Janis Joplin gave him head in the Chelsea hotel while their celebrity limos were waiting outside. We want to know all about Suzanne, Marianne, and the sisters of mercy (two traveling young women whom he gave chaste shelter one night). Cohen's many biographers are obsessed with his loves, depression, career ups and downs, Montreal Jewish origins, Buddhist practice and monastic retreats.

Recently, provoked in part by the album *Old Ideas*, and an ambitious, successful world tour, Cohen's public has shown interest in how he is dealing with aging, or more subtly, with the artist's meeting the challenge of the late career. Rather than focusing on Cohen's life (multiple biographies already exist) I want to think with him about the meaning—or more specifically meanings—of time, a theme he clearly addresses in the album *The Future* (1992). As the Christian philosopher Augustine said about time, we all think that we know what it is until we ask ourselves to define it.

## Meanings of Time

In *The Future* Cohen asks and finds some answers. Let's begin by looking at the first two songs, one about the end of time, the other about endless waiting, and then ask if these are the only ways of experiencing time in Cohen's universe. The title song evokes a vision of an apocalypse at the end of time. "Waiting for the Miracle" is a dark anatomy of a life based on deferral, on putting things off. We all want "Democracy" but when and how will it come? "Closing Time" is the hour when the bar closes, yet possibly time itself is closing. All lovers, Cohen says (covering a classic Irving Berlin song), should vow eternal love, love "always." These songs concern the experience—more precisely a range of various actual and possible experiences—of time. They deal with what philosophers call the phenomenology of time: sudden and startling change, interruption, boredom, anticipation of major events, and vows of eternal fidelity. Cohen invites us to think our way through a spectrum of ways of experiencing time ("temporalities," some would say). *The Future* consistently interrogates time. It explores and articulates different forms of temporality from religious, romantic, political, and artistic perspectives. It invites us to think about whether and how we can live these different times and how they are related.

## The Future as Apocalypse

In the lead song Cohen—or his prophetic persona—identifies himself as a servant of an unnamed higher power. His mission is to tell us of the vision of the future he's been granted. That future is murder. It teems with grotesque scenes of torture, fire, and phantoms. In this future we might as well abort fetuses and destroy the last trees. Readers of the Biblical Apocalypse will recognize imagery drawn from that story about the end of the world, yet it is updated and filled with our time's obsessive fears. Dehumanization, environmental disaster, loss of individuality and privacy, terror and humiliation are what the future has in store. Cohen's future gives a voice to our fears.

"The Future," speaks prophetically from the standpoint of a world lost or transformed—post-catastrophe, post-disaster (after the final turn, after the terrible misalignment of the stars). Whether through the emergence of the beast from the abyss and Antichrist (as in Christian tradition), or in more contemporary terms through war, environmental collapse, pandemic, domination by a society of total surveillance, or global capitalism, from this visionary site the dreadful has already happened. Everything is over. This is why Cohen calls for the restoration of the Berlin Wall, of Stalin and Saint Paul.

Yet why does the singer cry for the return of barriers and order, even those of tyranny, religious orthodoxy, and the Cold War? Christian theology offers a clue when it teaches that there is a "restraining force," in Greek a *katechon*, that holds back the coming of the Antichrist and the world's end. The Biblical source is the Second Letter to the Thessalonians attributed (doubtfully) to Paul; it speaks obscurely of a *katechon* in order to discourage premature expectations of the final tribulations and Christ's return. From the song's perspective, the *katechon* no longer works, the future we had hoped to delay is here: it is murder. Here is one perspective on time on the largest scale. Time as we know it can come to an end. In "The Future" there no longer is a future. It is a future robbed of futurity, of any sense of open possibility.

The song begins with regret for a time that has been lost, a world that no longer exists. The singer (or chanter) wants back what has been taken. But this is not the deep unease with "time and its 'it was'" that Friedrich Nietzsche analyzed as the deepest core of human resentment. It is a cry of distress at the loss of a specific kind of life that's no longer possible in the future. What disappeared was a private, secret life reflected infinitely in a mirrored room. The catastrophe involves the disappearance of walls and borders within which the singer could enjoy his former broken nights, including delights like anal sex.

Assuming a prophetic persona that owes much to both Jewish and Christian Biblical traditions (Simmons calls it "Jeremiah in Tin-Pan Alley") Cohen speaks (like Isaiah or Ezekiel) as a servant told to say with absolute chilling clarity that "it's over." Like Isaiah and Ezekiel he's seen nations triumph and decline. The "nations" are those peoples whose successions and relations constitute world history, the time of the world. That history comes to an end in "The Future." Whether we think of the tribulations of the last days foretold by Hebrew prophets or John's Apocalypse (which owes much to contemporary Jewish texts), or more recent fears of total disaster, it means that we are beyond measure, over the threshold, in a world of phantoms, road fires, your inverted and suspended woman, lousy Charles Manson–like poets, and the dancing white man. These can all be heard as rewritings of passages in Isaiah and Ezekiel (for example, see Isaiah 3:17–23 on the upside-down woman). The dancing white man surrenders his traditional position as privileged spectator and now becomes the spectacle. All that's left to do, the voice bitterly declares, is to join in the general murder and destruction, including abortion and ecocide.

The refrain exhibits Cohen's mastery of ironic ambiguity, not knowing what "they" meant by "repent." Does the prophet fail to understand his own instruction? Or is he channeling Spinoza, who said that "one who repents is doubly unhappy and weak"? And who's claiming credit as the Bible's Jewish author? Is it God, traditional author of the Pentateuch through Moses, the actual writers who severely edited and added to older texts, or Cohen himself, who here and elsewhere rewrites the Bible? Questions about time have yet to be answered.

## Waiting for the Miracle

The end-of-the-world scenario is only one form of time that Cohen sings of on this album. If the main point of view in the first song is theological and cosmic, the second, "Waiting for the Miracle," mercilessly reveals the very private life of lovers who've repeatedly postponed their union, perhaps until it's too late. No doubt we all dwell on those moments when "if only" we had responded to that invitation, taken that chance, or chosen a different path everything would have been better and different. It's all about missing the right time, failing to seize the opportunity, because we vaguely imagined that a miracle—something totally outside our power—would come along, resolving our life's uncertainties and indecisions. There may also be the suggestion that the poet too waits passively and too long for his inspiration. While Cohen speaks to a single person, the "I" and the "you" here could be anybody, could be you.

Stoic philosophers, like Seneca and Marcus Aurelius, harshly criticize the conventional time experience of waiting and deferral. Instead we should be alert for the opportune time, the temporary imbalance that provides an opening that could be seized to effect a major transformation of individual or collective life. In "Waiting for the Miracle" Cohen gives a stronger and more moving critique of waiting than do the Stoics. The song explores the dark side of delay and deferral, the time of the *katechon* in which we stretch out time to the maximum, fearing to take a chance or make a decision. The singer confesses to wasting his time, waiting for the miracle. Waiting here is the dark side of mere succession, of time as one damn thing after another, the devouring time that the Greeks call *chronos* and which the philosopher John Locke termed "perpetual perishing." The miracle would be (in Greek thought) the *kairos*, the transformative, decisive event or opportunity, the opposite of *chronos*. Cohen sometimes calls it a "transcendental moment," showing that he too can use a philosophical vocabulary. In this song the miraculous *kairos* is a wan hope, the dream of someone who's collapsed on the road of life, lying in the rain, drenched in regret.

Sylvie Simmons interprets this song and the album as Cohen's proposal of marriage to Rebecca de Mornay. This would surely be one of the most melancholy proposals imaginable, since he'd be asking the lover to adopt a life of parallel solitude with him while they continue to wait for the miraculous event. But if we understood the collection of songs from this point of view, we might be haunted by the suspicion that it is composed in a somewhat private lovers' language. In this light the album cover illustration—a bird, a heart, an open pair of handcuffs—invites speculation about binding and unbinding in several registers, and presents a number of interpretive options. Perhaps more specifically it's the emblem of ambivalence. Love (the heart) serves as a perch for either being proverbially "free as a bird" or the "bird on the wire," who, like Cohen, has no choice but to sing. Open handcuffs suggest the play of restraint and captivity, maybe an S-M bondage game, one that both highlights the theme and questions any simple opposition of freedom and bondage.

Whether or not the entire album should be construed as a marriage proposal, the one extended by the singer of "Waiting for the Miracle" invites much thought about love, time, and song. In this song it is always already too late. Life has been wasted and youth spent in the waiting process. The miracle is not the object of faith, which holds with passion to the coming event, or of hope, which still believes in possibility. But mere waiting for what may or may not come lacks both passion and a living sense of possibility. In the passive mode, giving oneself over to undifferentiated *chronos*, there's "nothing left to do." Pointless waiting and disappointed expectations are of course a major theme of the blues, which typically give voice to the downside of *chronos*, the feeling of futility, often announced by phrases like "Woke up this morning. . . ." In "Be for Real," one of two covers in this album, the singer who has a history of being hurt by his lover, fears being hurt again (and again) if she returns. "Waiting for the Miracle" differs from blues songs that lament a more or less datable loss (like your lover dumping you) because it records and regrets a failure to act, to seize the moment. Heard this way it reflects on the loss of time itself; it leads to thinking of an experience of time as loss.

We could read Cohen's song alongside Nietzsche's aphorism on "*The problem of those who wait*" in *Beyond Good and Evil* (section 274). Here Nietzsche writes like a Stoic, seeing most human beings as aimlessly waiting: "in every corner of the earth people sit waiting, hardly knowing how much they are waiting, much less that they are waiting in vain. And every once in a while, the alarm call will come too late. . . ." The genius of Cohen's song is its foregrounding the consciousness of waiting and realizing only too late that it is too late and time has gotten away from you irretrievably. "I didn't see the time / I waited half my life away." Waiting means that invitations or opportunities were declined. There was the passive expectation that "the great event" would simply manifest itself. The alternative, Nietzsche implies, is vigilance, readiness to seize *kairos* by the forelock. One of Cohen's most unusual pieces (on the collection *More Best of Leonard Cohen*) is a short statement, read by a robotic female voice, called "The Great Event," which says that time will be renewed "next Tuesday" when he/she plays the "Midnight Sonata" backwards.

Recall here the ancient figure of *kairos*. This personified image of opportunity has two pairs of wings, one growing from his back, one sprouting from his ankles. He is typically represented as holding a scale which is out of balance. That is, the time he announces is one in which things are shifting and rearranging themselves. Circumstances are open briefly to being mastered if we can read the signs of the times. We must literally seize the time, adroitly grasping the shock of hair at the front of his head. Otherwise, we'll be left in the lurch as we see the bald back of his head quickly speeding by. In contrast, a Cohen song about seizing *kairos* by the forelock is "First We Take Manhattan." There the singer declares that he was sentenced to "twenty years of boredom for trying to change the system from within." Rather than grasping the opportune moment when things are imbalanced, he submitted himself to the routines of the system, to the bureaucratic measured time that eats away at spontaneous life and keeps us going with promises of gradual change or the expectation of secure retirement.

## Happy Times: Let's All Get Naked

So is time coming to a terrible, final end or are we condemned (possibly self-condemned) to lead a life of eternal waiting in some limbo condition? This is the question posed by the two opening songs of *The Future*. With this question in mind, let's return to Cohen's three great interests—women, song, religion—seeing them from the perspective of prophecy and salvation (if we were to explore this from a biographical perspective, we could dwell on Cohen's close study of the prophet Isaiah with his rabbinical grandfather). These seem to coincide in an apocalyptic thematic of the glorified body and songs of divine praise and celebration.

Apocalypse is not only a final end it is also nakedness, a favorite Cohen theme. So, a brief note on language: in the Greco-Jewish translation of the Hebrew scriptures (known as the Septuagint) the Greek word *apokalypsis* was used as the equivalent of the Hebrew *gala*, which means uncovering or denuding. Biblical apocalypse and Cohen's frequent image of happiness, then, are both simultaneously revelation and denuding. I am less interested in uncovering the naked Leonard than in understanding Cohen's theme of nakedness (starker than mere nudity) in its full apocalyptic sense. When we are naked everything's been revealed and the final truth is unavoidable. Characteristically, Cohen says (adding his own words to his cover of a song by Frederick Knight) he is interested only in naked truth ("Be for Real"). The woman's naked body is a signature Cohen image, often expressed in religious language, as in "Light as the Breeze," where the lover's adoration is presented as a celebration of the glorious body. There he preaches adoration of the woman's body, prescribes a kneeling posture for devotion, and compares the sexual delta to the confluence of the river and the sea. The last image suggests a way of making contact with the oceanic or cosmic. This is the worship of the absolute, the alpha and omega (a phrase out of Apocalypse) or beginning and end of all things. Recording his own devotions, Cohen says he knelt like a believer, received something like a heavenly benediction, and achieved a glorious moment of peace. Theologically speaking, we might say he was participating in that life of salvation where all work is completed and there is nothing left to do but to give praise. If the choir of the saved and the angels sing hymns to God then, Cohen's "spiritual" addresses the naked body of the beloved.

This concatenation of questions around the theme of nakedness is especially strong in the verse of "Waiting for the Miracle" where Cohen says that he dreamed of his mostly naked lover, also waiting, as the sands of time ran through her hands. Yet some of her was light, perhaps the light, as he says in "Anthem," that comes through the cracks in everything and opens up another spiritual dimension.

## Beginning Again, Ending Again, Escaping Time

Let's consider the remaining songs on *The Future* which broaden the spectrum of temporal experience and provide alternatives to the dichotomy of terrible end or endless waiting posed by the first two pieces. "Anthem" is all about beginnings and persistence in a world where wars continue, the "holy dove" is caught and commodified, and there's no point in trying to make a "perfect offering" (this may allude to ritual sacrifices precisely specified in Leviticus and Deuteronomy). Every day at dawn the birds sing and begin anew. The singer not only heard them doing this, he heard them *saying* it. Song is a repeated litany of new beginnings, not just pointless waiting or a repeated round of suffering. Cohen provides his own version of those New World thinkers Emerson and Thoreau, who celebrate the promise of life in each fresh morning. Authentic beginning requires freedom from unnecessary, excessive concern with the past and future. In contrast to this mode of renewal through song, there are "signs" of the failure of governments and the continuing rule of hypocritical killers who disguise themselves through public piety. World history is a succession of ruins. And despite this, the world, as evidenced by the birds of dawn, is not a closed totality. The future is still open, but how? Somewhat enigmatically Cohen discloses that despite everything "There is a crack in everything / That's how the light gets in."

Here Cohen may be channeling a Gnostic thought: in this flawed world, created perhaps by a malevolent god (not God), some inkling of salvation or light nevertheless becomes evident through its very flaws and cracks. Contrast this with the framework of Jewish and Christian monotheism that give a sense to apocalyptic times in the lead song. These traditional religions see creation and salvation as involving the acts of a single deity. The world and its history are redeemed by the same God who created them. In Gnosticism—a philosophical and religious view that competed vigorously with early Christianity—the world is hopelessly irredeemable, the product of an evil or minor god (sometimes called a demiurge, following Plato). Yet there are uncanny cracks in the oppressive order of the created world, cracks allowing a metaphysical or spiritual light to appear. Escape from the miserable world is not through a sacred history developing within it (for example, from Adam through Abraham and Jesus and finally the end of days). Liberation depends on seizing the opportunity offered by the bits of light that get through the cracks. Deep down we are all sparks of pure light that can be awakened in the right circumstances.

So is Cohen a Gnostic? I prefer to think that he borrows a Gnostic metaphor to articulate the struggle to free oneself from the fallen world; perhaps Gnostic ideas filtered down to him from the Jewish Kabbalistic tradition. In "Anthem" he adapts the Gnostic motif of the cracks that let dazzling bits of light shine through the world's darkness. It is the anthem of a campaign or conflict, but of what kind? A struggle carried on without regard to time and future by those who sing, whether dawn's birds or midnight's poets? Or does the poet promise to engage with the world when he vows that the unnamed malevolent powers will hear from him? Yet he says this without much force and the march has no drum.

I have been suggesting that while the album *The Future* is about time, no single theory, view, perspective, or attitude with regard to time takes precedence over the others. Rather than taking this as a sign of incoherence, we might see it as a kind of *lyrical phenomenology* of time, in which an array of experiences and understandings of time is given voice. At some points shifts in tone invite us to think about shifts in temporal focus. "Anthem" ends by calling for a march, but notes that there are no drums; as if in response, the next song "Democracy" begins with a lively upbeat drumming march. If "Anthem" is ambivalent about activist engagement, the words and tone of "Democracy" are full of militant hope and enthusiasm. "Democracy" is coming, we're repeatedly told, although it's uncertain what its mode of being is: "it's real" but not "exactly there."

I would be surprised if Cohen were familiar with Jacques Derrida's idea of "the democracy to come" (p. 104), but I think we can use it to make sense of this militant, hopeful song. Derrida talks about the "e-vent," the unexpected, unpredictable, incalculable, surprising future which arrives, not in the form of a specific state of things (like a new constitution, governmental reforms, and so on) but that which is *always* to come.

Our vision of a full democracy should always be expanding as we respond to more calls for inclusion. Its shimmering spectral reality is the shadow that the future in process, always still to be determined, casts on the present and the past. It's not impotent waiting but enthusiastic expectation. Each verse of the song begins by declaring "It's coming. . . " and names fermenting, chaotic sites and provocations that elicit democracy from "a crack in the wall." The crack of course recalls the crack that lets the light in ("Anthem"). But now the crack is *in the wall*. Walls mark borders defining the power of states whose sovereignty restricts the spontaneous and autonomous activity of the people. Walls suggest social and political divisions that constrict democracy. Cohen deploys an extensive, varied set of metaphors summoning up visions of those cracks—homeless camps, the AIDS crisis, broken families—from which the democracy's light breaks in. If the future of the album's opening song is irredeemable disaster, the coming democracy is a paradigm of *futurity*, the openness to the radically new that cannot be predicted on the basis of the past. It is always arriving. Its reality is never complete, never fully determinate, always to come. We could describe this as the difference between apocalyptic and messianic—as in "messiah"—time. Apocalyptic time is that of the end, the final event. It announces the last judgment from which there is no appeal. Messianic time is a time of liberation and openness, as in "Democracy" where the heart opens, barriers are demolished, and a fresh future emerges, as in the Sermon on the Mount. It's a time freed from past restraints rather than a closing of time itself.

"Closing Time," by contrast, is honky-tonk eschatology, the end of the world in the alcoholic and erotic haze of a roadhouse Cohen might have frequented during his time in Nashville. We wonder whether it's just closing time in the tavern as dancers choose final partners for the night, or the closing time of a love affair, or could it also be a closing *of* time, an end of all things? In other words, is "closing" an adjective marking a specific time or a verb denoting the act or process of closing, completing, or finishing time? The second is suggested by the two times the dancers go successively crazy for both the devil and Christ. That sounds like the two moments of John's Apocalypse: first the catastrophe (devil), then Christ's kingdom on earth. Yet the site of "Closing Time" is also a bell tower that chimes "the blessed hours." Are these the bells that "Anthem" commands us to ring? As in other songs on *The Future*, uncanny cracks and thresholds appear. The scene at closing time may look like freedom, but feels like death. There is both a scene of revelry, a choosing of final partners, and the foreboding that the revels are now at an end. It must be something in between life and death, as democracy is real but not exactly there.

## Love Always

The original version of "Always" was written by Irving Berlin in 1925 and has been a standard tune ever since. Most versions take about three minutes. Cohen extends the song to eight minutes by means of a slow steady beat, choral backing, and playful interchange with the chorus, singing in one of his deepest tones, with repetition, framing, and his own additions. There's a heavy emphasis on the word "always." He adds a verse which could hardly have worked in the 1925 version comparing this true vow to lesser couplings, from flings in the shower to summer romances. The song expresses simply the lover's impossible yet necessary pledge of eternal love and fidelity. Can we seize the opportunity of love? Can love conquer time? Can a joyous eternity displace the stifling one damn thing after another of *chronos*? The final number on the album, "Tacoma Trailer," is a haunting, purely instrumental piece. As musical time flows calmly we are given an opportunity to think about questions like these that are raised in *The Future* and to meditate on the album's different takes on time.[1]

---

[1] Many thanks to Louis Schwartz who helped me to clarify many aspects of this essay and to Babette Babich whose work on music and contribution to our symposium on "Leonard Cohen and Philosophy" at the 2013 World Congress of Philosophy in Athens, Greece were invaluable stimuli.

# II

# Songs of Beauty

# 5
# Is Leonard Cohen a Good Singer?

Jason Holt

When Leonard Cohen accepted the Juno Award for Best Male Vocalist in 1993 for his album *The Future* (the Junos are like Canada's Grammys), he was characteristically self-deprecating, saying that "only in Canada" could he have won such an award. This remark evoked his well-known, ironically self-mocking verdict from "Tower of Song" that his voice is *golden*. While few would contest the substantial quality of Cohen's voice as an artist—that is, his figurative, nonvocal voice—many diehard fans will admit that he's not the *greatest* singer. Yet it seems reasonable to consider as a live question whether he ranks as a good one, and to explore in the process what it means to have artistic merit in such a role as singing. Though some detractors deny that he sings *at all* much less well, many fans would insist, on the contrary, that he's not just a good singer, but so much more.

Does it even make sense to consider seriously the notion that Leonard Cohen is a good singer when it seems pretty clear that he himself doesn't think so? Well, yes. He may not mean it, for one, and even if he does, he could be wrong. It's not just a matter of his opinion, or ours for that matter. Opinions differ widely on many questions, and Cohen's singing is no exception: some critics are too harsh, some fans too forgiving. In matters of taste it is often said "To each their own," and up to a point this is true. Say I like sleeping in, milk in my coffee, and listening to Leonard Cohen—and you don't. That's just fine, and if all people meant by championing or slamming an artist was "I like their work" or "I don't like their work," there would be no issue, no dispute. But that's often not where it stops. Taste tends to assert itself, to vie for dominance. Fandom wants company, and no dissent. Saying that Cohen is a good singer implies not just "I like him" but that *other people* should also so acknowledge him.

Since many fans will be at loggerheads with critics so harsh as to be *anti*-fans, how can we get beyond fandom and anti-fandom to achieve some sort of objectivity? Might we conduct an opinion poll? We could, but mere opinion won't do, as we've seen. Nor is it simply a matter of the numbers, of whether enough people (a majority?) self-identify as "Team Leonard." If it were a matter of popularity, then [*insert current pop phenom here*] would be better than Mozart, but clearly that's not so. Popularity determines neither truth nor quality, and supposing otherwise is fallacious, a reasoning error. Citing the fact that Cohen won a Best Male Vocalist Juno Award doesn't settle the matter either, for we may think—on independent grounds—that someone else should have won instead and that he shouldn't have been in the running. Because we need a real standard, tackling this problem, the problem of taste, will take us deep into philosophy from the shallows of the most egregious internet debates.

Beforehand, though, we should get a few things straight. When we talk about Cohen's singing, we should be clear *which* voice we're talking about: the early baritone (1960s–'70s), or the later bass (1980s–'90s), which are, if both recognizably Cohen, markedly different. The first period extends from *Songs of Leonard Cohen* (1967) through *Recent Songs* (1979), the second roughly from *Various Positions* (1984) to *Ten New Songs* (2001). The he-doesn't-really-sing complaint applies, if anywhere, to *Dear Heather* (2004) and *Old Ideas* (2012), and we should both forgive him this and dismiss the suggestion that such criticism applies in a similar way to his earlier work. The transition is gradual, but the difference is huge. The early voice has more range and urgency, the later greater richness, resonance, a gravitas won not from experience or cigarettes alone. Despite such changes, Cohen's voice admittedly has retained a slightly nasal tone and remained of narrowish range. It's not a generic voice, by any stretch, not generically beautiful either—it's way too distinctive for that.

## Cohen's Weight Class

Valid criticisms of Cohen's voice include its limited range and unconventionality, though more from a pop music than folk perspective. He's no Sinatra or Callas, to be sure, but it would be woefully unfair to set the bar that high. Good does not imply keeping pace with the great. It also would be unfair of us to judge Frank Sinatra by the standards of opera, or Maria Callas by those of jazz or pop music. Each is a great singer in their own domain or "weight class," and so too, I suggest, should we judge Leonard Cohen. In evaluating Cohen's voice, we should consider his weight class, which straddles the divide between folk and popular music. With one foot in each genre, Cohen weighs in—as we knew he would—as a singer-songwriter (for slightly different emphasis, songwriter-singer). Just as we "forgive" Sinatra for not writing songs, or Cole Porter for not being a singer, so too should we "forgive" singer-songwriters for lacking Sinatra's voice or Porter's writing chops. Being *good enough* at both is pretty impressive.

Perhaps, then, the question "Is Leonard Cohen a good singer?" isn't quite right. Maybe the better question, apropos of his Juno Award, would be "Is Cohen a good *vocalist*?" or, even better, vocal *stylist*. One strong influence on Cohen's musical style is often acknowledged to be the French *chanson* as exemplified by such artists Jacques Brel, where, as David Boucher observes in *Dylan and Cohen*, "the aesthetic sound of the voice determines the excellence of the work; for the *chansonnier*, it is style that matters and not perfect pitch or polished performance" (p. 137). Now the idea *isn't* that Cohen isn't a bad singer because he's not really trying to be a good one. Rather, knocking his voice for being in a particular musical style or tradition will count less as criticism of

Cohen himself and more as a complaint, whether just or prejudicial, about the entire tradition. Still, pigeonholing Cohen as a *chansonnier* seems to sell both him and his voice short. Cohen's distinctive, personal vocal style inherits from yet transcends folk, blues, country, pop—various traditions.

No discussion of Cohen's weight class would be complete without ranking him vocally relative to other singer-songwriters. We should note (along with David Hume) that this isn't mere opining, either, as such ranking can be an entirely objective matter where any dissent wouldn't be taken too seriously (pp. 40–41), as in the case of someone's hyperfandom moving them to proclaim [*insert current action movie star*] a better actor than Laurence Olivier. Among other singer-songwriters, it seems fair to see Cohen somewhere in the middle of the vocal quality spectrum, ranking below a Paul Simon but above a Bob Dylan; for a Canadian trifecta, let's substitute Gordon Lightfoot above and Neil Young below. Remember that as singer-songwriters, those tending toward the bottom of the vocal spectrum still have mediocre voices, which by implication means those like Cohen above are in the better-than-mediocre category: in other words, good.

Consider now what I'd like to call the great singer-songwriter argument, which goes something like this. Because being a singer-songwriter depends on two very different skill sets, such status implies a basic level of competence in both domains. In other words, you can't even *be* a singer-songwriter without being dually capable of writing songs as well as singing them. By extension, how highly one rates as a singer-songwriter has implications for singing and songwriting ability. An excellent singer might be a lousy singer-songwriter, but just as a great hunter-gatherer has to be a pretty good hunter *and* a pretty good gatherer—though not necessarily supreme in either—so too must a *great* singer-songwriter be, at the very least, a pretty good singer, even if, as with Cohen, the songwriting appears superior to the singing and allows us to forgive imperfections in the latter. In a nutshell, then, the argument is that because Cohen is a *great* singer-songwriter, he also, by implication, counts as at least a decent singer. Although Bob Dylan is unquestionably a great songwriter, one could argue, by contrast, that his voice limits his singer-songwriter rank to something short of great, the upper echelons of good.

## Style Prejudice

When we consider the role of experts in guiding our aesthetic choices, we naturally think of popular types of criticism: movie critics, food critics, literary critics, music critics. Although today's internet culture fosters what we may kindly call "democratic" approaches to criticism, where everyone's keen to assert their own taste alone, and it's always open season on anyone and anything, most of us still incline toward respect for certain expert critics. Good critics are able to discern, better than others, the qualities that make art—whether we're talking about a film, a singer, what have you—good, or worthy of attention. Being in a position to make those aesthetic judgments requires perceiving and responding to the relevant features of a variety of different examples, and doing so impartially (or, as David Hume put it, having a "strong sense, united to delicate sentiment, improved by practice, perfected by comparison, and cleared of all prejudice," p. 44).

That we should be "cleared of all prejudice" is something we should remind about 95 percent of all internet commentators. We sometimes associate such critical harshness, whether we find it on the internet or elsewhere, with justified opinion if not expertise. But such harshness can often conceal underlying prejudice. Take the following pre-internet pronouncement from critic Juan Rodriguez: "Although Cohen may have a private affinity for the vitality, ease and emotive qualities of pop music at its best . . . this does not automatically provide him with the talent to sing. Cohen plainly cannot sing. His voice is dull and monotonous and has little range" (p. 67). This reads like the sentence of a pretty uncompromising judge, who would be similarly tough assessing others and whose apparently principled stance commands our respect. However, the critic's evaluation unfolds rather surprisingly: "Bob Dylan, on the other hand, does know how to sing and he makes his own rough and unsweet voice an attribute, not a liability. Unfortunately, Cohen has been able to do nothing with his voice and this fact turns up in his melodies, which are slow, deadeningly similar, and wholly uninspiring." Ouch; the sting of it isn't the point, though. Rather, with this unexpected turn the critic has lost, maybe not all, but most of us. Whatever we might think of the relative merits of the two voices, they're not *that* different in terms of aesthetic judgment, not night-and-day different.

This passage also illustrates a significant and usually unacknowledged source of many negative impressions of Cohen as a singer: *style prejudice*. A lot of people simply don't like his style, any part of it, the way Cohen dresses, his poet-polished lyrics, his aesthetic sensibility, the ironic tone and dark, existential mood of many of his songs. Notice how the critic above linked what he dislikes about Cohen's voice with his dislike of the music itself, suggesting that melodic "disappointment" somehow reveals vocal inadequacy. Some don't like the romanticism, others the realism, others still the combination. To gloss any of these dislikes as "vocal inadequacy" is simply what philosophers call a category-mistake: a misattribution error. People who dismiss his singing are sometimes no more forgiving of more generically approved singers' covers (as with Jennifer Warnes's *Famous Blue Raincoat* tribute album), which indicates the issue isn't really Cohen's singing so much as the songs themselves. Preferring a cover to a Cohen original might also, but also might not, betray a style prejudice.

A similar style and content prejudice can be seen in attitudes toward the music of Tom Waits, whose voice is also unconventional and whose songs, next to Cohen's, are comparably nostalgic, gloomy, and depressing. There's nothing wrong with preferring, as I confess I do, the more conventional, smoother voice of Waits's early *The Heart of Saturday Night* (1974) to the roughed up vocals of his more experimental later work, but to transmute this preference into a negative *verdict* is again simply a style prejudice. Similarly, many who dismiss the folk baritone of the early Cohen probably haven't given his later pop bass a real chance, and those who deny that Cohen sings at all likely haven't really considered such early performances as "Stories of the Street" or "Sing Another Song, Boys."

## The *Je Ne Sais Quoi*

Although some take to Cohen's voice right away and others never do, still others come around after repeated or prolonged exposure. For some, in other words, Leonard Cohen is an acquired taste. To this extent, the pleasures of listening to Cohen are not unlike those derived from some alcoholic beverages, certain foods, and smoking, which typically require overcoming an initial negative reaction. Most people find their first exposure to the taste of beer, the texture of sushi, and inhaling smoke to be somewhere on the continuum between rather offputting and outright revolting. I suspect that Cohen himself would not find the comparisons insulting. Some people never get over their initial negative reactions, and that's fine. But the fans and critics who have managed to cross over, or who haven't had to, are able to enjoy whole spheres of experience, of pleasure, to which the rest of the world remains closed. To transpose a local beer ad into Cohen fandom terms, those who like him like him *a lot*.

To appreciate the importance of this point, that for many Cohen is an acquired taste, we should remind ourselves that, for Hume, part of being a good critic is sensitively discerning the relevant qualities, the aesthetic character, of the thing being judged. To the extent that Cohen is an acquired taste, his detractors might never be in a position to perceive the qualities that many fans and music critics enjoy. It's not that they *dislike* what the likers like, but rather that they've not managed to overcome their natural resistance to even experiencing, much less considering, what fans appreciate. As connoisseurs of beer or wine are able to discern qualities that dislikers simply can't, so too might the same be said for true Leonard Cohen aficionados.

What fans and many critics experience in Cohen, to the extent that this can be described at all, is a distinctive voice singing unique songs with genuinely poetic lyrics and that express a significant artistic vision. The distinctiveness of the singing matches the personal quality of the lyrics, which unlike almost all other folk or pop songs do more than gesture at poetry. Cohen's lyrics don't just gesture, they achieve, they *are*. Most generic voices are less distinctive and less distinct in expressing lyrics that seldom merit the emphasis of Cohenesque enunciation. Where some listeners might resent that Cohen's singing style betrays such an extraordinarily exacting concern with language, a loving exactitude, this care is part of what fans appreciate in his voice along with the sense of intimacy it suggests and explores with the listener. It's a voice rich with the attempt to share with the listener something both important and well-turned. Cohen's voice suits its poetic material.

As many critics, not just fans, see it, Cohen's voice has a mysterious, enigmatic quality, an undeniable *je ne sais quoi*. Critics observe in the DVD *Leonard Cohen: Under Review* that his voice has an "immense personal charm. You want to engage him when you hear his voice coming out of the speakers" (Robert Christgau). "It has a very hypnotic quality" (Anthony DeCurtis). But figuring out exactly why isn't so easy: "Is it the quality of his voice? Is it the way he dramatizes himself? I think that these things are very mysterious" (Christgau). Part of the answer might be found in a thought-provoking comment by Ronee Blakley, who also sang backup on *Death of a Ladies' Man* (1977):

> Leonard has in his voice a slight trembling from time to time which is extremely vulnerable and real and present and there. It's at the front of his head, though it almost has a rumbling sound, a biblical sound at times. It can also sound very sensitive and charming and this sound that he has in addition to the rabbinical quality . . . is almost what in Christian music would be called *bel canto* or *cantus firmus*: the kind that monks would sing. . . .

This comment suggests to my mind two very provocative things about Cohen's voice: first, that it succeeds in part by somehow tapping into our musical subconscious; and second, that it works not necessarily despite but also oddly *because of* its particular imperfections. A better voice just wouldn't be *Leonard Cohen's*. Would it make sense to wish him better endowed? I really don't think so. It seems we'd be missing the point.

## No Accounting?

As I write this I glance at a ticket stub propped up against my laptop: Section 37, Row J, Seat 2, not just a ticket, *my* ticket, for the Leonard Cohen concert at the Halifax Metro Centre, April 13, 2013. It reads "On stage promptly at 8 pm," which he was, and he played for three and a quarter hours. It was the second time I'd seen him live, the first also in Halifax in 2008 at a venue—and so he recalled in the 2013 concert—called the Cohn auditorium. Though I'd been a fan for very many years, I never thought I'd be fortunate enough to get to see him live, much less twice. The aura hasn't faded yet. But it gives me pause, this highly personal experience, shared with Megan (Seat 1) and thousands of others: communication as communion. It was, and remains, perhaps a perfect example of how art can—somehow, seemingly—personalize the universal, universalize the personal. Can I convey what it meant to me? Not exactly, though I can gesture at it. Could I convince someone who didn't like it that they should have? Probably not. "It's good but I don't like it" is no paradox. Good standards limit judgment without compelling taste.

This might remind you of the old chestnut, "There's no accounting for taste," a sensible but still ambiguous adage. It might mean that you can't explain why someone has the particular likes or dislikes they do, or that there's ultimately no justification for taste "beyond itself"—as the bromide goes, it is what it is. Hume, on the other hand, thought that there *is* accounting for taste, in terms of human nature, which he saw as uniform. That uniformity explains why there can be lasting consensus on great artists like Homer (p. 42). When there are aesthetic disputes, Hume thought, that's because some of the disputants lack true expertise, missing the right sensitivities or being subject to forgivable age- or culture-specific tendencies. In some cases, too, there will be unavoidable idiosyncrasies of personal taste that don't really touch on aesthetic disputes. Suppose, for instance, when it comes to Cohen, I prefer his realism, you his romanticism, though we agree that he's a great artist.

Can we confidently say that Hume-approved experts will agree that Leonard Cohen is a good singer? Not necessarily, though I've given some reason to suppose they may. It's actually pretty tough to figure out who, if anyone, the Hume-approved critics are. Given how vehement the disputes among critics, all of whom have some claim to objectivity, often get, and how rare consensus among them really is except in—fittingly—exceptional cases, perhaps human nature and aesthetic judgment aren't uniform but varied, pluralistic. Good critics then would be seen in terms of sub-universal but legit spheres of appropriate influence. But does this not just dissolve into utter subjectivity, an aesthetic of idiosyncrasy? Perhaps my enjoyment of Leonard Cohen's singing voice is mere preference after all.

Is that all there is? Maybe, and I'll tell you why. In my late teens I was depressive to the point of suicidal. My parents were naturally concerned, more so as the usual ways of addressing the problem proved ineffective. The depression and I were stubborn, lonely and painful as it got. My father did something totally counterintuitive but ultimately inspired: he bought me *The Best of Leonard Cohen* (1975) on cassette. Who would think to give their suicidal son "music to slit your wrists to"? And yet, as I listened, I resonated with the music, with Cohen's voice, all of it, with such immediacy, such intensity, it was so resolutive—it saved my life. How could that not cloud, in the best possible way, my judgment, biasing me toward the one voice that reached me through the darkness?

# 6
# Covering Cohen

Adam Auch

In the third verse of "Tower of Song," Leonard Cohen makes a joke at his own expense. In singing that he was "born with the gift of a golden voice," he makes a statement so clearly false that listeners are forced to understand it ironically. We know that Cohen doesn't have a beautiful singing voice, and here Cohen shows he knows it too. Appearing as it does in the midst of a song in which he reflects on his career in the music business, the line comes across as yet another example of Cohen's characteristic humor and humility.

Something interesting happens, however, when the song is covered by other singers, particularly when these singers have (or had) voices that could be plausibly considered "golden." Instead of a self-deprecating joke, the line takes on other meanings. For example, consider Marianne Faithfull's version of the song from 1999's *Vagabond Ways*. Unlike Cohen, Faithfull did once possess what I suspect many people would consider a beautiful singing voice. However, following years of drug and alcohol abuse, her voice hardened and coarsened considerably. As she sings it, the line comes across as a kind of lament—a reminder that something valuable has been irretrievably lost.

On the other hand, consider Tom Jones's version of the song (from 2012's *Spirit in the Room*) where he sings the lyric with fist-shaking sincerity. Like Faithfull, Jones had a beautiful singing voice in his youth, but unlike her, his voice is still in good condition (though tempered a bit by age). Aside from the bridge (the bit about widening rivers and how difficult they are to cross), the golden voice lyric is the only part of the song that Jones sings with his voice at full power. He performs the rest of the song in a muted, spoken-word style that approximates Cohen's own version of the song. There is no irony to Jones's performance—he wants us to know that, after all these years, he still has a (conventionally) beautiful voice. While a charitable reading of Jones's performance might take his version of the lyric as a statement of gratitude for his innate talent, it's hard not to hear it as a kind of boast.

Three singers, three different interpretations of the same lyric. How can this be? All ten words in the lyric have clear meanings. Why should it be a joke in one person's mouth, a lament in another's, and boast in a third's? What accounts for these different interpretations?

## Whose Voice Is It Anyway?

Another question: Just *who* is "Tower of Song" about? Who is it that was born with the golden voice? At issue here is the status of the golden voice lyric's first word: "I." "I" is an example of what philosophers and linguists call an "indexical": a word that refers to different individuals, objects, times, or places, depending on the context in which it is spoken. Other examples of indexicals include "now," "yesterday," "here," "left," "right," "today," and "tomorrow." The sentence "It is raining today" is true as I write this essay (I'm watching the rain through the window), but may be false when you read it. And a sentence like "I am over six feet tall" is true when I write or say it, but probably false if you say it. So our interpretation of the golden voice lyric is going to very much depend on who we take the "I" to be.

There are a lot of possibilities: it could be Cohen himself—after all, he wrote the song. But this would not account for the Faithfull and Jones interpretations of the lyric. So maybe the song is about whoever is performing it. When Cohen sings it, it's about Cohen, and when Jones sings it's about Jones. But this also isn't quite right. Not everything an artist writes or performs in the first person is meant to be autobiographical—after all, Johnny Cash never spent a night in Folsom Prison. So we shouldn't be too quick to assume that the song is about the person singing it. And yet our discussion of the golden voice lyric suggests that we do associate particular elements of a performance with the persona of the performer. But what is a persona anyway?

As an exercise, think about what immediately comes to mind when you hear or read the name "Leonard Cohen." You might think about the whiskey, the cigarettes, the fedora, and the impeccably tailored black suits. You might think of a poet or prophet, who while lacking a beautiful voice, makes up for it in the beauty of his words. These images and ideas that so easily come to mind when Cohen's name is mentioned make up his persona. It's this persona that audiences associate with Cohen's performances of his own songs, and it's this persona that shapes their expectations of the message he's attempting to convey. Something similar happens with Cohen songs written in the second person. When Cohen sings "Suzanne," you get the sense that he's addressing himself. When Judy Collins or Nina Simone sing it, they seem to be addressing the listener. At any rate, it seems clear that Cohen is aware of this persona, and he refers to it often in his songs (even addressing it explicitly in "Going Home" on 2012's *Old Ideas*). Cohen's performance of the golden voice lyric is just another example.

It's this playful engagement with his persona that can make many Cohen songs difficult to cover, as in the case of "Famous Blue Raincoat." But in this case, there's still enough space for other singers to make the song their own. Cohen isn't the only singer with a persona. We could run similar word-association exercises with Marianne Faithfull, Tom Jones, Elton John, Jeff Buckley, Lana Del Rey, or anybody else who's ever covered a Cohen tune. These associations will help to guide our interpretations of their performances. They help us to "fill in" the information we need to determine who the "I" is that's addressing us in the song. In other words, the artist's persona forms part of the context we need in order to understand what they're trying to say to us.

## Sincerely . . .

One of the reasons that the significance of the golden voice lyric changes depending on who's singing it is that Cohen has left an opening for other artistic personas to affect our interpretation of it. This is because Cohen doesn't explicitly tie his persona to the song. Although the song contains a number of references to his persona, they're only alluded to, hinted at (what philosophers call "implicated" but most people call "implied") rather than stated directly. A lot of Cohen's songs have this feature. Even something as personal as "Chelsea Hotel #2" (widely reported to have been inspired by Cohen's relationship with Janice Joplin) does not reference the Cohen persona directly. It does, however, hint at it through the claim that the singer isn't a handsome man (another self-deprecating joke that changes character when sung by somebody else). Things, however, aren't always so simple.

Let's look at another Cohen song that doesn't have the same openness to interpretation. "Famous Blue Raincoat" (from 1971's *Songs of Love and Hate*), written in the form of a letter, recounts a falling out and possible reconciliation between two (male) friends over the affections of a woman, Jane. In the last line of the song, the author of the letter is revealed to be none other than "L. Cohen." Let's call this line the "signature." The presence of the signature gives a particular identity to the person writing the letter—and by using his own name, Cohen explicitly ties the character in the song to his persona.

The presence of the signature poses a special challenge for anybody wishing to perform it. Because the song is tied so neatly to the Cohen persona, it's difficult for an artist to bring his or her own persona to bear on their interpretation of the song. Put another way, the signature forces artists to perform the song in character *as* Cohen. As a result, a would-be performer of the song faces a difficult choice: either don the Cohen persona yourself and perform the song as written, or retain your own persona and change the lyrics.

Both options have their strengths and weaknesses. Although the first approach, where you retain the original lyrics, has been by far the most popular choice of artists covering "Famous Blue Raincoat" in the years since it was first released (perhaps nobody wants to be accused of changing Cohen's words to suit their own performance), how successful this turns out to be will depend on how well one is able to inhabit the persona. Performers who regularly perform in character have an advantage here: chances are that the Tori Amos version of "Raincoat" (on the *Tower of Song* compilation from 1995) will seem to many to be much more successful than other straight covers, since Amos is well-known as someone who sings songs in character—especially when covering other writers' material (see, for instance, her 2001 cover album *Strange Little Girls*). At any rate, the second approach, where an artist changes the lyrics to weaken the associations with Cohen's persona, is much more interesting.

Now for a true Cohen fan, it might seem to be nothing short of sacrilege to consider changing the master's words. After all, if nothing else, Cohen is known for choosing his words carefully. Why shouldn't we respect his wishes? And yet, Cohen himself has revised his songs over the years (most notably the new lyrics for "Hallelujah" that appear on 1994's *Cohen Live*), and a few brave artists have made revisions of their own. On the title track of her 1987 album of Cohen covers, longtime Cohen collaborator Jennifer Warnes sings a slightly revised version of "Famous Blue Raincoat." Although it's difficult to determine exactly who was responsible for making the changes, it's worth noting that Cohen worked closely with Warnes on the album, and even performs with her on a track. Taken together with his tendency to revise his own work, this suggests that, in Cohen's mind at least, the second approach is an acceptable one.

The changes are small, but serve to the make the story

related in the song a great deal more ambiguous. In particular, the letter is now signed "a friend"—and the author is no longer explicitly claimed to have been Jane's lover. Removing Cohen's name from the ending helps to pry the letter-writer from his close identification with the Cohen persona. Warnes's version of the song is less specific—the central conflict may still be a love triangle, then again it could be a parent attempting to come to terms with their child's new relationship. As a result, Warnes's lyrical variations serve to multiply the number of possible interpretations of the song.

## The Rules of the Game

Up to now, we've argued that the ideas and expectations we form about a particular artist will inform our interpretation of his or her performance. So far so good, but we haven't said anything about how these different interpretations come about. After all, even if we are associating different personas with, for example, the "I" at the beginning of the golden voice lyric, the rest of the line remains the same. How can three people more or less saying the same thing produce three different effects?

Although most of us are certainly aware of the effect context has on how what we say is interpreted by others, there's a persistent belief that the meaning of what we say is fixed entirely by the meanings of the individual words we utter. After all, words have meanings, and they have those meanings regardless of who's speaking and what their intentions are. So while the claim made in the golden voice lyric may be (strictly speaking) true when Tom Jones sings it and (strictly speaking) false when Cohen sings it, we need some way of explaining why Jones's performance counts as a boast and why Cohen's counts as a joke.

When we talked about the personas that certain artists bring to bear on the material they perform, we talked a great deal about the assumptions that audiences are likely to make about those performers. There are, however, other assumptions we make that make ordinary conversation possible. The American philosopher Paul Grice attempted to catalogue these assumptions (which he called "conversational maxims") in an attempt to determine exactly what context contributes to the significance of what we say to each other.

One of the maxims Grice identified is that you shouldn't say anything you believe to be false (p. 27). Now Grice is not simply saying that you ought to always tell the truth—that would be a claim about morality, not about language. What Grice means is that, in ordinary conversation, we trust that people are being sincere in their dealings with us. This doesn't mean that you should believe everything someone tells you, just that most of the time we expect that people are telling us what they actually believe to be the case. Because these assumptions are in place, they can be used by savvy speakers to convey information that goes beyond what has actually been said. One way of doing this is to violate these expectations in such an obvious manner that one's partner in the conversation is able to work out what you're trying to convey.

To see this in action, let's return once again to the golden voice lyric from "Tower of Song." Why does it come across as a joke when Cohen sings it? Well, one reason is that the statement is quite simply false: the most natural interpretation of the lyric is that the signer has a conventionally beautiful singing voice, and Cohen certainly doesn't. What's more, Cohen is not deluded—he knows that his voice is in no sense golden. So here we have Cohen saying something that he believes to be false. This is a straightforward violation of the conversational maxim we've just discussed. And yet, there's no attempt to deceive—if this is a lie, it's a bald-faced one. We're forced to conclude that Cohen wants the line to be understood ironically. It's the mismatch between our expectations about Cohen (including our belief that he's not a conventionally good singer) and the claim contained in the lyric that makes the joke work.

*Adam Auch*

## Funny Voices and Angel Song

True story: I was recently at a service at a Roman Catholic Church where Cohen's "Hallelujah" was performed as part of the liturgy. Although the chorus remained the same, the verses were changed to something a little more unambiguously Christian. Though the song was well performed, I found myself annoyed at hearing the song in that context. First, because the song has become overplayed to the point of becoming an emotional cliché (*see also*: "Grace, Amazing"), and second, because the change in lyrics didn't accomplish anything that couldn't have been accomplished by a change in musical approach.

I suspect that I'm not alone in my annoyance with the near-ubiquity of "Hallelujah" in the years since it escaped from near-obscurity through covers by Rufus Wainwright (on, of all things, the soundtrack to *Shrek*) and Alexandra Burke (who released her cover as a single shortly after winning the British version of the *X-Factor* in 2008). The success of the Wainwright and Burke versions of the song (and the tsunami of other versions that have followed in their wake) illustrates another interesting effect of context on interpretation. Most versions of the song that have been released since the boom aren't that different lyrically from those (such as John Cale's 1987 version) that preceded it. The difference is largely one of performance. The versions of the song recorded since the boom have tended to perform the song as a hymn or anthem, while the ones that preceded the boom (including Cohen's own recording) tended to take a more ambivalent approach.

This shift in approach suggests that in thinking about the interpretation of a song, we must pay attention to not only *who* is singing, but *how* they sing it. The way something is performed can affect how we are meant to take it. This is something we are all familiar with. Consider the difference a sarcastic tone can make to the interpretation of a sentence like "That was a *lovely* evening" (or consider how difficult it is to convey sarcasm online). The same idea can be applied to musical performances: In the late 1990s and early 2000s, there were simultaneous vogues for pop-punk covers of 1970s soft rock ballads (Me First and The Gimme Gimmes covering Carly Simon's "Nobody Does It Better") and for lounge covers of contemporary hardcore punk and heavy metal songs (Richard Cheese and Lounge Against the Machine's version of Disturbed's "Down with the Sickness"). These performances were clearly intended to be funny—the humor originating not so much in the lyrical content of the songs, but in the mismatch between that content and the performance style. Tom Jones's performance of the golden voice lyric from "Tower of Song" is another example of performance informing interpretation, since it's his decision to sing the line with the full volume and power of his conventionally beautiful singing voice that makes it seem like a boast.

On a lyrical level, "Hallelujah" seems utterly ambivalent about religious faith. This ambivalence is reflected in Cohen's vocal performance, where the verses are almost spoken in a flat, dispassionate voice. Where any emotion does seep in, it's anything but reverent (consider the extra bite Cohen puts on the "do ya" and "to ya" in the first and third verses of the original version). The chorus, on the other hand, would not sound out of place in a church. The juxtaposition of the plainness of the verse and the elaborateness of the chorus suggests a tension between earthly and heavenly desires.

This tension is conveyed in a very different way in Jeff Buckley's version from 1994 (which may be the highest profile pre-boom version of the song). Buckley's performance is spare and ethereal, suggesting at the same time a chilly remoteness and something quite carnal. If Cohen's version of the song is the sound of us forgetting "to pray for the angels," Buckley's version is the sound of the angels forgetting "to pray for us."

In contrast, Wainwright goes out of his way to bring out the song's anthemic character, a similar approach to the one k.d. lang took in her version from 2004. Wainwright's version of the song features a fluid vocal line throughout, and he replaces the almost-sneering "ya" in the verses with the far less confrontational "you." This isn't particularly surprising given the generally operatic character of his own compositions. Burke uses her version of the song to show off the range and power of her voice, perhaps appropriate given that she rose to prominence through a singing competition. Because these approaches use the song to demonstrate technical mastery over lyrical content, they tend to favor singing the verses in the same way as the chorus. As a result, the tension that marked the Cohen and Buckley versions is lost, and the song comes across as a straight hymn.

## An Unanswered Question

You may have surmised from the discussion in the last section that I prefer the pre-boom versions of "Hallelujah" to those that came later. You may have also noticed a hint of snarkiness in my description of the Tom Jones version of "Tower of Song." In making these observations you may have begun to wonder just what makes for a good cover version. This is a difficult (perhaps impossible) question to answer, and I'm afraid that attempting to do so would take us too far off the track we have pursued so far. Having said that, we can at least conclude by remarking that sometimes we ourselves are part of the context of an interpretation, and our own histories and the associations we form with a piece of music will inform both our preferences and our understanding of its content.[1]

[1] I would like to thank Jason Holt, Susanne Marshall, and Jan Sutherland for providing the conversation, the encouragement, and the enthusiasm that helped bring this chapter into being.

# 7
# Leonard and Lorca

EDWARD WINTERS

I was once playing Cohen's first album, *Songs of Leonard Cohen*, when my younger sister entered the room and asked why I was listening to such depressing music. I replied that I listened to his songs because they're beautiful, and that while I found them almost unbearably sad, I didn't feel the least bit depressed by listening to them. Indeed, I found them heartening. This chapter is an extended reply to her question more than forty years on.

In his lecture, "The Secret Life of the Love Song," delivered at the Academy of Fine Arts, Vienna, on September 25, 1999, Nick Cave remarks,

> All love songs must contain *duende*. For the love song is never truly happy. It must first embrace the potential for pain. Those songs that speak of love without having within their lines an ache or a sigh are not love songs at all but rather Hate Songs disguised as love songs, and are not to be trusted. These songs deny us our humanness and our God-given right to be sad and the air-waves are full of them.

Of this specific sadness he says, "Leonard Cohen deals specifically in it," but notes that such genuine sadness—that expression of longing—is rare in contemporary rock music. Not so in flamenco. Flamenco music always aspires to *duende*, even when it disappoints. But what is *duende*? It concerns a kind of aesthetic response to works of art that resist the temptation to excessive sentimentality.

In addition to listening to Cohen's music, I also read his novels at the time of their publication, and I found in them a certain conception of the aesthetic that I have held throughout my life. I offer you this snippet from *The Favourite Game*. Breavman, the narrator and autobiographical voice of Leonard Cohen, is at university with Shell, whom he sleeps with but does not love. They have been driving all day and put up in a cheap rooming house. Shell wants him to help her move the bed.

> Breavman was furious. He didn't want to move the bed.
>
> "What does it matter where the damn bed is? We'll be out of here by eight in the morning."
>
> "We'll be able to see the trees when we wake up."
>
> "I don't want to see the trees when we wake up. I want to look at the dirty ceiling and get pieces of dirty plaster grapevine in my eye."
>
> The ugly brass bed resisted her. For generations of sleepers it had not changed its position. He imagined a grey froth of dust on the underside. (pp. 136–37)

## A Short Address in the Second Person

You, reading this chapter in a library or on a train or at a bar, have fallen in love and suffered accordingly; you have been torn up like wind-borne ticker-tape; like betting slips in the gutter outside the track; or worse: you have grown tired of love and it no longer perturbs you. You lie awake at four in the morning ordering your regrets and counting your sins, sorting the deep from the shallow, the immensity of some trivial remark, its embers burning slowly still. This is your life and you did it. You wonder how you might be saved and by what or by whom. You have drunk from the top-shelf with its famous brands—the good rum with its Baroque label and its gold medals; but you have also swallowed the nameless liquors from the well and you know their bottles inside out. In bars you nursed a drink alone, overwhelmed by hopeless desire; summoned by the gleaming obsidian eyes of a boy or a girl who returned the pleasantries, softly, in a foreign accent, and who poured your drinks and smiled courteously. You squandered time in squalid apartments doing drugs (both soft and hard). You've had your uppers and downers. And when death comes you shall have left too many things undone and unsaid. And you, in this library, or on this train or at this bar, shall surely die. And everybody knows. . . .

Love, loss, utter dejection, abject boredom, regrets (both small and large), bouts of binge drinking (both brief and protracted), desire, fear, and defeat—all forms of longing: what has philosophy to say about any of these as they cast their shadow over our lives? How might we reason within these realms? Better, perhaps, to treat of them in song, as Cohen does, where the passions can be suitably expressed and left aching and dark, unilluminated by the light of reason.

## *Duende*

In his 2004 book of that title, author Jason Webster is introduced to the concept of *duende* and later discusses it with Pedro, a Spaniard with whom he takes in a concert.

> One of the fat women stood up, the low hum-like song began, and the audience fell silent.
>
> "Did you feel it?" Pedro asked again when the piece was over.
>
> "Yes," I said.
>
> "No," he said. "Did you really *feel* it?"
>
> I couldn't speak. The performance had filled me with something I had never felt before, and didn't know how to describe.
>
> "That was *duende*," he said. (Webster, p. 31)

A couple of pages on the concept calls out for explanation if not definition. Not all concepts need be defined. Game is one such. There are many forms a game can take and it is hard to think of one feature that all games must have in common and by which they are defined as games. Nevertheless, the term is used confidently and successfully. However, the same cannot be said for *duende*.

> "Pedro," I asked as we walked back to the car, the narrow streets crawling with people as they headed off, "what is *duende*?"
>
> He didn't reply at first, but waited until we had emerged onto the esplanade.
>
> "*Duende*," he said. "*Duende* is *duende*. More than this you will have to find out for yourself, *mi querido*. . . ." (p. 33)

That reply is inadequate, unhelpful. In the case of terms such as "game," we can muddle along knowing more or less what activities count as games, and communicating on that basis, without having to give a precise definition of the term. It looks as if the concept *duende* is different and resists even vague characterization. There seem to be no criteria by which we can sanction its use as a meaningful term in our language, in which case, we could never know its correct application. We must look elsewhere for clarification.

Nick Cave, in his "Love Song" lecture, refers to Federico García Lorca, who as we know was a major influence on Cohen. While Cave gives a well-informed characterization of *duende*, there's still no real way to sort candidates into clear-cut cases of *duende* and non-*duende*. In listing artists who he thinks have *duende*, Cave includes Bob Dylan, Lou Reed, and Leonard Cohen, equivocates over Van Morrison, and rules against the Tindersticks who "desperately want it." We need to grasp the basis on which some artists, but not others, are included in the *duende* class.

Lorca, in his *In Search of Duende*, expresses the intractability of the concept but begins to describe how we might nonetheless recognize its presence. The "black sounds" of melancholy in music—and how many Leonard Cohen songs fit this description?—and presumably in poetry and the other arts too:

> Manuel Torre . . . pronounced this splendid sentence on hearing Falla play his own *Nocturno de Generalife*: "All that has black sounds has duende." And there is no greater truth.
>
> These "black sounds" are the mystery, the roots fastened in the mire that we all know and all ignore, the fertile silt that gives us the very substance of art. "Black sounds," said that man of the Spanish people, concurring with Goethe, who defined the duende while speaking of Paganini: "A mysterious power which everyone senses and no philosopher explains." (p. 57)

Philosophy is charged here with the crime of trying to imprint rationality on that which lies outside the jurisdiction of reason—think of academics generally, as Breavman observes in *The Favourite Game*, as having "hands bloody with commas" (p. 101). A great many people in the arts think of criticism as an unwarranted intrusion of reason into a realm where emotion should reign unencumbered. However, the philosopher's task here is to examine the ways such emotions are to be themselves understood.

Lorca was a surrealist poet. (Despite his profound influence on Cohen, and despite occasional flashes of surrealism, Cohen himself isn't usually characterized as a surrealist.) The Surrealists attempted to make work that engages the viewer with thoughts that lie beneath the surface of appearance as that might be explained by science. The attempt of the Surrealists is to bring out the nature of the uncanny in the ordinary things of everyday life. Magic and irrationality, dream and mystery, were to be features of the dark character of life cast in shadow by the cleansing light of reason and science. That is to say the Surrealists wanted to find aspects of life untouched by the relentless march of science and rationality—somewhere for the soul to take refuge.

Lorca identifies three spirits that move the artist to create (pp. 58–60). These are the angel, the muse, and the *duende*. "The angel gives lights" and inspires visionary art—art that looks forward. The muses are the nine daughters of Mnemosyne, goddess of memory, and the half-sisters of Apollo, god of beauty, poetry, and music. The muse inspires an art of memory—based upon experience, both perceptual and emotional. The angel and the muse operate outside of us, whereas "one must awaken the duende in the remotest mansions of the blood" (p. 59). The *duende* is a demon; it wields a dark power whose energy is emotional, primordial, and "in the moment." As such, Lorca attributes to it Dionysian characteristics, as Nietzsche would call them.

Of philosophical importance to an appreciation of *duende* both in itself and in the work of Leonard Cohen is a conception of aesthetics that includes life rather than forms a gulf between life and art. A problem for much so-called modern art derives from the apparent separation of art from life—a separation that did not figure when art belonged to the enchantment of life by religious belief. Immanuel Kant thought of the aesthetic attitude as a kind of disinterested attention implying a separation, a distance between perceiver and artwork. The spectator looks at, listens to, or watches a painting, a concerto, or a dance. But the festival participant *engages in* the festival. The opposition is shaped for us by Nietzsche, in his *Birth of Tragedy*, who ascribes the two views to the symbolic character of the Greek gods Apollo and Dionysus.

The Apollonian conception of art involves only passive contemplation, whereas the Dionysian claims our *participation* in the art we are experiencing. Music is Dionysian when, for instance, a religious composition is enmeshed in the religious ceremonies for which it was written. Indeed the concert hall with its Bach recital, its concertgoers sitting in an audience, is on this view a degradation of the original intention, which was for music to be integrated into, and not simply accompany, the liturgy of the Mass. Music, perhaps more than the other arts, provides an idea of what enchantment means in terms of religious feeling. Many of Cohen's more spiritual songs reflect this tendency quite clearly. It is this that is missing from the secular world and it is this that needs to be replaced by art if art is to re-enchant the world.

Here the notion of magic is used to fill out the idea of an emotional engagement with the world. Dionysian magic, we might think, is not the audience we give the conjurer; nor is it the belief in some causal power that cannot be explained by science. It is the emotional coloring that we are able to give to the world in virtue of some activity we are engaged in. Think of the war dance of the warrior about to engage in battle. The war dance is undertaken in order to summon up courage and to bind the warriors together as a fighting unit, and to identify a people against its enemy. This form of magic can be found in the singing of national anthems before international sporting events, where it is again engaged in by nationalists to focus their unity and patriotism. The role of music in religion, then, can be seen as the magical engagement that colors emotional responses to the ceremony underway. You can hear Cohen calling to us in his "There is a War" and commanding us in "Dance Me to the End of Love." It is to be heard as part of the activity that provides the ceremony with its celebratory force. Moreover, its contribution is integrated into the ceremony not as a mere adjunct, but as an internal constituent. (The ceremony wouldn't be the ceremony it is without the music.)

## *Sol y Sombra*

*Sol y Sombra*, literally "sun and shade," is the name of a drink comprising equal measures of anise, a clear aniseed liqueur, and Spanish brandy, a dark spirit—the concoction served in a small brandy snifter. The name derives from the distribution of seats at the bullring. *Sol* designates the cheapest seats that are in sunshine throughout the *corrida*; *sombra* designates those that are shaded throughout. *Sol y sombra* are those that are in sunlight at the beginning of the afternoon and become shaded as the sun passes over. *Sol y sombra*, however, is also used as an epithet for the Spanish character—the two sides of the collective soul of a noble race. And we are well acquainted with the cliché of someone having a dark side.

The *duende* is surely Spanish. Nevertheless it entered Spain via Gypsy or, to use the contemporary term, Roma culture from Egypt, most probably originating in India—as did "deep song" whose prototype is the Romani *siguiriya*. Deep song prefigures flamenco in Andalusian culture and, as such, claims a greater authenticity. It is unaccompanied and has the sound of a cry or a wail. Flamenco introduces the guitar and with it the possibility of harmony and polyphony. As Lorca tells us,

> The Gypsy siguiriya begins with a terrible scream that divides the landscape into two ideal hemispheres. It is the scream of dead generations, a poignant elegy for lost centuries, the pathetic evocation of love under other moons and other winds.
>
> Then the melodic phrase begins to pry open the mystery of the tones and remove the precious stone of the sob, a resonant tear on the river of the voice. No Andalusian can help but shudder on hearing that scream. (p. 4)

We might wonder how this helps us to understand Leonard Cohen, a Montreal Jew—removed by thousands of miles and many degrees Fahrenheit from Andalucía. We should note that in 2011 Cohen was awarded Spain's Prince of Asturias Award for Literature. In his acceptance speech he remarked that he had brought with him his guitar, a forty-year-old Conde from Madrid; and that as a young poet he had studied the English poets but he was searching for a voice of his own. When he discovered Lorca he felt that Lorca had given him permission to find a voice. He also remarked that one day, early in the sixties, he was visiting his mother's house and that in the park overlooked by the house was a young Spaniard playing flamenco guitar to a group of boys and girls. Cohen hired the young guitarist to teach him to play. The Spaniard tuned Cohen's guitar and taught him six chords. Those six chords are not only the basis of many flamenco songs, they also were to become the basis of all Cohen's songs. Everything, he told his audience, came from Spanish soil and he expressed his gratitude to the country to which he owed so much.

So much for Spanish *duende* and the national character of Spain. However, we might recall that Torre, discussed by

Lorca above, concurs with Goethe. In a footnote Lorca refers us to *Conversations with Goethe*, in which the author Eckermann finds it "a suitable occasion to speak of that secret, problematic power, which all men feel, but no philosopher explains, and over which the religious help themselves with consoling words. Goethe names this unspeakable world and life-enigma the Dæmonic (dämonisch)" (p. 357).

A page earlier Eckermann comments that Goethe seeks an all-encompassing Deity, whose nature includes the demonic as part of His greatness. Some artists use this energy to make an art that speaks more for the whole than for the merely agreeable. This is familiar Cohen territory. According to Goethe, it is to be encountered more often with musicians than with painters. Goethe was writing from an abstract point of view; and so he wasn't concerned with any particular nation but with the conditions of human existence. So far as Torre drew upon sources external to his native Spain, we can assume that he spoke of a more universal concept, such as the demonic, when giving shape to the *duende.*

Nietzsche, late in life, was so taken by Bizet's *Carmen* as to call it "perfection." Perhaps as an example of international interest focusing upon a Spanish narrative, and taking Spanish musical themes within the score, the story of a beautiful Gypsy girl who worked in a Seville cigarette factory deeply affected the philosopher who looked for and championed the Dionysian in art: a German listening to a Frenchman's music that captures the tragic life of a poor working girl in Andalucía. *Carmen* is *duende*.

## Art and Genius

Surrealists like Lorca rejected the saccharine and duplicitous nature of bourgeois culture. Its sweetness they found sickening, a lie. Life is not sweet. Our sexual relationships are messy, painful, achingly insecure and sometimes catastrophic. That is the nature of the love song that celebrates what it is to be a vulnerable person reaching out to another. Leonard Cohen writes about the loneliness that each of us must feel at some time or other—unless we systematically fabricate some convoluted deception, not just of others but of ourselves as well. Bourgeois culture, to the Surrealists, is nothing short of such a deception. And so art, according to these artists, is a search for a certain kind of truth; a truth that, without the revelatory power of art, would remain undiscovered.

In Kant's *Critique of Judgment* there are much-discussed passages on artistic genius. Contrasted with science, which always involves rule-following, there are no rules that govern making art. Rather, it is as if nature speaks through the artist to provide us with original ideas that stand alone as original. They do not imitate previous works of art but serve as standards of taste for others to follow. Consider an art class in which students are asked to copy a master work. The professor looks at a number of them describing them as adequate copies. Then he sees a piece by one of the students and deems it promising. In this last case the student shows some originality. Their work is not a mere copy.

Or consider the image from *The Favourite Game* with which we started this chapter. Shell expresses the view that nature, as represented by the trees, is the proper place to find beauty. She wants to look through the window at them when she wakes. This is the standard representation of a picture as a window we look through. But Breavman wants a different kind of beauty. He takes the room in which they will spend the night as the place for thinking about the world as something we're just "passing through." The ephemeral nature of the one-night rooming house is contained in the sadness of the image, as is the thought of a "froth of dust" under the bed—to be disturbed by achieving the saccharine niceness Shell desires. There is something more honest and truthful in Breavman's acceptance of the "dirty plaster grapevine" that might fall in his eye.

It is not that we cannot say what it is that we hear when we recognize *duende*, as for instance in "deep song." Rather we should notice that in this original incantation we hear the originality or the integrity of the singer in her interpretation of the flamenco song she performs. Similarly, in Cohen's work, we recognize an original and perceptive characterization of our world, unsweetened by the niceness that otherwise we might crave. The world is not sweet. It is full of yearning and bitter sadness and it is ours. If you add to this the remarkable influence that Spain, Lorca in particular, has had on his work, we can see why the dark tones of *duende* provide a valuable perspective on that work. During his acceptance speech in Spain Cohen tells us of the voice Lorca helped him to find: "As I grew older, I understood that instructions came with this voice. What were these instructions? The instructions were never to lament casually. And if one is to express the great inevitable defeat that awaits us all, it must be done within the strict confines of dignity and beauty." Leonard Cohen, in his poetry, in his novels, in his songs, and also in his humility, achieves this. That's why it's a mistake to think of his work as depressing. It's shoddy, flimsy, easy, light, pretty art that's truly depressing. Cohen's work, by contrast, is dark, serious and, above all, beautiful in its candor. It lifts the heart—tears at it—as does the scream of deep song. It has *duende*.

# III

# Songs of Love

# 8
# Irony as Seduction

CHRISTOPHER LAUER

Leonard Cohen's lyrics are undeniably seductive, but what exactly makes them so can be difficult to pinpoint. For the most part they lack the youthful exuberance of a Keats or the sustained passion of a Donne, and they occasionally toy deliberately with disgust: witness the line in "Closing Time"—"She's a hundred but she's wearing something tight"—or the one in "I'm Your Man"—"I'd howl at your beauty like a dog in heat." If such lyrics flatter, it's not by highlighting anything particularly worthy about the listener, and if they seduce, it's not by promising an otherworldly experience.

Cohen somehow manages to flatter and seduce us by indicating that these are not his aims at all, and, even if they were, he would be incapable of succeeding anyway. But far from blunting its impact, the obliqueness of this approach makes it all the more powerful. We feel a sense of intimacy with Cohen that would not have been possible if he attempted to express his ardency in more conventional terms. Rather than aim directly at intimacy, Cohen's most affecting songs take a circuitous route, denying that intimacy is possible at all and seeking to make the listener complicit in this denial.

## Get a Personality!

To understand how Cohen can pull off this trick of making us feel close to him by telling us again and again that he'll no longer let anyone close to him, it is useful to turn to Søren Kierkegaard's first major work, *The Concept of Irony* (1841). The book turns its attention to Socrates, a man who was executed for, in addition to alleged heresy, "seducing" or "corrupting" the youth of Athens. Kierkegaard barely mentions the possible sexual connotations of this alleged seduction, but he does argue that, for all his virtues, Socrates was not entirely innocent of leading those around him astray. Indeed, leading others astray was central to his method of philosophy. In ancient Greek, this method came to be called "irony" (*eironeia*).

In Socrates's time *eironeia* was a relatively uncommon word. It would have been intelligible enough as a modification of *eirō*, an ordinary word for "speak," but its unnecessary suffix would have made it sound to Greek ears something like how "speechifying" sounds to us today: as a mockingly fancy term for speech that was too fancy to be trusted. When writers like Plato used it to refer to Socrates, it came to mean something like "dissembling."[2] When Socrates claimed to be ignorant, there was a sense in which this was *merely speech*. Just as Cohen has made a career of being simultaneously confessional and reclusive, Socrates always seemed to be hiding something of himself, even when his language sounded straightforward.

All speech hides far more than it reveals. To say anything meaningful at all requires us *not* to say countless other things. But Socratic irony elevates the concealment built into all speech by making hearers conscious of the distance between the speaker and what he says. In everyday conversation, when you ask how I am doing and I give only a vague, conventional answer, I allow the conversation to flow right past the divergence between my words and my feelings. If, however, I reply with an especially curt "Fine" and turn my head away, I am letting you know that I am not fine at all and that there are depths to myself that I am refusing to express. You can choose either to ignore my curtness or to question me further about my true feelings, but in either case I have made plain that something about me cannot be conventionally expressed.

Such ostentatious self-concealment makes us more attentive not only to the speaker's motivations, but to our own as well. When Cohen asks dismissively, "But you don't really care for music, do you?" we can't help but think about both what he's hiding and what we're hiding. Socrates made an art of this approach to conversation, continually drawing his friends in by saying both less and more than he seemed to intend. In the process, Kierkegaard argues, Socrates made it possible for everyone who associated with him to develop a "personality." Kierkegaard uses this term in a technical sense to mean far more than when we now say, "She has a great personality," or even confrontationally, "Come on, get a personality!" In the modern casual sense, when we refer to someone's "personality," we refer to a consistent pattern of interacting with others that is in some way unique to the individual. When, in contrast, Kierkegaard uses the term, he is referring to a kind of self-awareness that *cannot* be found in casual interactions with others. Socrates's philosophical genius lay in challenging his contemporaries to realize that who they were could not be reduced to their engagement in the life of their community.

His irony was thus not merely a matter of words, but of interpersonal relations. Ordinary verbal irony takes a statement to mean its opposite, as when the hackneyed sitcom character goads a friend who has just disclosed too much, "Why don't you tell us what you *really* think?" We find comfort in such scenes—albeit a dull, anesthetizing sort—because irony is generally an unthreatening way of cultivating intimacy. An ironic turn of phrase points to a meaning beneath the surface, and when the speaker acknowledges that we grasp this meaning, we share with her an open secret. According to Kierkegaard, Socratic irony operated on a similar principle, but it was much more enlivening, since what was hidden behind everyday language was not just an opposite meaning for the sentence but an entire self-understanding. Appreciating Socratic irony meant grasping not just the hidden meaning of a sentence, but that all meaning involves a certain amount of hiding.

The meaning of the word "irony" has continued to evolve since Socrates's time to the point where we can now call facts of nature "ironic." When I can't help giggling at the church sign that quotes Psalms 16:11 ("In your right hand there are pleasures forever") or Cohen titters at the stubborn persistence of sexual desire in the old and frail, we are marveling at what Kierkegaard calls "nature's irony," the notion that nature itself seems to be screwing with us. Just as an act of verbal irony hides a true intention behind an opposing sign, nature seems to conceal its intentions behind the obstreperous or absurd appearances it puts before us. No doubt, there is often consolation to be found in this approach to nature, but when we try to locate irony either in words or in states of affairs, we lose sight of the ways that the practice of irony in the Socratic fashion builds personalities and holds a promise of intimacy. Kierkegaard's interpretation of Socrates helps us understand that irony is not just a relationship between a speaker and his words, but a relationship between subjects who share a private meaning. What makes this sharing so freeing is that it does not bind us to all the ordinary implications of our statements. The ironist affirms neither the literal meaning of his words nor the opposite, but merely recognizes that the hearer is capable of understanding the gap between words and intentions—between the social order and an individual personality.

While the recognition of this gap can open up the possibility of greater intimacy, such intimacy cannot be sustained forever. The sitcom character whose only goal is to entertain can get by indefinitely on such a lack of commitment, but someone who wants to disclose a personality through irony has the much more difficult task of being serious about connecting with others on a foundation of unseriousness. The latter type cannot be merely a joker who mocks all seriousness, including his own, but must keep alive a promise even as he acknowledges that nothing really can be promised. In this regard Leonard Cohen's best work not only keeps alive the Socratic project, but renews and improves upon it.

## Cohen's Sexy Irony

One of the reasons many of Cohen's songs are so affecting is that, even when they fall into our modern fixation with nature's irony, they quickly return to the kind of Socratic irony that seeks to restore a one-to-one connection. From "Suzanne" to "Ain't No Cure for Love" to "Democracy," Cohen's songs frequently feature alternations between the third and second person that allow the song's narrator to take a bird's-eye perspective in one breath and attempt to reestablish an ironic connection in the next. "Closing Time" finds a great deal of irony in the mating rituals of adults past their primes, but these impersonal musings give way to the second person: "I loved you for your beauty / That doesn't make a fool of me. / You were in it for your beauty too." Here Cohen initially seems to offer a half-apology for the superficiality of his earlier attraction, but he retracts it with a challenge: who we are inevitably evades what convention says we must be. The connection may have been superficial, but because what was superficial was also shared, it was a connection nonetheless. When, however, Cohen proceeds in the next line to mock himself for the "voice that sounds like God to me / Declaring that your body's really you," he calls both his original cynicism and its romantic cancellation into doubt. The supposition that our true selves are driven by biological urges that exceed the strictures of culture is itself a delusion, though a not entirely unhappy one. This admission of self-deception is both an offering to the listener to share a secret about the narrator's true self and a suggestion that this true self does not really exist. Unlike the fascination with the lover's beauty, the "voice that sounds like God to me" is apparent only to the narrator. Cohen has given us a clue about his true feelings and yet made clear that it is not a reliable clue—and, in any event, he's not sure these feelings exist in the first place.

In this oscillation between offering up a hidden meaning and suggesting that there might not be any hidden meaning at all, Cohen follows the contours of Socratic irony, which is a large part of what makes his lyrics so inviting despite their coldness. Even in moments of brutal cynicism, as in "Everybody Knows" and "The Future," he makes clear that his goal is not to prove the impossibility of genuine intimacy, but to *cultivate* the same sort of intimacy he has just claimed is impossible. In many of Plato's dialogues, including the *Meno*, the *Republic*, and the *Theaetetus*, Socrates shows a similar commitment to pursuing shared wisdom with his friends even as he voices suspicions that such wisdom is impossible. His clear-headed rejection of apparent points of agreement encourages his friends to seek a higher truth with him, and his moments of skepticism about this higher truth only heighten their desire. Because he refuses to accept superficial agreement, they know that any points of agreement that do emerge will not be superficial. Like Cohen, he makes us see the value of commitment by denying that present circumstances meet its stringent conditions. Yet though there is undoubtedly far more philosophical range in the Socratic reflections that have been passed down to us by Plato, what makes Cohen's songs *sexy* is an additional element not found in Kierkegaard's account of Socrates and at best underdeveloped in Plato's depictions of Socrates.

This extra element, it should first be noted, is not sex itself. Though our modern term "platonic love" can be traced back to Plato's depiction in the *Symposium* of a chaste and high-minded Socrates, previously in that same dialogue Socrates is seen flirting openly with the host of the party, and there is clearly an erotic element to Socrates playing with Phaedo's hair in the *Phaedo* (section 89b). Like Cohen, Socrates is capable of being entranced by both superworldly concerns and tactile immediacy. Yet what gives Cohen's songs an additional erotic charge is their tendency to dissolve their own ironic distance. In its allusions to the AIDS crisis, the breakdown of social bonds, systematic oppression, and casual infidelity, "Everybody Knows" is thoroughly cynical about the possibility of love in the modern world, and yet the song's third verse steps out of the omniscient, scornful third-person perspective to call out an unfaithful partner in the second person. Cohen's words, "Everybody knows you've been discreet, but there were so many people you just had to meet without your clothes" are a clear example of verbal irony, but this is not the sort of knowing irony that seeks to disengage entirely. The tone is hostile, but this very hostility is a sign that Cohen has stepped out of the ironic stance that makes his personality inaccessible. When the rest of the song returns to its ironic stance, it thus has a tone of disoriented pleading rather than resignation at the modern evils it catalogues. Cohen's irony allows him to avoid committing himself to the position of either the distant sage or the bitter lover, and this refusal to make a commitment implies that he would be open to encountering us on such an ambiguous basis as well.

"Democracy" makes a similar appeal for an imperfect love amidst a backdrop of disaffection with the modern world, but in this case the second-person address is kinkier and less wounded. Because the rest of the song is concerned with grand social and political themes, the "Ah baby, we'll be making love again" stanza appears with something of a jolt. The sexual metaphors that follow seem intended more to make the listener blush and giggle than to arouse, but this mixture of the political and the sexual also adds a new sense to Cohen's direct political claims. When he concludes the stanza with the chorus, "Democracy is coming to the U.S.A.," it becomes clear that by "democracy" he does not just mean that those in power will take into account the needs of the poor and disenfranchised, but that the immediacy of human connection will not be subordinated to alien powers and standards. Our obsession with sex, he seems to be suggesting with his overwrought erotic language, can appear trivial when considered alongside the greatest dilemmas of our time, and yet the perspective that judges it trivial only does so by laying claim to an established set of values—which is exactly what democracy helps to undermine. The stanza is sexy not because there is a direct erotic appeal in the image of "going down so deep / the river's gonna weep," but because Cohen shows a willingness to consider the full ridiculousness of sex and still conclude that it nonetheless *matters*. Here, as in "Everybody Knows," the irony is turned back on itself, so that dissembling serves the purpose of emphasizing the possibility of a speech that also expresses something sincere.

## The Crack in Everything

This pattern of interrupting the distant with the immediate can be seen in so many of Cohen's songs that it might seem to be an unconscious tic, but the explicit themes of "Hallelujah" and "Anthem" show that Cohen is well aware of what he is doing. "Hallelujah" features a similar narrative structure to the songs we have been considering, shifting from the third-person observer to the second-person accuser-forgiver and then back to the third-person observer, but even its third-person reflections are about the centrality of irony in love. The song draws an analogy between religious and sexual ecstasy, but it posits that what makes both so transporting is not their ability to bring us to a completely alien land, but rather their inherent incompleteness. The original studio version of the song includes a verse that makes irony central to every such experience of ecstasy: "There's a blaze of light in every word / It doesn't matter which you heard / The holy or the broken 'Hallelujah.'" The "brokenness" of any particular instance or expression of love is not a sign that lovers have failed to come to terms with one another, but the space in which love is allowed to develop. Thus when Cohen recalls a failed relationship with a mix of disappointment and certainty that it was destined to fail, he acknowledges the presence of intimacy even in the impossibility of intimacy. This resoluteness in the face of breakdown is even clearer in the verse, "And even though it all went wrong / I'll stand before the lord of song / With nothing on my tongue but 'Hallelujah.'" Here Cohen makes explicit his affirmation of love in spite of its failure to live up to its own promises. Song itself is a kind of promise that makes no promises. The singer does not really bare his true self or commit himself to any particular line of action, and yet willingness to sing passionately anyway commits him to pursuing love even where its conditions are absent. This insight can only be conveyed by someone who is willing to embrace the role of the ironist with all its contradictions, which is perhaps why so many artists who manage to cover the song with more sustained passion (k.d. lang deserves special mention) nevertheless seem to be missing something. Cohen's renditions of the song can't help vocally winking through lines like "Now you never even show it to me, do you?" but such unseriousness avoids yanking us out of the song's emotional power and, indeed, only pulls us in further. Only someone able to appreciate the comedy of his own desires can take the tragedy of love seriously without becoming resigned to it.

Perhaps Cohen's most systematic assertion that the impossibility of intimacy is no obstacle to continuing to strive for it appears in "Anthem," which treats music as a fitting mode of expression not just for love, but for all hope in a broken universe. One who rings "the bells that still can ring" does not assume that song can ever provide a perfectly adequate offering to whoever might be listening, and yet she chooses to make this offering anyway. She does so not because she deludes herself into thinking that this time might be different or even that the mere attempt is all that can be asked, but because the imperfection of the offering of song is part of what makes the song an intimate art form. The most intimate singer would thus not be one who manages to spackle over all the flaws and inconsistencies in her position, but one who lets the light get in.

## The Bleak Side of Irony

This sets a pretty high bar for the successful songwriter. In order to hold together all of these thoughts, Cohen relies on a great deal of multiply embedded irony. In a typical verse, a surface expression of disappointment with love incompletely hides a willingness to forgive, and for this irony to work Cohen must assume the listener can perceive both the disappointment and the forgiveness at once. At the same time, in order for the sincerity of this expression of forgiveness to be apparent, Cohen must also make clear that he still feels wounded by the experience, and yet that this woundedness is not an absolute obstacle to a genuine connection. Moreover, to avoid putting undue pressure on the listener or appearing too ardent, Cohen must also recognize that there is nothing special about his reaction—that's just the way love works—at the same time that he insists that he still finds *this* connection important or even sacred.

With all this weight put on a single ironic expression, we should not be too surprised that Cohen at times allows his irony to collapse under the weight of its own contradictions. This bleaker side of irony can be found in "Tower of Song." The song begins with its irony in full force, as the narrator acknowledges his desire while simultaneously trying to eliminate every hint of a request: "And I'm crazy for love, but I'm not coming on." But as the narrator continues we realize that he is really not offering any kind of connection at all apart from the pure dissemination of feelings through song. The song is strikingly earnest in its acknowledgment of the pain previous romantic failures have caused him, but it refuses to acknowledge any vulnerability in the present. Cohen is, to be sure, his usual charming self, modestly acknowledging his lowly position in the Tower relative to such greats as Hank Williams, but the Tower is less a symbol of phallic incompleteness than a fortress from which he can only observe the world passively. When the song shifts from the lofty third-person perspective to the intimate second, it fails to betray Cohen's customary vulnerability. He finds himself stunned that the gulf between him and his lover has grown so wide and despairs, "All the bridges are burning that we might have crossed, but I feel so close to everything that we lost," but he catches himself and ruefully observes, "We'll never have to lose it again." From his new position in the Tower, love is merely the raw material of song. His love will thus persist indefinitely in its present form: "You'll be hearing from me, baby, long after I'm gone. I'll be speaking to you sweetly from a window in the Tower of Song." Here the notion that love is inseparable from its simulation, which such songs as "Closing Time" and "I'm Your Man" merely leave open as a possibility in order to solicit further intimacy, is acknowledged as an insuperable fact. He has been telling us all along that every promise of genuine intimacy had to be false, and yet we were innocent or stubborn enough to believe these promises anyway.

This collapse of irony into bare-faced cynicism is a danger present in all irony, since irony works by giving only a hint that there is more meaning hidden in a personality than what can be conveyed in words. This promise seduces us because it conveys that we, like the speaker, can contain an entire life that is unable to be expressed in words, but it also cancels itself as a promise. The ironist can always say, "What, you didn't take me seriously, did you?" and we have no grounds for a valid counter-claim, since we were warned from the very beginning not to take everything too seriously. The ironist can betray us without leaving proof that we have been betrayed.

Socrates, too, sometimes rejected friends and demanded solitude, and in Plato's depictions of him his assertions that he just wants to be left alone sometimes sound sincere. And yet in the *Phaedrus* Plato was also careful to have him denounce writing as a departure from the true activity of philosophy. Like the painter—and for that matter like Cohen's singer from whom we'll be hearing long after he's gone—the philosopher who is present to us only through his writings is one who is no longer open to our appeals and challenges (section 275d). Like the writer who refuses to be held to account for his philosophical assumptions, the singer who refuses all desire for the return of his love has yielded to the temptation of making his irony absolute.

This is a large part of what makes Cohen so rare. The modern world has no shortage of ironists, and many, like

Socrates in the ancient world, succeed in speaking on multiple levels at once and enlivening us to the possibilities of personality. Yet Cohen's songs show a commitment to establishing and renewing direct personal connections in spite of their ironic tendency to undermine such connections. For Cohen, it has never been "the gift of a golden voice" that allowed him to connect with listeners, but his acknowledgment of the limitations of this voice.

# 9
# The Mystery of the Mirror

LISA WARENSKI

The room is small, but the window faces the river and the light is good. The floor, made of fine burnished wood, is uneven. A dancer's space. It's here that the story told in the song "Suzanne" begins.

Leonard Cohen's muse, Suzanne Verdal, was a modern dancer and choreographer. She was the wife of Armand Villaincourt, a sculptor of some renown who was fifteen years her senior and Cohen's friend. After her relationship with Villaincourt ended, Suzanne rented an apartment in a rooming house along the Saint Lawrence River in Old Montreal, where she lived with her child by Villaincourt. There were few cafés in the area at the time, so Suzanne would have her friends come to her home, where she would serve them tea and mandarin oranges. She had a practice of lighting a candle to invoke the "Spirit of Poetry" and invite quality conversation when she and Cohen had tea together. (I found helpful details about the inspiration for "Suzanne" in *I'm Your Man: The Life of Leonard Cohen* by Sylvie Simmons.)

As the story of the song unfolds, it exhibits a certain conception of self-awareness and of relationships between conscious subjects that is embraced by psychologists and those philosophers who work in the tradition known as phenomenology. Phenomenologists are concerned with the structures of consciousness as they are experienced from a first-person perspective.

A key element of the view portrayed in the song is the idea that our bodies shape our minds: we experience the world through our bodies, and we're implicitly aware of ourselves in our experience. A second, related component is that we come to appreciate ourselves and others as being "minded"—as having beliefs, desires, and emotions—through our interactions with each other. Psychologists take our capacity to understand ourselves as minded, as well as our capacity to understand others as having minds of their own, to be part of the process of maturation. This maturational process is activated in the context of a parent-child relationship in which the adult "mirrors" the developing mind of the child in such a way that the child experiences his mind as his own. The child will likewise come to understand other people as having minds of their own. Through this process, the child acquires the ability to represent and respond to the mental states of others—a process that is sometimes referred to as reflective functioning.

## The Body Self

To begin to understand what it could be to "touch a perfect body with a mind," we must first consider what it is to be embodied. Persons are conscious, and they have bodies, as Leonard Cohen notoriously reminds us. But you don't just possess your body: your body *is* the perspective in space and time from which you understand the world. Your body structures your experience of the world, including your experience of other people. We can consider our bodies as objects that can be observed, examined, or represented in paintings or sculptures, and when we do, we're considering our bodies as objects from a third-person perspective. But from a first-person perspective, our bodies *constitute* our point of view. We perceive the world with and through our bodies. Our experiences have the qualitative character that they do because of our sensory capacities. There is something that it's *like* for you, from your perspective, to walk along a misty waterfront, to hear the boats go by, and to see the chapel of Notre-Dame-de-Bon-Secours. From a first-person perspective, the body is "lived" as opposed to experienced as an object. The lived body is the body as an embodied first-person perspective that structures our experience. This type of theory originates in the work of Edmund Husserl (as explained in *Husserl's Phenomenology* by Dan Zahavi) and is developed by Maurice Merleau-Ponty *(Phenomenology of Perception).*

A key dimension of the first-person, embodied perspective that plays a crucial role in our experience of ourselves and others is what phenomenologists call pre-reflective self-consciousness. Pre-reflective self-consciousness is a kind of awareness of ourselves that we have *before* we engage in any form of reflection. It's implicit in our experience; indeed, it constitutes the distinct first-personal character of experience: my experiences are unmistakably mine in that it's *I* who is having them. For phenomenologists, pre-reflective self-consciousness is embodied, and we are pre-reflectively aware of our bodies *in* experience.

Perception isn't mere passive reception. It involves bodily action. The bodily actions may be so subtle and small that they aren't noticed by the perceiver. For example, the tiny movements of our eyes, called saccades, that take place when we read a book or watch a basketball game typically go unnoticed. In other cases, we are tacitly aware of our bodies when we explore and experience the world. If I reach for a cup of tea offered by Suzanne, I'm tacitly aware of where my body is as I perform this action, and this tacit awareness enables me to judge how far I have to reach in order to pick up the cup of tea. As I draw the cup of tea to my mouth, I know where the cup is in relation to my mouth. I may slow the movement of my arm as I bring the cup near my lips, and I'll tip my head to make contact with its thin china rim in anticipation of sipping the hot tea. I have a sense of where my body is and how it is moving as I perform the action (proprioception), and I know where my body is in relation to other things (kinaesthetic awareness). But I don't ordinarily reflect on my movements as I reach for a cup of tea; I simply reach for the cup.

The tacit bodily awareness that I have when I reach for the cup, draw it to my mouth, and take a sip of tea, is a form of pre-reflective self-consciousness. When I perform these actions, I'm not aware of my body as an object. My body isn't "given" to me in experience as a spatial object in the way that it is when it's perceived by another person. As Husserl observed, originally, my body is experienced as a unified field of activity, a potentiality of mobility and volition, an "I do'" and "I can" (*Husserl's Phenomenology,* p. 101).

When I do sip the tea, I experience the tea as being hot, and there is something that it's like for me to have this experience, which is to say, the experience has a particular qualitative character. The tea feels hot in my mouth, but I may also experience it as warming my body. My experience of the hot tea is unmistakably *mine*. This sense of "mineness" is also a form of pre-reflective self-consciousness.

My attention will likely be drawn to my experience of the hot tea, in which case I will become reflectively aware of my experience. I may say to Suzanne, "The tea is hot." When I'm aware *that* I'm having an experience of a certain kind, I'm *reflectively* aware, which is to say, I'm reflectively self-conscious.

We are aware of our bodies in various ways and to varying degrees when we perform particular actions. We sometimes deliberately guide our bodily movements, but we're often not fully aware of our bodily movements in the reflective and self-conscious sense of "aware." For example, when I peel a mandarin orange, I may look for a spot near the top of the orange where I can insert the top of my thumb to pierce its skin, and I deliberately insert my thumb in the chosen spot. I am aware *that* I am inserting my thumb in a particular spot. I may also be self-consciously aware of the movement of my thumb as I begin to peel away the skin. But I'm not reflectively aware of the kinetic melodies of my fingers and hands as I remove the skin of the orange in its entirety and pull away the excess fibers. A given action will often involve both reflective and pre-reflective elements of self-awareness.

## The Role of the Other in Self-Awareness

Philosophers and psychologists alike have recognized the importance of relations with other conscious beings—intersubjective relations—in our capacity for reflective self-consciousness. We become aware of ourselves when we're perceived by others. As I will explain, the very possibility of your becoming a fully human person and acquiring an awareness of yourself as such depends on this kind of social interaction.

The way that another person can make you aware of yourself is nicely illustrated by the following example from the chapter entitled "The Look" in Jean-Paul Sartre's *Being and Nothingness*:

> Let us imagine that moved by jealousy, curiosity, or vice I have just glued my ear to the door and looked through a keyhole. . . . But all of a sudden, I hear footsteps in the hall. Someone is looking at me! What does this mean? It means that I am suddenly affected in my being and that essential modifications appear in my structure—modifications which I can apprehend and fix conceptually by means of the reflective *cogito*. . . . I see *myself* because *somebody* sees me—as it is usually expressed. (pp. 347–49)

Imagine that you are the person who has just looked through the keyhole. When you hear the footsteps in the hall, you are made aware of yourself in the way that Sartre describes. For this to be possible, you must be aware that you exist in such a way that you can be seen by another. But this sense of your own visibility is immediately linked to your pre-reflective, proprioceptive-kinaesthetic awareness of your body ("Phenomenological Approaches to Self-Consciousness," by Gallagher and Zahavi, p. 24).

Imagine that you see the person in the hallway who is capable of seeing you. You see the other because the other is embodied and so is an object for you. But when you look at the other, you experience the other as an experiencing *subject* as opposed to a mere object. You don't, of course, experience the other in the same way that the other experiences herself; you experience the other as a subject whose perspective isn't directly accessible to you. You're able to recognize the other as an experiencing subject only because you, too, are an embodied subject. Leonard Cohen exploits this facet of perception in "Take This Longing" when he says that "your body like a searchlight" his (Cohen's) poverty reveals.

Our capacity to recognize our mental states—our beliefs, desires, and intentions—as ours, as well as our ability to understand another person's state of mind, originates in the context of social interaction. Developmental psychologists understand this process as having its roots in early social interactions, and in particular, in the context of parent-child relations. A developing infant will eventually come to experience her consciousness as distinctively her own by being exposed to the reactions of others to herself.

When responding to an infant's changing needs, a parent plays the role of a mirror to the developing infant. In *Playing and Reality* (p. 151), Donald Winnicott asks, rhetorically, What does the baby see when he or she looks at the mother's face? Winnicott answers that ordinarily, what the baby sees is himself or herself: the mother is looking at the baby, and what she looks like (to the baby) is related to what she sees there. If the mother is attentive and responsive to the baby's expression, the baby will see himself or herself reflected in the mother's gaze.

In this metaphor of the mother as mirror, the mother doesn't merely reflect the infant's behavior; instead, she anticipates and reflects the developing mental states of the infant. The mother is thus something of a "magical" mirror in that she facilitates the infant becoming a person. In her 1998 article "Having a Mind of One's Own and Holding the Other in Mind," Susan W. Coates explains the sense in which the mother should be understood as a magical mirror. The mother sees in the infant something that is still only potential—something that she both recognizes and shapes. The mother's ability to see the unrealized potential in the infant is what allows the infant to find it in the face of the mother, and to experience the reflected state of mind as his or her own.

Dr. Coates offers us the following example by way of illustrating how a child can come to discover something new about his mind through his mother:

> A young toddler, barely two, is playing in the backyard; he excitedly pulls at and sniffs some flowers while making excited but unintelligible utterances. His mother can see his pleasure, a pleasure that differs from her own, and smiles in recognition saying, "You really love those colors, don't you? You are a guy who loves flowers." Now in addition to the flowers and the child's excitement, there is a third space (Ogden 1994) where the boy moves from a spontaneous sensory experience to a discovery of the experience (of his enjoying colors and the flowers) in the intersubjective space as it is held in the mind of the mother. The child looks at the mother, sees himself, and smiles; there is a recognition and a discovery of a part of the self held by the other. By virtue of being sensitively met, the child comes to experience loving colors and flowers as a part of his notion of himself, and this notion has emerged in the transitional space created by the mother's attuned response. (pp. 122–23)

By being attentive and receptive to the child's responses, the mother has enabled the child to experience his responses as his own. The child thus experiences his mind as his own. In time, the child will come to appreciate the mother as an autonomous, separate person, and he will develop the capacity to experience some of her responses as expressions of love.

The need for the other in establishing the self is paradoxical: in order for you to differentiate yourself from the other and to experience your own agency, you need to be recognized by the other. This is "the paradox of recognition." Psychologist Jessica Benjamin, who has examined the implications of this need for the other, writes "At the very moment we come to understand the meaning of 'I, myself,' we are forced to see the limitations of that self" (p. 33). The paradox was first recognized as such by Hegel in 1807 (p. 178), who understood recognition to be essential to our development as social beings, and self-consciousness to exist in and for itself when, and only by the fact that, it is acknowledged by another. Some version of the paradox may be alluded to in Cohen's song "Who by Fire," which is based on a Hebrew prayer that is chanted on the Day of Atonement. The prayer recites the various ways in which you might leave this world: some will go by fire, some by water, some by sword, and so on. In "Who by Fire," Cohen asks, "Who in solitude, who in this mirror / . . . And who shall I say is calling?".

As many psychologists have pointed out, fathers and other primary caretakers—not just mothers—can be magical mirrors for young children. Moreover, other adults and older siblings who are capable of responding to young children in this special way can serve as mirrors. In Leonard Cohen's song, Suzanne possesses and exhibits this special sensitivity when she holds the mirror for the children who "are leaning out for love" and perhaps, as "Our Lady of the Harbour," for the rest of us as well.

## The Epistemic Value of Love

Being experienced and reflected by others in the way that I described above is essential to the maturational process, but the value of such reflection doesn't diminish upon reaching maturity. On the contrary, true and accurate reflection is a central component of friendship and love, and it's a primary reason why we value these kinds of relationships. Love in its various forms is one means by which we can acquire self-knowledge or self-understanding, and in particular, knowledge of our values, dispositions, and concerns. *Episteme* is the Greek word for knowledge, and to say that love is a pathway to self-knowledge is to say that love has, among other benefits, epistemic value. Our ability to see and accurately reflect each other is central to love in that it enables us to form relationships based on mutual trust and respect, without which genuine love isn't possible.

In her discussion of the epistemic significance of love, Neera K. Badhwar reminds us that Aristotle thought that friends served as "mirrors of the soul" for each other. She then draws a parallel between the mirroring that takes place between friends and the mirroring that occurs in a parent-child relationship. For a friend to be such a mirror, he or she must reflect the person accurately and without distortion, and do so reliably over the course of the friendship. Love relationships, whether of friendship or romantic love, reveal ourselves to ourselves in that we are seen and affirmed in the eyes of the other ("Love," p. 57). This mirroring seems to be an essential part of the friendships at the heart of Cohen's two novels: between Breavman and Krantz in *The Favourite Game* and between the narrator and F. in *Beautiful Losers*.

A friend or lover does not merely reflect you as you are in the moment. As in the case of a parent-child relationship, the gaze of the one who is the mirror does more than reflect the beloved truly and accurately: the mirroring person also shows the beloved what he or she as mirror sees. Cohen's poem "Beneath My Hands" quite explicitly expresses a lover's desire to act as such a mirror ("I want my body and my hands / to be pools / for your looking and laughing"). Like a sensitive parent, the friend or lover is a magical mirror who offers you an interpretation of yourself in which you may discover or construct an aspect of you. In this sense, the friend or lover reflects the person you are becoming as well as the person you are and have been.

As Badhwar and others have observed, the acknowledgment of a person's potential by a friend or lover can help to bring about that very potential. This idea is given to us in Plato's *Symposium*, where love is seen as the power by which we bring forth the beauty of another by recognizing it. The possibility of bringing out a person's potential rests on an acknowledgment of that person's inherent value as a human being and the valuing of his personal qualities for their own sake. "To love is not only to respond to value but also, thereafter, to seek value and to expect to find it. This optimistic, value-seeking spirit makes love imaginative and discerning, thereby enabling the lover to perceive potentials that even the beloved cannot see" ("Love," p. 55).

In a love relationship or friendship, a union is formed through the history of interactions between two people that potentially transforms them both. Love is not just an emotional state that is present at a particular time; it represents a complex pattern of interactions between two people involving emotional interdependence and appreciative response. As the philosopher Amelie Rorty notes, love exhibits *historicity*: it arises from and is shaped by a pattern of dynamic interactions between people. The pattern of interactions that constitutes the relationship shapes and transforms the lovers (*Friendship*, pp. 73–77). You are who you are in the relationship because of the particular other, a particularity that is known and experienced by you in virtue of the ways that it is expressed.

## The Mystery of the Mirror

We can imagine Suzanne as Leonard Cohen might have seen her, sitting across the table from him in her apartment in the late afternoon. The fading light through the window beside her illuminates her face: undertones of rose and terre verte. During a pause in the conversation, perhaps she gets him on her wavelength. Then she lets the river answer.

Leonard Cohen and Suzanne Verdal did not sleep together. But in a 1994 radio interview with the BBC, Cohen admits to touching her perfect body with his mind "because there was no other opportunity." Although her relationship with Villaincourt had ended by the time she moved to the Montreal waterfront, circumstances didn't permit a romantic relationship with Cohen (*I'm Your Man*, p. 129).

As a professional dancer and the object of Cohen's desire, Suzanne no doubt had a "perfect body." The facts and circumstances together initially suggest a somewhat literal interpretation of the line of the song in which Cohen says, "you've touched her perfect body with your mind." But this objectified physical appreciation of Suzanne can't be the basis for her trust, which is what the other line of the couplet asserts as having been secured by your (his) touch of the mind. Nor is the body-as-object plausibly what "perfect body" refers to in the lines where first Jesus, and then Suzanne, touches *your* perfect body. The body-perfect must ultimately be understood as the embodied subject, in other words, the person incarnate.

When Jesus touches your perfect body with his mind, and so you come to think maybe you'll trust him, the body that he touches is the mortal you. The trust that is thereby engendered is the result of Jesus's true and accurate reflection of you—not just certain aspects of you, but the "perfect" you. In this context, perhaps you as you were made in the image of God and you as you might come to be realized through fellowship with God. This touching of the body by the mind would be a form of seeing and understanding; if it is an expression of love, it is an expression of *agape*, the Greek term for a kind of love that is unconditional and spiritual. In God's eyes, people are intrinsically valuable, and they have equal worth. *Agape* recognizes the inherent value of persons as such, and to be seen in this way by Jesus is to be understood and valued for your own sake as a person. (On the other hand, there is textual evidence for both a Christian interpretation of Jesus and an understanding of him, by Cohen, as a fellow anguished Jew. If Jesus is taken to be the latter, his touching of your mind may be an expression of *philia*, that is to say, brotherly love.)

In the case of friendship or a love relationship, however, people value each other not only for their intrinsic worth as persons but for their individuality. When Suzanne touches your perfect body with her mind, she sees and appreciates you as a unique human being. What makes you unique are your abilities, dispositions, values, and concerns, and their concrete style of expression ("Love," p. 64). Suzanne reflects truly those qualities that make you who you are. You know that you can trust her because she values and respects *you*.

Suzanne touches the embodied you with her mind. The body that is touched is not merely the body taken as object; it is the body *as* the field of physical activity *and* the vehicle of expression of the "I" as subject. When she touches your perfect body with her mind, she sees your beauty as it might be physically expressed in erotic love. She sees you through a history of shared perceptions, imaginative thoughts, and feelings—a history that bears traces of your past experiences and which portends the future. And she holds you in her mind. To touch someone's perfect body is, among other things, to play the role of the magical mirror, the mirror that reflects not only what is but what can be.

Suzanne sets her cup of tea down on the table. Daylight has vanished, and in its place is the flame of the candle that she lit for you when you arrived. As she lifts her head, her eyes meet yours. In her gaze, you find what you will always want again.[1]

---

[1] Thanks to Peter Julian, Maria Kowalski, Nicholas Pappas, and Barbara Pizer for helpful conversations. Special thanks are due to April Selley for interpretive assistance with the Judeo-Christian elements of "Suzanne" and to Jason Holt, the editor of this volume, for many helpful editorial suggestions.

# 10
# Leonard Cohen on Romantic Love

SIMON RICHES

Leonard Cohen offers a conception of romantic love from a distinctly spiritual perspective. With characteristic emphasis on the poetics of love and relationships, we might say that Cohen worships female beauty to the extent that people of faith encounter a religious experience. Juxtaposed with this spiritualization of love, Cohen's songs also embody a conflicted picture of relationships, where his protagonists enter into relationships with each other that are, somewhat paradoxically, at once both distant and close. In his songs, military metaphors abound and the conflict Cohen depicts is dark, solitary, and often underpinned by degrees of irrationality and self-deception.

The topic of self-deception raises a paradox about rationality that has long perplexed philosophers, namely: *how is it possible* to lie to yourself? After all, how can we concurrently hold one belief and another that contradicts it? Cohen's songs express a spiritualized conception of romantic love and show that Cohen addresses the paradox of self-deception by offering an understanding of romantic love that goes beyond reason; it is based instead on faith. In doing so, he rejects a pessimistic determinism in relationships and embraces freedom, authenticity, and irony. The irony in Cohen's songs is the natural consequence of the conflict.

## The Erotic and the Spiritual

There's a striking case of ambiguity in "Night Comes On" where he recounts an episode of being locked in a kitchen, taking to religion, and wondering about the length of time "she" would stay. One possible clarification of this rather suggestive line is that religion is a woman, or even women in general. In other words, his relations with women—and indeed female beauty—engender a kind of religious experience, albeit of a more hedonistic kind, which is to be accorded something approaching worship. In so doing, Cohen follows a tradition in the history of art, literature, poetry, and cinema, bringing to mind, for instance, the goddess Venus, Helen of Troy, and the idea of the femme fatale as a contemporary goddess. We might look no further than "Light as the Breeze" to see this played out in full. In this song, Cohen is literally worshipping a woman on his knees, in an encounter that appears to eventually bring about salvation. In the early 1990s, Cohen said: "I don't think a man ever gets over that first sight of the naked woman. I think that's Eve standing over him, that's the morning and the dew on the skin. And I think that's the major content of every man's imagination. All the sad adventures in pornography and love and song are just steps on the path towards that holy vision" (quoted in Simmons's *I'm Your Man*, p. 20). Countless Cohen songs concern a woman as the central subject; and, through endless *eulogizing*, Cohen invokes the idea of something transcendental in his appreciation of female beauty. The reference to blessings from heaven in "Light as the Breeze" is matched in songs like "Our Lady of Solitude," where Cohen describes light emanating from a woman's body. Notably, Cohen's biographer Sylvie Simmons remarks on his "flair for fusing the erotic and spiritual" (p. 493), and goes on to recount how this has been an enduring theme right through to his advanced years.

## There Is a War

Ultimately, however, Cohen's fusion of the erotic and the spiritual comes at a cost. Even a song like "Came So Far for

Beauty," despite the protagonist's persistence, is about all that is left behind. There's a sense in which Cohen finds his view of female beauty almost overwhelming, even unsustainable. In "Hallelujah," he places female beauty in the spotlight once again, this time observing it under the moonlight, and explaining how we can be simply overthrown by it. This idea is a recurring theme in Cohen's love songs. A notable example occurs in "The Traitor," in which Cohen draws a distinction between dreamers and men of action, and clearly aligns himself with the former camp. These are presented by Cohen as mutually exclusive categories in terms of one's attitude to love and beauty. The dreamers and men of action are described as being at war; and, for a while at least, the dreamers seem to be winning the battle. Cohen is the great champion of the poet's perspective and, here, we find him celebrating the prominence of the romantic idea of the dreamer; but, as the song goes on, the celebration wanes. By the end of the song, stung by his own falsity, Cohen tells us that he has been openly labeled a traitor.

Cohen's distinction between dreamers and men of action brings to mind those who fantasize and entertain "higher" concerns, on the one hand, and those who take a pragmatic stance with tangible outcomes, on the other. We might broadly think of this distinction in terms of the philosophical conceptions of rationality and irrationality. Cohen's protagonists, in their role as dreamers, can be taken to be endorsing something irrational in their transcendental appreciation of romantic love and beauty. However, the cost is a fragmentary picture of relationships, where things don't run smoothly, despite Cohen's apparent immersion. Often Cohen's songs leave us with a beautifully captured but ultimately conflicted sense of distance and loss. Think of the bittersweet "thanks" in "Famous Blue Raincoat," with so much conflict beneath the surface of simple gratitude; the resentment with which Cohen mocks the master in "Master Song"; and the weariness with which Cohen warns against the dealer in "The Stranger Song." Cohen can cast himself as both close confidante and distant outsider, where the outsider is often also the victim, as in "Death of a Ladies' Man," or in "Master Song," which, like so many of Cohen's best love songs, is about a love triangle, this time employing metaphorical characters of master, pupil, and prisoner. The distance, here, provides Cohen with the space to reflect, but it also yields safety.

So, despite Cohen's protagonists' all-encompassing faith in romance and beauty, their irrationality can also leave them blinded by beauty and, as he describes in "The Traitor," literally among the enemies of love.

## Self-Deception of the Dreamer

The irrationality of Cohen's dreamer accounts for why he is able to occupy positions of both closeness and distance within these relationships. This irrationality may sometimes seem to veer into cases of self-deception. There are clear-cut cases of contradictory thinking in Cohen's songs: the needing and not needing of "Chelsea Hotel #2," and in his poem "You Do Not Have to Love Me," where he writes, "I prayed that you would love me / and that you would not love me."

But the self-deception Cohen depicts often probes much deeper into the heart of relationships. In "Chelsea Hotel #2," Cohen conjures up a beautiful sense of reminiscence as he remembers the woman he was with, but the final verse contradicts our notions of love. Cohen suggests that despite the "love," she was essentially just another. This is confirmed in the final line where he tells her that he doesn't think of her that often. Despite the heightened sense of spiritual love, it appears to still be disposable.

Perhaps even more significantly, in "Famous Blue Raincoat," Cohen has a striking relationship with his "brother"—who he also describes as his "killer"—one that appears so contradictory given the way Cohen seems at once to want to appreciate his killer, despite the fact that there's so much underlying doubt, deliberating whether he misses or forgives him, even oddly approving of his rival's thwarting him. Here, Cohen captures the uncertainty of a complex relationship beautifully. Crucial to this is the way he suggestively depicts his wavering protagonist as a self-deceiver: as someone who holds contradictory beliefs at the same time; or, as philosophers have sometimes put it, as being able to lie to yourself.

In so doing, Cohen draws our attention to the paradox of self-deception. How can we lie to ourselves, since that would mean holding one belief and at the same time holding another that contradicts it? It might seem natural to think that there is—or ought to be—an underlying unity to the human mind, to a person's overall system of thoughts and beliefs, a unity characterized by consistency and coherence. Following the ancient Greek philosopher Aristotle, who characterized human beings as rational animals, the possibility of concurrently held contradictory beliefs doesn't seem to fit with this intuitive picture of our minds. After all, surely I can't be in a position where I'm genuinely able to lie to myself, can I?

The conflict here parallels the conflicted representation of God as caring yet distant, and all-forgiving but punishing. Given this fact, perhaps it is no wonder the man of faith experiences conflicting emotions, like hope and fear, or trust and guilt. One might even argue that there is something in the conflict that intensifies the experience.

But clearly there is an issue over how the philosophical problem of self-deception should be resolved. In the rest of this chapter I will argue that Cohen's conception of love can explain away this paradox if we take seriously the dreamer's view of romantic love and beauty as fundamentally transcendental and beyond reason.

## True Love Leaves No Traces

In Plato's dialogues, the philosopher Socrates asks his interlocutors for definitions of key concepts; for example, he asks: What is justice? What is piety? In this regard, we might equally ask: What is love? It's important to bear in mind that what Socrates sought in each case was a universal and essentialist definition, one that describes the *essence* of the thing in question, and according to which any given concept has a set of necessary and sufficient conditions. This endeavor presupposes what is known in philosophy and cognitive science as the classical theory of concepts.

Given Cohen's poetic and transcendental approach, it is clear that Cohen would reject any classical theory account of love. In other words, he would reject the very idea that love could have a definable essence in the sense described. For a philosophical exponent of this view, we might turn to the later work of the Austrian philosopher Ludwig Wittgenstein. In his *Philosophical Investigations*, Wittgenstein characterizes his position in terms of "language games" and instead of claiming that there's one thing in common to all things we call games, he says that there is a whole network of similarities and connections, rather like the idea of family resemblances:

> Consider for example the proceedings that we call "games." I mean board-games, card-games, ball-games, Olympic games, and so on. What is common to them all?— Don't say: "There must be something common, or they would not be called 'games'"—but look and see whether there is anything common to all.—For if you look at them you will not see something that is common to all, but similarities, relationships, and a whole series of them at that. (section 66)

So, according to Wittgenstein's anti-essentialist view, there's no one common factor connecting all instances of things we call games, or any concept for that matter.

This position can be developed further if we think of love as an essentially *subjective*, rather than objective, concept. According to this view, love will differ in subjective experience from person to person because it is shaped by our cultural norms and attitudes. Psychologist Robert Sternberg argues that we *construct* our love stories. Our constructed love stories draw on our histories and experiences, and we can't see outside of these stories. This view denies the singular and universal definitional approach we see in the classical theory of concepts and casts doubt on certain evolutionary accounts, which view love as a mechanism for survival and genetic replication. Instead, this view suggests a relativized notion of love. In other words, there are no objective truths about love, and love has no objective reality.

Cohen's transcendental account of love is ultimately subjective and won't conform to the essentialist idea of love as being definable. So, if the concept of love has no objective reality—and we reject the idea that there are objective truths about love—and love is instead constructed by the stories and songs born out of the subjective experiences of individuals, then Cohen can describe love in ways that incorporate the contradictory beliefs we find in self-deception.

## Love beyond Reason

One historically popular way to help us make sense of the self-deceivers we find in Cohen's songs is to think of the mind as somehow divided. This is a view that we find in various thinkers, from Plato and Sigmund Freud, to the recent American philosopher Donald Davidson. Davidson puts the idea like this:

> The point is that people can and do sometimes keep closely related but opposed beliefs apart. To this extent we much accept the idea that there can be boundaries between parts of the mind; I postulate such a boundary somewhere between any (obviously) conflicting beliefs. Such boundaries are not discovered by introspection; they are conceptual aids to the coherent description of genuine irrationalities. (p. 211)

This isn't to endorse a physical idea of compartmentalization or division. Rather, as Davidson explains, such division is a conceptual tool to allow us to make sense of self-deception.

One might argue that this "divided mind" explanation of self-deception allows us to make sense of the conflict that the protagonist feels towards Jane and his rival in "Famous Blue Raincoat." Potentially, it's a way to account for such "genuine irrationality." But I think the way Cohen fuses the erotic with the spiritual means we can go a step further than this idea of mental division and irrationality; I think there's a more fundamental explanation that means we can reject the premise that love must have some coherent definition and see Cohen as giving an account of romantic love that goes beyond reason.

In understanding Cohen in this way, we can return to the work of Wittgenstein, this time on religion. In his biography of Wittgenstein, Ray Monk characterizes Wittgenstein's view of religion in the following way: "Religious beliefs are not analogous to scientific theories, and should not be accepted or rejected using the same evidential criteria" (p. 410). So, following Wittgenstein, if Cohen's stance on romantic love and female beauty is akin to religious experience and belief, as I have claimed, then the claims he makes of it need not be subject to the same level of evidential criteria that we reserve for the truths of science. Rather Cohen can endorse a faith-based approach to the truths of love, with all the inconsistencies and contradictions such an approach may entail.

## Sincerely, L. Cohen?

Two consequences emerge from Cohen's standpoint on the relativity of the truths of love. His position becomes both liberated and ironic. With both of these consequences comes yet greater authenticity.

Ultimately, Cohen rejects a pessimistic determinism about love; there's no ultimate path for love to follow but instead a range of narratives about potential love stories. From the conflict, then, we find freedom; and it's in affirming this kind of freedom that I think Cohen reveals his authenticity as someone able to capture in song certain truths about love and beauty.

This emancipatory element to Cohen's work leads him to reject what the philosopher Richard Rorty calls a "final vocabulary." A final vocabulary is a kind of expression that can't be superseded by other alternative descriptions. To reject a final vocabulary of love means that love can be remade and reconstructed through new stories but never definitively articulated.

A songwriter like Cohen, who rejects a final vocabulary for love, is poised to become an ironist. According to Rorty, an ironist fulfills three conditions:

> (1) She has radical and continuing doubts about the final vocabulary she currently uses, because she has been impressed by other vocabularies, vocabularies taken as final by people or books she has encountered; (2) she realizes that argument phrased in her present vocabulary can neither underwrite nor dissolve these doubts; (3) insofar as she philosophizes about her situation, she does not think that her vocabulary is closer to reality than others, that it is in touch with a power not herself. Ironists who are inclined to philosophize see the choice between vocabularies as made neither within a neutral and universal metavocabulary nor by an attempt to fight one's way past appearances to the real, but simply by playing the new off against the old.

Rorty goes on to explain that ironists have a "realization that anything can be made to look good or bad by being redescribed" and are "never quite able to take themselves seriously." They're "always aware that the terms in which they describe themselves are subject to change, always aware of the contingency and frailty of their final vocabularies, and thus of their final selves" (pp. 73–74).

Irony has always been part of Cohen's fusion of the erotic and the spiritual. But, with Cohen's advanced years, the later work embodies an increasingly ironic and self-deprecating tone. Witness songs like "Everybody Knows," "I'm Your Man," "I Can't Forget," "Tower of Song," and "Going Home." These songs are laced with irony. Furthermore, this increased irony is the natural consequence of the rejection of reason that underpins his fusion of the erotic and the spiritual because Cohen is no longer able to take himself fully seriously. And yet something about this only adds to the authenticity. We see more vulnerability; Cohen with his guard down. In doing so, Cohen toys with his relation to his listener, making us consider how much of his lyrics are a reflection of his genuine experience and how much they are employed for romanticized, artistic effect.

This is a reflection we can apply to his entire body of work. We know that Cohen himself was the owner of the famous blue raincoat (*I'm Your Man*, p. 72) and was often described wearing it in his early years. So is he the undersigned or the recipient of the letter? Was his woman stolen from him, or did he do the stealing? If the truths of love are relative, then perhaps both versions of this love story can be true. If we dispense with final vocabularies, we can dispense with final selves—and, in doing so, we dispense with the distinction between protagonist and artist and bring about a fusion of the two. Perhaps the two fuse together most prominently in the deeply personal and confessional lyrics of "In My Secret Life," where we find Cohen seemingly relating his own propensity to be deceptive.

In conclusion, the notion of being overthrown by beauty that we find in "Hallelujah" and so many other songs provides the basis for Cohen's transcendental account of romantic love. So depicted, love and relationships can be an unrelenting struggle. But with Cohen's fusion of the erotic and the spiritual, this conception of romantic love is one that's not constrained by the usual modes of reason. While the relativity of Cohen's view leads to an ironist position, there is a liberating effect that allows him to reach and express greater authenticity.[1]

[1] Thanks to Katerina Alexandraki, Fern Day, Sonja Delmonte, Malcolm Devoy, Jason Holt, Matthew Mayhew, Jill Riches, and Andrew Watson for helpful comments and suggestions on earlier drafts.

# 11
# Hallelujah and Atonement

BABETTE BABICH

Poet that he is, Leonard Cohen's songs come to live within us. Indeed, Cohen's observation that there's "a crack in everything" resonates in popular culture and even echoes in the title of a book about not Cohen but spirituality: *How the Light Gets In* (Schneider).

In his own songs, Cohen often seems to address us directly, his words expressing soul-wrenchingly dark feeling, desire, sometimes heartbreakingly keen. The erotic themes often include a constant dialectic, asserting (thesis) and countering (antithesis), and sublimating (synthesis) the claims of others, including the deity. In this way, his songs of love include not only the promise of grace, salvation, and blessing, but also conflict and abandonment, as well as affirmation and letting be.

## You

This asserting and countering is ambivalent, echoing as it does in Hegel and in Plato's terminology and indeed even before Plato in the turn from love to strife in the Pre-Socratic thinker, Empedocles. And there's ambiguity too. Hence in Cohen's "Hallelujah" we hear the ambiguous play between the "you" the singer seems to address—the one who isn't really a music fan—and the "you" who seems to be David himself (could that be Cohen?). This is the David of the secret song, the one who finds himself undone by "her beauty in the moonlight," and who later winds up bound to a kitchen chair, of all things, by some unnamed "she." Associations run riot in the song (Babich, *The Hallelujah Effect*). With this poetic ambiguity there's a suggestion of erotic sadism, sexual play, and a disturbing hint at an ultimate unmanning gesture. Everything falls into place, the domestic binding of strength, which shatters the locus of power, along with the special significance of a woman cutting an incapacitated man's hair, and now we're no longer talking about King David and any song, however pleasing to the Lord, but old Samson and the temple he brought down around him.

Cohen's ambiguity works between the lines of the song. The "you" addressed is lover and king and champion in one, and we remember that in addition to writing psalms, David was a warrior: one who knew how to keep his distance for the sake of triumph. Calculated distance adds to the sense of ambiguity. Still the flag that "you" would seem to have placed on some marble arch in the interim, complicates the dialogue. This "you" is the one who doesn't really care for music, but at the same time it's clear that "your" flag, however displayed, can't hold a candle to the singer's tale. It is of sublime irrelevance (this is the consummate synthesis of the song) as the "you" in question, whichever "you" hears the holy or the broken Hallelujah.

Plainly, the song is only incidentally about David; it's really about Cohen and his lovers, and it lets them know his singer's disappointment, a lover's resignation. The dialectic works because Cohen begins the song in his own voice: the first word—after "now"—is "I."

Both sympathy and ambivalence are possible from this perspective and in this same sense, Cohen asserts a sovereign interpretation of his own claim, partly sung to himself and partly sung to (and for) the listener who identifies with Cohen, the singer, and partly sung to his lovers. For his own part, what singer wouldn't want a share in whatever secret King David knew, a sovereign secret to living large, with intrigues and battles, the secret of a series of lovers to sing to and a reputation as a lover and a singer exceeding nearly anyone in the Bible. Rather like Cohen himself.

## Ambiguity

Lovers are more than fickle. The lover makes a promise to the beloved and seemingly always, nearly immediately breaks his word: it "breaks in his mouth," as Nietzsche says (*Genealogy of Morals*, p. 60). Am I, can I be, the same person who promised in the past? Can't I say: that was then, this is now? Everything changes, especially feelings. Feelings change, we change. Those who know us today often ignore the past, a distinct advantage for those who prefer to see themselves as able to reinvent, reconstitute themselves every day.

Descartes reminds us that "because I was in existence a short time ago, it does not follow that I must now exist, unless in this moment some cause create me anew as it were,—that is, conserve me" (p. 95). Derrida echoes this point in the context of making promises: "in a promise, when you say 'yes, I agree, I will' you imply, 'I will say "I will" tomorrow and I will confirm my promise,' otherwise there is no promise. Which means that the 'yes' keeps in advance the memory of its own beginning" (p. 27).

In practice, of course, promises and contracts are sometimes broken but that means only that they simply "stop," so Derrida argues. Cohen seems to express a perspective on this stopping, addressing the "you" who changes from generosity to refusal ("but now you never show it to me").

And thus Cohen illuminates the ambiguity of the human condition: challenging us with his "Hallelujah": "It doesn't matter which you heard." The thing about ambivalence is that Cohen can give his claims away again and again. The poet's license takes it either way, has it both ways, in a nonexclusive disjunction, as the song goes.

Ambivalence, having things both ways, having anything both ways, even when it comes to religion but especially when it comes to intimacy, is consummately erotic. At the same time, ethically speaking, it can be the essence of forgiveness and forbearance, even love. As Simone de Beauvoir highlights in *The Ethics of Ambiguity*, the ambiguous is emblematic of the human condition, existentially described as a lack of being: a person is what they are not, both their past legacy as well as future projects and plans.

For the existentialist, the key turns on a life in time: the life lived by who you used to be and are no longer, as no longer young, innocent, trusting, foolish, and so on. At the same time, there's the life you currently live and have to live. This having to live is both obligation and condemnation. The past, even if it haunts you, is no longer an option; the future takes its own good time and, ultimately contingent, may turn out other than expected. A person is "freely obligated" to be, and may succeed or fail. And only for such a being *can there be* an ethics:

> One does not offer an ethics to a God. It is impossible to propose any to man if one defines him as nature, as something given. . . . This means that there can be a having-to-be only for a being who, according to the existentialist definition, questions himself in his being, a being who is at a distance from himself and who has to be his being. (*Ethics of Ambiguity*, p. 10)

Cohen's broken "Hallelujah" seems to sing of the failure that proves a higher order, even without God. One might call this higher ideal the "Empedocles effect" in Cohen as it retraces the alteration of love and strife as the cycle of cosmic time. As Empedocles describes the eternal cycle, "In Anger all are different forms and separate, but in Love they come together and are desired by each other" (*The Presocratic Philosophers* by Kirk, Raven, and Schofield, p. 293) according to the epoch in question. Parmenides is relevant to the extent that both Cohen and Parmenides would seem to share a vision of women as angels or messengers, as these guide the adept in the first part of Parmenides's *Proem*: "The mares that carry me as far as ever my heart ever aspires sped me on, when they had brought and set me on the far-famed road of the god, which bears the man who knows over all cities. On that road was I borne, for that way the wise horses bore me, straining at the chariot and maidens led the way" (p. 473).

For his own part, Cohen's youthful idealization of women as poets (recollecting he supposed "that all women were poets," and hence as we will see that he further reflects their language was the language of poetry) leads him to his own poet's vocation. But where Parmenides is raising the question of Being, that which is and at the same time that which is impossible not to be (p. 245), Cohen himself expresses a vision of the divine. In keeping with his typical attention to ambiguity, Cohen includes Jewish, Christian, and even Buddhist elements. He refers to Buddhism not simply as an idle practice but from the perspective of an ordained monk.

Cohen's "Hallelujah" can be heard in this fashion and even in his "Suzanne" Cohen moves between religious confessions. As Judy Collins, who made "Suzanne" a hit with the recording on her album *In My Life* (1966), reflects on this ambiguity in Sylvie Simmons's biography of Cohen, it almost seems "that a Jew from Canada can take the Bible to pieces and give the Catholics a run for their money on every story they ever thought they knew" (p. 150). As Dionysus, transcending the male, the female, the bourgeois, the counterculture, as well as the banal-exotic and ecstatic-erotic, perhaps above all we hear redemption as Cohen sings "Suzanne" with intimate pathos, a ballad of fascination and captivation, longing and rebuke, and this works, no matter whether Cohen sings it himself or Judy Collins does. Listening to the song, we're almost there in our minds as Cohen describes the harbor with the sun like honey. This recalls the "honey sacrifice" we read about in Nietzsche's *Thus Spoke Zarathustra*, which alludes not only to the generosity of Zarathustra and echoes Empedocles's own gift to the people of the sacrifice of an ox made of barley and honey, but also to the erotic significance of honey (*Reading the New Nietzsche* by Allison, pp. 165–68). Recalling the cycle of love and strife, we remember Empedocles and his honey sacrifice of the same love ruling the world of commingling, combining different elements. But what about difference? How does love engender strife? In Empedocles, when different things come together, it is by means of that coming together that they must eventually recoil and separate again.

Thus we wonder about the "ladies of the harbor," and if we listen to Nina Simone's cover of "Suzanne" we can hear echoes of St. Augustine. Still we ask, as this tells us about the ladies, who is the "you" who receives the "tea and oranges"? "She" brings these to you. Is that "you" the singer remonstrating with himself? Is that "you" the listener? Both? Who—which you?—has always been her lover? Who's speaking? Again, thinking of Nina Simone, we can note the impact of different covers of Cohen's songs. In some covers—this is true well beyond Cohen—the singer seeks to channel the original voice (like singing along with the radio in the car for the karaoke effect) while other singers take their revenge on the song or seek to take it over for the sake of a hoped for new hit, an appropriation which sometimes brings back the song itself.

In the case of Cohen, as in the case of a lot of pop music, just how much philosophy do we need? We're able to identify the "she" in "Suzanne" (because the song carries her name: it's *about* her). But in the case of other songs, like, Carly Simon's "You're So Vain," who the "you" is is still a debated topic, a referential issue charmingly, humorously, embarrassingly, illustrated in Carly Rae Jepsen's "Call Me, Maybe." We may ask what such a song really means, but hearing the song turns out to be insufficient: we have to see the video to disambiguate the reference. Given a culture of acknowledgment and support of sexual difference, we get it and with the video, we get to see that the songwriter gets the point herself: her song is about open-mindedness, forswearing bias. Meaning is a little more problematic in the case of Psy's "Gangnam Style." Do we take that with or without Korean?

## Feminism and Nietzsche

Are such questions of meaning more a matter for cultural or media studies than philosophy? Posing the question in this way can be convenient in Leonard Cohen's case as it saves us the trouble of overthinking his songs. And then there are the questions of feminism. Both "Hallelujah" and "Suzanne," but also quite a few others (even "Dance Me to the End of Love"), are characterized by a fond dissonance. May we call Cohen a feminist given his declared "love" of women? Like most such love interests, Cohen's love of women, like Shakespeare's talk of love in his sonnets, tends to be undone by its own, and almost immediate, distraction, and Cohen himself dispassionately tracks his own dissipation. Interest in the other sex as with the identification of being a ladies' man traditionally betrays self-interest. Some authors make this point over on Cohen's behalf: Cohen isn't misogynistic because he's really not talking about women, so goes the argument, but just about himself.

As Nietzsche reminds us in *Beyond Good and Evil*, we are, as he was, caught coming and going, beyond correction, beyond change. For Nietzsche, and I would argue for Cohen too, the projection, the supposition, the fantasy that women could constitute the fairer or as Goethe supposed the "higher" sex, is also a way of dis-imagining their humanity: Simone de Beauvoir describes how the "other" sex, like the Jim Crow laws in the American South, does not merely distinguish, it diminishes, it distances. Nietzsche sees this "stupidity" in himself analyzing his own "convictions" as he speaks of incorrigible personal prejudices, set off in scare quotes, as so many "footsteps to self-knowledge, signposts to the problem which we *are*—more correctly to the great stupidity which we are, to the *unteachable* 'right down deep'" (pp. 143–44). But Nietzsche also discredits the misogynistic basis of the ideal of the "eternal feminine" in both Wagner's operas and Goethe's *Faust*. But even Nietzsche himself projects himself upon "women," seeing them from a distance and imagining that there can be discovered a better or a higher self, as Nietzsche writes in *The Gay Science* (his book titled for the tradition of courtly love). Cohen's projections are steeped in this same ideal poetic tradition, and one can hardly refrain from pointing out that this tradition was a convenient refuge for him, as he tells Tim Footman: "I thought that all women inhabited this highly charged landscape that poetry seemed to arise from. It seemed to be the natural language of women and it seemed to me that if you wanted to address women . . . you had to do it with this highly charged language" (p. 184). The distance Cohen underscores here between himself and women is the same distance Nietzsche highlights in the title of his *The Gay Science* aphorism, "*Women and their action at a distance*" (p. 123). It covers alienation, fascination, ambivalence: all of which may be heard together with a wonder that runs throughout "Suzanne" and which together with a high religious tonality also forms the heart of "Hallelujah."

Formally, the referent for the second person singular pronoun "you" varies as it functions in "Suzanne" and "Hallelujah." The "you" who speaks in Cohen's "Suzanne" is the singer's own self, sung between the singer and the selves of his compatriot listeners who know what he means: "you" meaning you the (male) listener and the singer, you who are and have been subjects of desire, subjects of salvation. So the "you" who sings and the "you" who hears "you have no love to give her" is also the one Suzanne gets "on her wavelength," not through what she says, since she doesn't really speak, *half crazy* as she is, which is also the reason the "you" who is Cohen, or the listeners who identify with him, can wish to "spend the night beside her." Cohen's listeners have been there and understand, they also understand how, at least for the space of the moment (but this is how we have Eros in the first place, this is how Penia seduces Poros), it's already a given *that*, as the song continues, "you've always been her lover."

At the same time, Jesus was a sailor—as Cohen says—and again we may refer to Nina Simone to help us here and we remember too that it can be no accident that Cohen's backup singers are often gospel singers.

The erotic moves through the exotic to the divine and then, over-familiar—but what else is it to love?—Cohen, just as he will in "Hallelujah," seems to take the side of the divine. Suzanne, as she speaks in the shadows of the song sung to the "you" who is addressed, has the audacity to claim compassion of us, not for ourselves, but for Jesus, broken "before the sky would open"—specifically, Good Friday at 3 PM on Golgotha hill in Palestine.

As a Jew, Cohen reminds us to feel for Christ, not to be a Christian necessarily but to get the point about Christ, and even Nietzsche, that consummate anti-Christian, gets that too, writing as he does in *The Antichrist*: "There was only one Christian, and he died on the cross" (p. 151). And we're at Golgotha again.

Ecumenicism has its limit however, most particularly when it comes to the erotic and "Suzanne" makes this point as clearly as "Hallelujah"—especially as Nina Simone sings it. And this can work—this is a point Beauvoir makes in *The Second Sex*—because male and female, male or female, gender here and gender there, all of us listen with *men's ears*. And that's the point, again, of "Call Me, Maybe" (this is exactly why the song works) and it's why Psy's "Gangnam Style," offensive as it should be, works for listeners across the board, blowing viral video stats out of the park.

Thus Cohen's "you" in "Suzanne," even as this refers to the singer himself, taking the perspective of Jesus's touch, of Suzanne's touch, isn't the same "you" invoked when we get to his "Hallelujah" where he sings of David's secret chord and then reproaches some other "you" for not really caring for music.

The "*do ya*" stings. This "you" is a target, the object, and is neither the singer nor the male listener. This is another Other, one who in time undergoes unwanted changes from the "time you let me know," to the time, now, when "you never show it to me." This one flies a flag on a victory arch, or wants to, wears its heart on its sleeve, tells others too much, especially when the singer himself is already justifying other conquests by appealing to higher ideals, since love isn't "a victory march."

This "you," who doesn't care for music, withholds, being at the same time a "you" who overreaches, a female. Her desire is the desire of the one who desires desire, who doesn't desire any object as such but desires instead to be desired: to be the loved object, and who wishes to announce the fact of that desire, the facticity of being loved, to all and sundry, a "you" who needs diamonds and wedding parties (or at least a marble arch) to do it. At the same time, this is the woman who "only speaks poetry" and who, of course, suffers what happens to anyone who only speaks poetry. Let's remember T.S. Eliot's Cumaean Sybil, who gets "old and wrinkled" while Cohen stays (and pushing eighty he's still, wonderfully, thankfully, there in his mind) "seventeen."

The point to be made can be rephrased via the sweet spirit of Jonathan Richman's "I Was Dancing in the Lesbian Bar," and in this same gendered sense, now necessarily so, it can't be any woman's voice that can take over and sing "Hallelujah," of all of Cohen's songs. But and arguably beyond Cohen's own voicing, even beyond the late Jeff Buckley—the usual saint of the song—and beyond even Rufus Wainwright, father of Cohen's granddaughter, yet another Canadian singer, k.d. lang, has achieved just this, not just once but again and again. When lang sings "Hallelujah" we get clear hints of other versions, the beauty of Buckley's rendering of John Cale's indispensable phrasing of the song and Wainwright's recollections of the same modalities (*The Hallelujah Effect*, p. 79). But it's k.d. lang who lets us hear the chords that are the key to the song (she sings so that both words and chords are there to be heard) to the extent that listening to the crafted structure of the song, Cohen's poem as a poem, which is to say, Cohen's music as music, turns out to make all the difference.

## Who

Like the Hallelujah psalm praising the name of God, Cohen's "Who by Fire" recounts the New Year prayer, *Unetanneh Tokef—who will be inscribed*. This is the meaning of the blessing of the New Year Greeting, *L'shanah tovah—may you be inscribed.* To be inscribed in this sense means that the name of the person so greeted might be added to the Book of Life for the coming year. The ultimate issue is fate, one's fate, one's destiny, and the destiny for each and every one of us.

The judgment of the high holy days, the judgment of the New Year, is the judgment of the Lord, as all are brought before the Lord. As a prayer to grace the holiest days of the year, it is attributed to the medieval rabbi Kalonymus ben Meshullam who, in good traditional fashion, reports hearing it in a dream from Rabbi Amnon of Mainz, a moving liturgical psalm, but I quote only that part of it that bears on what Cohen sings:

> On Rosh Hashanah it is written,
> On Yom Kippur it is sealed,
> How many shall pass away and how many shall be born,
> Who shall live and who shall die,
> Who shall reach the end of his days and who shall not,
> Who shall die by fire and who by water. . . .
> (*The High Holiday Prayer Book*, pp. 189–90)

*Unetanneh Tokef* recounts the judgment of the Lord, between salvation and doom. What is decided in the new year is fate. And because this is a prayer what's also emphasized is hope: the chance of mercy. As the logic of the high holy days sets Yom Kippur, the day of atonement, to answer the conclusion of this Rosh Hashanah New Year prayer: "But *Teshuvah*, *Tefillah*, and *Tzedekah*, Penitence, Prayer, and Deeds of Mercy annul the severity of judgment."

Cohen's "Who by Fire" repeats this and we may find in it echoes of Anaximander, Heraclitus, and therefore, as Nietzsche tells us, also a *tragic* ethics, as Cohen hears all the ways of coming to one's own death, such as poets and songwriters like to count these kinds or modes of judgment. These disjoint ways of life and death aren't the flower-power, petal plucking, "she loves me, she loves me not" of more pragmatic (and one might say justly unattributed) rot-gut verse: "For if she will, she will, you may depend on't; And if she won't, she won't; so there's an end on't."

The beauty of the love disjunction, in all its insight and all its calm (a calm no lover ever concedes or seems to believe for a moment: the beloved will or won't, loves me or doesn't) is its illustration of both the principle of contradiction and the same principle of identity which is yet more fundamental to logic and mathematics, namely tautology—as if one needed that. In the same way, different in spirit and accent from Derrida's reflection that every promised yes is affirmed again, "yes, yes," the philosopher Sidney Morgenbesser proved the value of counting positive statements twice, *yeah, yeah*, as taken twice they make a negative, the Beatles already one step ahead when it came to love, sing "She Loves You"—count the yeahs—*yeah, yeah, yeah*.

The Judeo-Christian world is fond of threes, and if the Lord decides who is inscribed and who not, there is mercy, forbearance, what Hegel's dialectic saves (*Aufhebung,* usually translated as "synthesis," also means what is preserved): "Penitence, Prayer, and Deeds of Mercy annul the severity of judgment." But Cohen's "Who by Fire" echoes not only the Rosh Hashanah prayer but the words of the American poet Robert Frost's "Fire and Ice" as Frost himself alludes to judgment and the end of days and what he remembers of the touch of "desire." Frost's "desire" resonates with Cohen, who always holds with passion even if from the same first-person perspective Frost emphasizes, and there's the doom once again. "Who by Fire" echoes this favoring, it also speaks desire (echoes of "Ring of Fire") but the high tone is wholly prayer, the prayer of the days of awe.

## Towards Death

Cohen's verse tells the various ways of perishing, as if there's a simple list of the ways to go. Inside Cohen's lyrics is a recognition of the singularizing solitude Nietzsche emphasizes in *Philosophy in the Tragic Age of the Greeks*: "To walk along a lonely street is part of the philosopher's nature" (p. 66). This is why Heidegger can tell Hannah Arendt that thinking is a "lonely business," as such solitude can account for both the destiny and the obscurity of the philosopher. The distinction may also be made with regard to the arch-lonely Heraclitus as Nietzsche writes: "The feeling of solitude, however that pierced the Ephesian hermit of the temple of Artemis, we can only intuit when we are freezing on wild desolate mountains of our own" (p. 67).

We can sense this then only when we, too, belong to what Nietzsche, alluding to Schopenhauer, calls "the republic of creative minds: each giant calling to his brother through the desolate intervals of time" (p. 32). Nietzsche emphasizes solitude here, the same solitude that may be heard in the first-person focus of Cohen's reflections.

The song's coda—"who shall I say is calling?"—is quasi-Augustinian. The same eros of desire holds between the creature and the creator, where what's to be noted is the attunement of creator to creature, the call is issued not from the abandoned soul, crying out for his god in the wilderness. This isn't Elijah, this is a post-Christian Jew, who keeps all his piety in the space and in the midst of every advantage of Western, all-too-Christian culture. As Nietzsche reminds us in *The Antichrist* (and we always need reminding, jealous as we are of our sectarian differences), "A Christian is only a Jew of a broader confession" (p. 159).

The conclusion of "Who by Fire" alludes to awe as it lists, again and again, the various ways to be called from life. The solitude ("Who in solitude . . . ?") is the "who" that Cohen changes from the original Rosh Hashanah prayer, transposing this musical liturgical poem to the tonic rhythms of today's music, speaking, as surely as the tradition itself, to our hearts. What Cohen sets to music is not the subject "you," not the object "you," but rather the singularizing "who," the who that we are in our uniqueness, as death, as Heidegger reminds us, cannot but singularize each one of us in its claim, at the hour, at the moment of its claim.

# IV

# Songs of Literature

# 12
# Politics in *Beautiful Losers*

STEVEN BURNS

A few years ago I was on a bus. I was re-reading *Beautiful Losers*. A stranger got on, and took the seat beside me. I looked down at my page, flipped to another page, and then found myself closing the cover. I didn't want the stranger to see that I was reading so much "fuck" and "shit." There's no doubt that the book could be charged with obscenity. One critic wrote, "I have just finished reading *Beautiful Losers*, and I've had to wash my mind." People who just saw the book as obscene wanted it banned from libraries and bookstores. That is one way of reading Cohen's novel, but it is not a very good reading. I'll call it the Obscenity Reading.

When I first read the book in the 1960s, its obscenity did not bother me at all. I was excited to learn what one of my favorite poets was thinking about Canadian politics. My purpose in this chapter is to recover that excitement. But first let me introduce another way of reading it. One way to move past the Obscenity Reading is to note that famous court cases in 1960 had made it legal to publish D. H. Lawrence's 1928 novel, *Lady Chatterley's Lover*. And many readers were finding "redeeming literary merit" in Henry Miller's *Tropic of Cancer*. Cohen was already known as a poet, and some readers were quick to find graceful metaphors and insightful turns of phrase in *Beautiful Losers*. A saint is someone who "rides the drifts like an escaped ski" (p. 95); or "the old people gathered at the priest's hem shivered with a new kind of loneliness" (p. 82). It is easy to find individual moments of redeeming beauty, and thus a better way of reading the novel. I'll call that the Poetical Reading.

But a reader should not be content with disconnected moments of delight. A good reading of a novel should explain how the various moments hold together, how they form a unity. When a reader offers an interpretation, he or she cites many details from the text and tries to show how they form a coherent story. There are many better ways of reading *Beautiful Losers* than the Obscenity Reading or the Poetical Reading. I am going to advocate a Political Reading and will claim that it can shed light on other, less satisfactory readings.

## Best Readings

I have a philosophical theory that I want to put on the table right away. It is a commonplace in discussions of literature to claim that the greater a piece of writing, and the richer a work, the more interpretations it will sustain. I claim that there is a mistake in that idea. True, it is important to keep an open mind, and to try to imagine various interpretations and different ways of reading a work of literature. But some interpretations are better than others, and if that is so, then it is likely that one interpretation will be best of all. I call that the *best reading* of a work, and I think that that is what we are all looking for when we argue about how to interpret a novel. In what follows I offer some steps in the direction of the best reading of *Beautiful Losers*. (I also discuss this theory in my article, "Best Readings.")

I don't want that to be an arrogant claim. Here is an argument that supports it. Let's accept that I am wrong. If there is no best reading, then a work can support more than one equally good reading. Consider the well-known duck/rabbit drawing.

It is a drawing that does sustain more than one equally good interpretation. There is no more reason to believe that the protrusions are rabbit ears than that they are a duck bill.

It can be a duck, or a rabbit, but it cannot be both at once. Either explanation is as well supported as the other. I claim, however, that the ambiguity only exists because the drawing is so oversimplified, so schematic. If we were to add feathers or fur to the drawing we would make it richer, make it a better portrayal. But at the same time we would reduce the ambiguity of its meaning. So it goes with greater art. The richer and more detailed a work, such as either of Leonard Cohen's novels, the less likely it is to sustain ambiguity, and the more likely it is that an interpretation will prove to be the best one. That conclusion, of course, is just the opposite of the one we assumed when we began.

Why does a more detailed work reduce ambiguity? Because there's more evidence, more detail about plot and character, for instance, that will support one interpretation over the others. I shall attempt with my Political Reading of *Beautiful Losers* to give the best explanation of the greatest number of details in the novel. I'll start with the question, "Who are the losers, anyway?"

## Who Are the Losers?

Almost everyone mentioned in the novel is a loser. This includes the defeated tribe called "A——s" whom the Historian is studying (p. 4), it includes the New Jews of Montréal (p. 160), it includes the male prostitutes and drug addicts on Blvd. St. Laurent (p. 189), and it includes Mary Voolnd, who nurses F. and is mutilated by police dogs (p. 226). In fact I think that all Canadians are being called losers. But there are four main losers. The novel starts and ends with Kateri (Catherine) Tekakwitha. Here are the opening words:

> Catherine Tekakwitha, who are you? Are you (1656–1680)? Is that enough? Are you the Iroquois Virgin? Are you the Lily of the Shores of the Mohawk River? Can I love you in my own way? I am an old scholar. . . . I fell in love with a religious picture of you. You were standing among birch trees, my favorite trees. God knows how far up your moccasins were laced. . . . Do I have any right to come after you with my dusty mind full of the junk of maybe five thousand books? I hardly even get out to the country very often. . . .
>
> Catherine Tekakwitha, I have come to rescue you from the Jesuits. (pp. 3–5)

We learn some things in this passage about the first two losers. One is Catherine, who died in 1680. The second I shall call the Historian. He is first of all an old scholar who is writing "The History of Them All." That's what Book One of *Beautiful Losers* is called. He is also a dirty old man—he is thinking of what is under Catherine's skirt as well as of her fame and her sainthood. Moreover, we learn something from this opening passage about the style of the novel itself. It has constant comic turns and one-line jokes: as if getting out of the city were a qualification for befriending a 300-year-old Aboriginal woman.

On the second page the Historian tells us about "my friend F." who "died in a padded cell, his brain rotted from too much dirty sex" (p. 4). F. is the third of the beautiful losers. The fourth is then introduced. She is the Historian's Aboriginal wife, Edith (she is a descendant of the A——s). She has committed suicide, by crouching at the bottom of an elevator shaft in their apartment building until the descending machine crushes her beyond recognition (p. 7).

So the Historian is going to tell us a story about himself and three others. Those are the four main losers. Three are already dead. The Historian is writing their history. The second part of the book is called "A Long Letter from F." (p. 143). Writing from his death-bed, F. gives another view of the same characters and their story. Finally there is a short section called "Beautiful Losers: An Epilogue in the Third Person," which concludes the story about the four losers.

## A Psychological Reading

The 1960s in particular were a period of revived nationalism in Canada. The reading of Canadian literature from the 1960s naturally requires some acquaintance with how the country was at that time conceived and conceived itself. Not to see that the book is deeply embedded in Canadian politics is to miss something essential. This has to be at least part of a good reading of the novel. I hope to get you to agree with me about that, but let me first introduce a very fine reader who does not agree with me.

When *Beautiful Losers* appeared in 1966 it was immediately reviewed all over Canada, but especially by distinguished poets. One of the most impressive of those poet reviewers was Michael Ondaatje, now best known as the author of *The English Patient*. He published a short monograph, *Leonard Cohen*, in 1970.

*Beautiful Losers*, writes Ondaatje, "is a gorgeous novel, and is the most vivid, fascinating, and brave modern novel I have read." On first reading he was struck by some powerful scenes, but thought that "nothing linked them together," and that it was "simply too sensational." That suggests that his first reaction was a Poetical Reading. A second reading revealed to him "superb writing, structure, and themes that are very basic to Cohen" (p. 45). That last phrase is important, for Ondaatje sees the characters, at least the Historian—whom he calls the Narrator—and F., as "a powerful extension of several of the traits of Leonard Cohen" that are also to be seen in his early poetry. So he writes:

> What makes the style and technique of the book so valid and effective is the way Cohen uses it to characterize and juxtapose F. and the Narrator. The Narrator is always being defeated by Art, History, Language; F. uses language like a sword, illogically, excessively, and unrealistically—his speech is riddled with invalid and brilliant images. . . .
>
> The Narrator's "book," is therefore the most tortured piece of writing imaginable. . . . Book Two, "A Long Letter from F.," shows a

> remarkable change of style, a calm that is gracious after the diatribes and uncertainties of the Narrator. . . .
>
> We therefore find the essential drama of the novel in the styles Cohen uses, for F. is trying to break down the restrictive laws and values that limit the Narrator, to become the Narrator's Mephistopheles and lead him through madness and total freedom into sainthood. (pp. 46–47)

I call this the Psychological Reading, because it claims that the book is mainly an account of the author's personality and that the two main "authors," the Historian and F., are warring aspects of Cohen himself. There is much that is right about this, and another fine critic, Stephen Scobie, develops the idea further. But I do not agree with the main assumption—that the novel is best seen as portraying aspects of Cohen's psyche

Ondaatje reinforces his claim by comparing *Beautiful Losers* to Cohen's 1963 novel, *The Favourite Game*. The earlier novel clearly was autobiographical—the story of a young, talented Montréal Jewish boy, with his sidekick friend and his girlfriend, making their way into adulthood. So Ondaatje says "as Breavman (the hero of the early novel) separated himself into lover and artist," in *Beautiful Losers* "the role of the lover is played by F. The Narrator struggles along after them, watching, discovering . . ." (p. 50). Cohen, that is, has separated himself into Historian and F., and the drama of the novel is the struggle of one part of him to liberate the other part of him from his hang-ups, his mental constipation. But this does not fit *Beautiful Losers* all that well.

The Psychological Reading misses some very important things. First of all it treats the Indian women, Catherine Tekakwitha and the Historian's wife, Edith, as secondary characters. But Catherine's importance cannot be reduced to an example of the Historian's incompetent interest in history, and an example of sainthood for F. to emulate. Nor is Edith just a dead Indian. She is loving, ambitious, experimental, and tries until the end to make a living husband of the hopeless Historian. Even her suicide is presented as a desperate attempt to save their love by teaching him that the living are more important than the dead. In my reading the women are as central as the male characters. They are important in their own right, and not just because they might patch together the broken men (a recurrent theme in Cohen's poems and songs).

Second, Ondaatje's reading does not explain the fact that F. is French. Leonard Cohen is not French. But F. is undoubtedly French. Why, then, should F. be one of the two sides of Cohen's personality? One of the stories that F. tells in his long letter is the story of his losing a thumb while blowing up a statue of Queen Elizabeth, monarch of England and of Canada. The famous statue, on Sherbrooke St., was in fact a target of separatists, Québec nationalists, on the occasion of the Queen's visit to Canada in 1964. I think that Québec separatists were part of the Canadian landscape that Cohen was portraying, rather than a part of his own personal psyche.

Perhaps I exaggerate this aspect of F.? He is introduced as "my friend, F.," so F. could stand for Friend. Stephen Scobie thinks it could stand for Frankenstein (*Leonard Cohen*, p. 99). It could also stand for phallus; think of the Historian as a desperate, once-rational mind being led about by his penis. But F. says: "It is not merely because I am French that I long for an independent Québec." In the course of the ensuing political manifesto, he makes a telling political remark: "The English did to us what we did to the Indians, and the Americans did to the English what the English did to us. I demanded revenge for everyone" (pp. 186–87). The Indians, the French, and the English are all losers. Canadians are all losers. That, I think, is a strand in the narrative of *Beautiful Losers* that reaches from the first page to the last. It is also, I am sure, a significant fact that in those two passages, and in various places elsewhere in the novel, Cohen makes use of the official Canadian practice (developed in the 1960s) of proceeding in two languages, alternating French and English. Finally, F.'s long letter ends with "Signé F." (p. 226).

## A Political Reading

So if the Psychological Reading is too private and personal, and leaves out significant aspects of the novel, what do I think are the important ingredients in my Political Reading? In 1962 Canada had a national election. The governing Conservative party under John Diefenbaker had quickly become unpopular. The newly-elected John F. Kennedy in the USA was getting all the trendy headlines. Kennedy sent campaign help to the opposition Liberal party, led by Lester Pearson. The Liberals, whose policies were friendlier to the Americans, won the election. George Grant responded in 1965 with a book, *Lament for a Nation*, that turned the country on its head. He argued that John Diefenbaker was the last of the nationalist Canadian leaders, and that the recent election marked the end of an independent Canada. The Liberals had accepted what he called the continental model of development. In future, Canada would not build its own railway line from East to West, and strive to control its own economy. It would seek deeper and deeper integration with the American economy. The Canadian project of building a separate nation on the northern half of the continent was finished. Grant wrote about what Canadians were losing. I think that Canadians are also Cohen's losers.

My reading of *Beautiful Losers* must now be becoming clearer. It is not a portrayal of Cohen's psychology as much as it is a portrayal of his city and his country. That is why Catherine's conversion by French Jesuits is so important, that is why F. is French. Let me say more about each of the main losers, and how they represent aspects of Canada in the 1960s.

The nation of Canada begins, of course, with its original inhabitants, and with their confrontation with Europeans. The first major confrontation was between the French and the Indians (as they were called by Europeans who thought that in sailing west they were on their way to India). Catherine Tekakwitha was a girl of the Mohawk First Nation. When she was four, she and her whole village contracted the European scourge, smallpox. Catherine's body was weakened by the illness, she was partially blinded and her face was disfigured. She was also orphaned when the rest of her family all died of the disease.

A Jesuit missionary, Père de Lamberville, came to her tribe when she was eighteen, and impressed her with the stories about both Jesus's love and his suffering. She began to try to suffer as he had, and undertook acts of great self-denial, self-punishment, and self-mutilation. The missionaries warned her that she was taking these signs of penance too far, but she persisted. She vowed to remain a virgin forever. She prayed for hours in freezing temperatures. She whipped herself. She lay on a bed of thorns. She refused most food. So she died, weakened by her religious practices, at the age of twenty-four (in 1680). But she had had visions. She had wandered the forests placing small wooden crosses as reminders of prayer and penance. Others had visitations from her after her death. Miracles were performed in her name. The Roman Catholic Church had declared her venerable in 1943, but she was not made an official Saint until 2012, long after Cohen's novel demanded her "official beatification" (p. 242).

We see here the story of a Native North American child whose life was devastated first by the disease and then by the religion of the invading Europeans. Much of the novel's obscenity, the blood and pain, the flesh and sex, begins in Cohen's honesty about Catherine's life. "I have come to rescue you from the Jesuits," his Historian announces. But the novel ends with her still in their hands. Catherine represents Canada's Aboriginal people, who were losers in their confrontation with European invaders.

The Historian confesses already on the second page that he suffers from constipation. It helps to think of his constipation as his essence. He is cramped, inhibited, full of anguish and regret. I think he typifies English Canadians, inhibited by rules for being good, and rules for being rational. F. is indeed his opposite, and Catherine's opposite, too. He is sensuous, lively, witty, and elegant. He is also successful as a businessman; at one point he pays a million dollars for a factory. Later he becomes a Member of the national Parliament in Ottawa. Some readers thought at the time that F. was modeled on Pierre Trudeau (who became a Member of Parliament in 1965, and became Prime Minister in 1968). He even drove a Mercedes convertible like Trudeau, and like Trudeau he brought glamour and passion to the project of dragging English Canada into a new era. But the comparison fades away; F. fails in his mission, and he dies in an asylum, apparently of a sexually-transmitted disease.

The fourth main loser is Edith, a reincarnation of Catherine. She had a hard childhood, and was raped at thirteen. We learn that life with her husband, the Historian, gets less and less interesting for her. She and F. conspire to save the Historian from himself. But if she represents contemporary Aboriginals, she too fails to save English Canada from its dismal fate. Notice too that Mary Voolnd, who becomes important as F.'s nurse in his final days, is from Nova Scotia (p. 150). I see no reason for this detail except that it helps to establish that the book is about the whole country.

These episodes underline the central metaphor: Canadians are constipated and have trouble reaching orgasm. The Quiet Revolution Francophones have tried to show them a better way. But despite F.'s example and tireless efforts, Edith and the Historian continue to be mired in frustration. We have a standoff. None of them succeeds. All are losers.

My point is twofold. First, the four Beautiful Losers are not just aspects of the author's consciousness. Second, one of its obvious aspects is that the four characters include a representative of the situation when the Europeans arrived, and three contemporaries who represent the three founding peoples of the nation of Canada: Aboriginals, French, and English. *Beautiful Losers* is all about Canada on the eve of the 1967 centennial of its founding.

At this point, you may be feeling the need for a more sophisticated argument concerning the idea that there is one interpretation of a novel that can be defended as the best one. One argument that still holds its own was given in 1968 by Anthony Savile to the distinguished Aristotelian Society in London, England. Savile presents in that paper an account of best explanation in aesthetics. The search for the best interpretation is another way to describe my project. T.S. Eliot called it "the common pursuit of true judgement." Savile argues that the correct reading of a work of art is the one that accounts for the greatest number of relevant features of the work, while being as simple and unitary and appropriate as any competing readings. This is what my reading of *Beautiful Losers* aspires to do.

## A Sexual Reading

My Political Reading is not the only one left standing. There are other contenders to deal with. Since sex and religion go so closely together, let me introduce a sexual reading by offering a religious reading. You can see a resurrection story in *Beautiful Losers*. All the main characters die in Books One and Two. In Book Three those losers all reappear, transformed. Cohen himself called the book "a liturgy . . . a great mad confessional prayer" (as quoted by Ondaatje in *Leonard Cohen*, p. 44). Douglas Barbour outlines this reading in his penetrating essay, "Down with History." He discusses the metaphysics of time, showing the contrast between the Historian's sense of time and F.'s—who defies the limits imposed by history by trying to live wholly in the present. And he finds deliberate confusion in the chronology of the novel which reflects this religious dimension.

Another aspect of this reading is the way systematic thinking is attacked. The Historian is trying desperately to be rational. F., in contrast, tries to teach him to "connect nothing" (p. 16). Religions often insist that direct experience and faith are to be preferred over reason. In a telling symbol, the System Theatre is a movie theatre in Montréal where several scenes take place. But the "Sy" letters are broken, so that the neon sign says "stem Theatre" (p. 221). Stephen Scobie makes insightful remarks about this rejection of rigid, systematic thinking in favor of the organic pattern of a stem. And F. proclaims in his letter: "God is alive. Magic is afoot" (p. 157). But let me move on to sex.

William Blake suggests the following connection between religion and sexuality: "Priests in black gowns were walking their rounds / And binding with briars my joys and desires" ("The Garden of Love"). This is what happens to Catherine Tekakwitha when she meets the Jesuits. I see the sexual metaphor that dominates the novel this way. European colonizers convince Catherine to embrace the briars, and she chooses virginity and self-flagellation. The Historian also has trouble having sex with his wife, Edith. He is usually too preoccupied with his research to respond to her love. And in a wonderful scene at a Separatist political rally, he is excited by a woman who presses into him in the crowd, but is distraught in the end: "I didn't come. I failed again" (p. 123). And Edith, in turn, is deeply frustrated.

Their friend F. tries to help them. He has sex with both Edith and the Historian, and with almost everything else that moves. He embodies liberation from the hang-ups of his friends, and, in contrast to Catherine, seeks sainthood through self-indulgence rather than self-denial. The climax of this story, if you will pardon the word, is a great orgy scene in which F. introduces a tireless Danish Vibrator in his attempt to bring Edith to orgasm (pp. 164–83). But he, too, ultimately fails. Edith commits suicide in order to teach her husband that the living are more important than the dead. Yet her husband remains a constipated and dirty-minded old man. The unexpected liberation comes at last in Book Three, to which I shall return.

The Religious Reading and Sexual Reading of the novel are mostly symbolic. It is not a pornographic novel; the point of all the sex is to serve as a metaphor for a more general liberation or salvation. So we must ask the question, who are the people to be liberated? And this brings me back to my Political Reading—for the four main characters represent Canada.

When I try to remember what I loved about this novel when I first read it, I realize that I thought of it as a kind of *Lament for a Nation*. The Canada that I had grown up in, that had been the territory of my political imagination, was being deconstructed. However, while Grant was lamenting the loss of something he treasured, Cohen is dreaming of a radical transformation of the country.

There are commentators who vigorously disagree with my reading. Scobie is one example:

> It is certainly possible to read the whole of *Beautiful Losers* as a political work, and to argue that the personal victimization of the central characters can be read as an allegory of Canadian society. But I am not sure that the tone of the book allows this interpretation to be primary; the tone is obsessively personal, and politics are absorbed into private vision. (*Leonard Cohen,* p. 113)

To this I reply: however private the vision, it is still Cohen's vision of Canadian society, its main founding peoples, its persistent character, its problems, and their potential resolution. These are the subject matter around which the nightmares of self-destruction and the pornographic allegory of desperately striving for orgasm are woven. So I maintain that this interpretation, although it may not be the first one you'd think of, is a fundamental one. It is the necessary framework for a "best reading" of the book.

## The Future of Canada

The novel ends with a short third section. This is a test case for my account. What sense can we make of Book Three, a short epilogue written in the third person? The constipated and filthy Anglophone Historian from Book One has been living in a tree hut through the winter. The other founding people are dead, and there is not much left of him. Then "Spring comes from the West." He stands by a road, trying to hitch a ride into Montréal. In what seems to me a key image, a blonde young woman in an Oldsmobile stops to pick him up (p. 234). Remember, he was trying to save Catherine Tekakwitha from the Jesuits. He wanted to make her not just a dead virgin saint, but a living object of passion. Well, it seems to me that the blonde may be Catherine updated, or Catherine's successor. She is wearing moccasins. And the old Historian can see how far up they are laced. She drops him off at the System Theatre (p. 235), where he blinks in time with the frames of the film, so that both the film and he become invisible.

I read the beautiful, uninhibited, sexually demanding woman in the Oldsmobile as Joni Mitchell, but that's my fantasy. Spring, new life, has arrived. She says "ισισ εγω," which means "I am Isis." Isis is an Ancient Egyptian goddess of fertility. Isis has a great many other attributes, as well, but virginity and self-punishment are not among them. She is Catherine transformed, she is the spring, she is the future. She is not self-denying, not virginal, not "hung-up." She eagerly demands an orgasm from her passenger. Canada after Expo 67 will be a different place. Montréal will be a different city. And those who live on will be very different people. They will not be candidates for martyrdom or sainthood. They will not be trapped by their own history and their inhibitions. Catherine will be completely transformed. Perhaps that will be the final miracle, her sainthood achieved.

The old man now goes into The Main Shooting and Game Alley (the bottom of Montréal's desire apparatus, as Cohen puts it). A mob forms to attack the old man. And what does he do? First he turns into a combination of F. ("the Terrorist Leader that escaped tonight") and the Historian ("the pervert they showed on TV they're combing the country for") (p. 239). And then *he dematerializes*. For the first time in his life he relaxes totally. And he simply disappears. Mobs of ordinary Montréalers assemble. They are seeking a revolution, a second chance, a new future. Cohen does not tell us what will happen next. Perhaps the old man rematerializes as the lens of a movie projector and shows a vision of what may come. But we know that the old Canada is past. The future will be for people who are not inhibited by History, whose bodies are not tortured but liberated, and whose minds are not bound by the mythologies of the past.

Those of us who have lived into the Harper era (Stephen Harper became Canada's Prime Minister in 2006) may fret that we've now reverted to the Canada of Cohen's Historian. But for Cohen, in 1966, the future is an open promise. Catherine Tekakwitha is long dead, and Cohen pleads for the sanctification of a transformed Catherine. There are three other Beautiful Losers: They, too, are all dead. One Aboriginal, one French, one English; one crushed by the machinery of the modern world, one shriveled by the madness of his lively passions and ambitions, and a confused and constipated one who finally relaxed and just disappeared. The novel is Leonard Cohen's assessment of the state of his country, and his dream of its future.[1]

---

[1] I first wrote about *Beautiful Losers* for a lecture series I gave to Canadian Studies and Philosophy students at the University of Vienna in 2006. I am especially grateful to those students, who loved Leonard Cohen and taught me many things about him and this novel.

# 13
# Writing Poetry after Auschwitz

PAWEŁ DOBROSIELSKI AND
MARCIN NAPIÓRKOWSKI

The debate about the role of the Holocaust as a model for modern ethical understanding of memory was reflected in a proverbial way by philosopher and sociologist Theodor W. Adorno, when he claimed, "There can be no poetry after Auschwitz" (the actual line from p. 162 of "Cultural Criticism and Society" translates as "To write poetry after Auschwitz is barbaric"). Modern Western culture is characterized by a particular obsession with the past as an object of moral concern. The Holocaust plays a crucial role in this artistic, literary, and philosophical trend. Many philosophers have written on the topic of the Holocaust, which has been dubbed a defining event for Western culture.

The Holocaust clearly plays this vital role in Leonard Cohen's *Flowers for Hitler*. Actually, the book can even be interpreted as a literary embodiment of the ongoing philosophical debate. What Cohen does is to prove Adorno wrong. What does it mean to write poetry that self-consciously highlights the fact that it's written *after* the supposed end of all poetry?

## Images and Dreams

Let's start by asking a very basic, even naive question: What is the poet's world made of? What are the basic elements that Leonard Cohen uses to create his poetry? The cover of the first edition of *Flowers* suggests an answer. The cover contains a number of odd symbols which, despite the date of publication (1964), resemble weird icons on a computer desktop: flowers, food, a castle, a plane decorated with hearts, an arrow-pierced heart, a parachutist, two naked women, a dog, and finally the eponymous Adolf Hitler himself.

Even a cursory glance inside the book reveals the importance of such symbols. The repertoire of images used in this relatively big collection (over 120 pages) seems disturbingly repetitive. There are relatively few recurrent motifs that reappear in almost all the poems, as if the poet had used a pile of cards, shuffled and dealt them out over and over again. What's even more intriguing than the very limited number of motifs is their apparent incoherency. Some of them come from Cohen's spiritual repertoire, while others can be easily assigned to the common 1960s fascination with drugs and altered states of consciousness. There are also many historical and geographical references. But there are also some very unremarkable items that reappear again and again: telephone, radio, green grass, and, of course, flowers. Together they are like an annoyingly infectious song we hear in the morning and can't get out of our heads throughout the whole day—a good enough way to start a horror.

Some of the most strikingly recurrent images and symbols, grouped in basic categories in a random order, are as follows:

- (Astronomy) planet, star, moon, sky
- (Drugs) opium/poppies, junkie, (alcohol) to be drunk
- Burning (a body, oneself, books)
- Concentration camp
- Ashes
- Oven and smoke
- Telephone and radio
- The Nazis: Hitler, Goering, Eichmann
- (Hydrogen) bomb, mushroom (cloud)

- (Family) father, grandmother, mother, sister (also:) house, room
- (Geography) Ganges, Canada (Montreal), Cuba, Poland, Russia, America, Japan (and more . . . )
- (Religions) Judaism, Christianity, Buddhism, rabbi, priest, Zen-master, Jesus
- Flowers, grass
- Suit
- Hair/naked body
- History, museum
- City Hall

Sigmund Freud, the father of psychoanalysis, whose theory of dreams influenced deeply both modern philosophical debate on memory and Cohen's more surrealistic poetry, claims that an analyst should distinguish between the "material" of dreams and their meaning. "What are dreams *made* of?" then, is a basic question, preceding any possible attempt to explain them. In dreams it isn't the images themselves that are significant (we may call them the *vocabulary* of dreams), but rather the relations between them, the *grammar* of dreams. Let's consider, then, possible relations among the symbols Cohen uses.

We could reorganize the list, randomly combining elements, and that is actually what Cohen does throughout the whole volume. At least one of the above images appears in almost every single poem. Many of the poems are so saturated with recurring motifs, that they seem entirely built from some prefabricated building-blocks, or "poetry bricks." Think of creating a do-it-yourself *Flowers for Hitler* generator that would produce an unlimited series of new poems by randomly juxtaposing these motifs (like: "Naked Goering enters a City Hall full of ovens, where he receives a phone call from Jesus," and so on). Although it may seem odd to a devoted fan of the Canadian bard, this is exactly what the structure of the collection suggests. And it would not be, in any case, *diminishing* the value of Cohen's poetry! Just the opposite: we should rather admire the book as an *open collection*. To be honest, it seems that no single poem taken separately is a true masterpiece, but taken as a whole, the volume makes a "system" capable of expressing a lot.

Just think of *Flowers* as if it were not a collection of *poems*, but a kind of *machine* programmed to produce them. (We don't think the poet himself would take offense.)

## Repression

We know already what Cohen's poetic world is made from. Let's try now to enter it. First of all, the world Cohen invites us into is *normal*. Despite being gravely influenced by surrealism, the landscape of *Flowers* is furnished with surprisingly typical items in more or less trivial configurations. And this is exactly where the horror begins! The world is *awkwardly* normal, given *what has recently happened*. It had been just two decades since the Holocaust, and yet everything looks as if all the atrocities of the two world wars had never taken place.

More than anything else, perhaps, it's the apparent *normality* of everyday life that seems to horrify Cohen (or rather, that Cohen uses to horrify *us*): "It never happened / There was no murder," repeats the voice of the poetic narrator in a frantic search for any evidence that will overturn this assumption. But the grass is not red—as we read in "The First Murder"—it's just green, as it should be. The fact that the world goes on, that the grass *is* green, that people continue to be born, married, and buried in peace, makes all the atrocities of the past seem highly "improbable."

But what happened, happened. There are *ashes* under the surface of the green field. Continuing the rhetoric of this horror, we may say that the dead are *not fully* dead. "I can't get their nude and loving bodies out of my mind" reads "A Migrating Dialogue," while "The Music Crept by Us" provides us with a Titanic-like picture of life as a party where "the band is composed / of former SS monsters." "For My Old Layton" presents a similar picture of people living close to "the breathless / in the ground." The image culminates in "The

Invisible Trouble," where we see a man covering up numbers on his wrist that appeared there as a hallucination, a side effect of watching too many Holocaust movies. There are no numbers on *our* forearms, yet there is a burden—as we may interpret this metaphor. An author analyzing the image of the Holocaust in *Flowers for Hitler*, Sandra Wynands, accurately writes about "the inability to reconcile normality with the knowledge of horror" which is at the same time "the inability to imagine such horror in the presence of normality" (p. 206).

It all "just happened" suggests the title of one of Cohen's poems ("How It Happened in the Middle of the Day"), causing *no change* in the way the world turns. Life still goes on, and people pass by the mass graves not even noticing their existence. There's no difference, "not a single alien tremor / in the voices crying: tomatoes, onions, bread"—notes a disbelieving Cohen, unconsciously(?) paraphrasing a famous verse by Polish poet and Nobel prize winner Czesław Miłosz whose poem "Campo di Fiori" (1943) juxtaposes the burning ruins of the Warsaw Ghetto with the execution of Giordano Bruno burned at the stake in 1600. Even before the flames had died, observes Miłosz two decades before the publication of *Flowers*, life went back to normal, and merchants were selling such ordinary things as lemons and olives at the very same square the horror had taken place.

"How come the buses still run? / How come they're still making movies?"—asks "A Migrating Dialogue." The fact that the life goes on *despite* all the atrocities seems somehow more horrifying than the atrocities themselves. At the surface there are flowers, and grass, and music—people eat, drink, play, they even make love. But all this normality is founded on a kind of dark lie which, since Freud, we call *repression*—the lie we tell ourselves not to have to face the truth that will be too terrifying to bear.

## The Discovery of Guilt

The Western world "rediscovered" the Holocaust only in the 1960s, more than fifteen years after the ovens in Auschwitz went out. Until then the postwar boom was in full swing. In the 1950s rapid economic development, mass production of goods and babies, as well as the emergence of new lifestyles seemed much more important than facing the recent horror. The memory of the Holocaust was repressed in various ways. Survivors' narratives were not particularly welcomed and often misunderstood. Western societies decided to turn their backs on the past and look hopefully towards the future.

During the war Germany had been perceived as the archenemy and Russia as an indispensable ally; afterwards, for political reasons, the roles shifted. As a result, the few depictions of the Holocaust produced during that time were particularly striking. For example, *The Diary of Anne Frank*, a 1955 Broadway box-office hit play adaptation of the Dutch text (adapted in turn into a film in 1959) was structured as a universal melodrama with a moving and uplifting ending—a quotation from the diary that read: "In spite of everything, I still believe that people are really good at heart."

Among various notable events that sparked widespread public interest in the Holocaust in the early 1960s, and finally resulted in what we see as the contemporary obsession with memory, one seems to be of particular importance not only in general but also to Cohen himself—the capture, trial, and subsequent death sentence for Adolf Eichmann, eponymous subject of one of Cohen's poems. Although this event caught both the CIA and the American public by surprise, it coincided with favorable political and social conditions. With the death of Stalin, the Krushchev thaw, and the end of McCarthysim, the Cold War entered a new era. The need for a clearly defined enemy diminished. The West was now ready to face both the victims of the Holocaust and its perpetrators.

The court proceedings, which lasted for a few months, were broadcast on television and radio throughout Europe and in the US—a historical first. This had also been the first time since 1945 that the Holocaust received widespread newspaper coverage, including daily analyses, editorials, contextualizing articles, and so on. People gathered to watch and listen to both Eichmann, the bureaucrat who logistically organized the destruction of European Jews, and an endless procession of witnesses who described the horrors they endured in minute detail. It was a spectacle—directed as such by Israeli authorities—through which the atrocities inscribed themselves in the Western collective imagination. Peter Novick has observed: "As part of this process there emerged in American culture a distinct thing called 'The Holocaust'—an event in its own right, not simply a subdivision of general Nazi barbarism" (p. 144).

The most influential interpretation of the Eichmann trial was the concept of the *banality of evil*, coined by Hannah Arendt (recently famous thanks to von Trotta's 2012 biopic) in *Eichmann in Jerusalem* (1963), a book collecting her reports from the courtroom proceedings for the *New Yorker*. She presented the accused as a bland, shallow, mindless man—"thoughtless and speechless"—motivated not by ideological zealousness, but by private ambitions and the principle of obedience. Eichmann's ordinariness—which seems to have made a deep impression on Cohen as well—was underlined by the fact that he excelled at nothing prior to the Final Solution—he was a mediocre violinist, a poor student, and a boring companion. Contemporary evil—according to Arendt—is banal, because even deeds that are horrifying and committed on a gigantic scale are not a result of pathology or ingenious wickedness, but rather petty motives and seemingly meaningless people.

These reflections coincided with the results of the famous psychological experiment by Stanley Milgram, conducted in 1961 in an attempt to resolve the "Eichmann question" posed by Arendt. It showed that ordinary people would willingly and voluntarily administer pain and suffering to others when pressured by an authority figure. Although the social diagnoses of Arendt and Milgram have been modified and subjected to critical scrutiny since, they played a crucial role in the development of the collective sense of guilt for the Holocaust in the 1960s in Western culture.

The concept of the *banality of evil* is directly alluded to by Leonard Cohen in the poem "All There Is to Know about Adolf Eichmann," where Eichmann is described—in the form of a personal survey—as a perfectly normal and ordinary man without any distinguishing features. At the same time our expectations towards this embodiment of evil are targeted and questioned—we anticipated a madman, a demon, someone who would relieve humanity from blame for the atrocities of the Holocaust. However, parallel to Arendt's concept, the horror prevails, because—as Adorno would put it—the social and psychological conditions that enabled the Holocaust still flourish in today's world. The role played in *Flowers* by supreme Nazi officials and architects of the Holocaust—Eichmann, Goebbels, Goering, and finally Hitler himself—is therefore paradoxical. On the one hand, they engage in seemingly ordinary activities and are placed within images and descriptions of normality (even if these are filtered through the poetic imagination): the yawning summer, the rusting harbor, normal physiology, and so on. On the other, their very names are necessarily associated with atrocities, which are then extended, by association, into every corner and walk of life.

## Global Memory?

*Flowers for Hitler* is at the same time a product of the 1960s' tendency toward collective memory and a distinctive voice within that discussion. Again, somehow paradoxically, Cohen's understanding of the Holocaust—encompassing the atomic bomb, ecological catastrophes, and so on—transgresses the historical event, making it rather a metaphor than a strictly literal object of discussion. It may be said, then, that for Cohen the Holocaust is rather a means to than an object of poetic description.

Jeffrey Alexander, a leading sociologist from Yale, investigated how it is possible that this one specific historical event could become transformed into a universal symbol of human suffering and moral evil. Alexander answers this question by pointing to a phenomenon also present in Cohen's *Flowers*. He shows how the "cultural transformation," as he calls it, was possible because the original historical event, traumatic in the extreme for a particular group of people, was *redefined* as a traumatic event for all humankind. "Now free floating rather than situated—universal rather than particular," writes Alexander, the Holocaust "lives in the memories of contemporaries whose parents and grandparents never felt themselves even remotely related to it" (p. 6). Isn't this exactly what strikes us so much about Cohen's *Flowers*?

How did this universalization happen? Alexander shows how important the development of new media was for establishing this memory firmly in the global consciousness. The same intuition is present in Cohen's repertoire of symbols. Just look how far his sight reaches! The narrator of his poems seems to live simultaneously in Canada, Cuba, and even Poland. It seems that the radio could be taken as an important symbol of this point of view (or, point of hearing). Just look how Cohen uses his radio to listen to the whole world! Among the static he's picking up America, or Russia, or "the end of a Mexican song" ("I Had It for a Moment"), even a Polish lullaby ("Waiting for Marianne"). Despite being global, the way he uses the radio as a poetic image and symbol still remains personal, even intimate. It is he, the lonely poet, carefully listening to the pulse of the globe.

Similar to the radio, another recurring item in the poet's world is the telephone, which represents interpersonal communication. In the new, post-traumatic reality, however, every attempt at such intimate communication seems futile. The communication is never successful. You call somebody, although you don't want to. At the other end of the wire a telephone is ringing, but nobody answers. Isn't that the paradox of the telephone? As with any medium, it separates by giving an illusion of being closer.

So the poet-protagonist is trying to look into the mysterious past, using the means available to him (media and images). What exactly does he see? What does he hear on his radio and through his telephone? Well, that's where the most controversial part of the new, global memory begins. For many people Arendt's *Eichmann in Jerusalem* was an outrage. Many critics claimed that by diminishing the horrifying image of the perpetrators and openly disputing the guilt of some victims, she blurred the moral line dividing the evil from the good. If Adolf Eichmann had some human qualities, and if the Jewish Councils (*Judenrats*) were said to collaborate with the Nazis, then why not to ask about the moral guilt of the Soviets, the Americans, the Mexicans, the Poles? Had everybody really done *everything* possible to prevent the Holocaust?

What Cohen sees when he projects his imagination back into the past, is this very confusion. He sees himself both as a victim and as a perpetrator. One day he wakes up as a survivor from a concentration camp, staring at a number on his forearm. The next day he feels like a Nazi, burning his books ("Millennium"), or even feels that "Hitler the Brainmole" remains inside his head. This troubling identification seems to anticipate the reflections of Zygmunt Bauman, who claims that the most unsettling knowledge that we can infer from the Holocaust is not that we could also have been the victims, but rather that we could well have been the perpetrators.

## The Return of the Repressed

Let's go back to the image of grass that grows on ashes. Let's try to think of it geologically, in terms of layers, following an image from "Another Night with Telescope," where the world seems "an eternal unimportant loom / patterns of wars and grass." A cross-section of history shows a constant stratification of ashes and grass, age after age, surface after surface.

What if grass is green not *despite* all the murders, but *because* of them? If we are all both victims and perpetrators, then life *is* a concentration camp. If the postwar world is grown on ashes, all the flowers *are* flowers for Hitler. The day is beautiful. One sees "flowers all over . . . new grass," reads "Folk," there is "a little church," we read, a school, some waving flags, even "some doggies making love." But what is *behind* this curtain of pleasant appearances? There's always more than meets the eye, or rather, there's more than we want to meet the eye. *Flowers for Hitler* presents a Gnostic vision of the world, one that conceals a dark mystery. It's a vision of a sham as the building material of "reality," so familiar thanks to the Wachowskis' *The Matrix.* But in the real world (in the matrix of memory) it's not machines that are to blame for erasing humanity's remembered sense of reality, but humanity itself.

In *Flowers* the whole culture is exposed as a fraud. There is no innocence anymore. Even comic book heroes are implicated. As commentator Sandra Wynands puts it, "Disparate figures of contemporary Western culture are listed as collaborators in the Nazi crimes . . . no peculiarly German form of authoritarianism or mentality produced the Holocaust but rather Western culture as a whole, including exponents of ostensibly 'innocent' popular culture" (p. 203). As in a horror movie, *Flowers for Hitler* reveals the concealed by showing *the uncanny* in everyday life, in two senses: first, the *normality* of life that returns after atrocities; second, a dark *mystery* lurking beneath ordinary life, threatening at any moment to erupt on the surface. Leonard Cohen forces us to face the *uncanny* and ask: If normality functions only to cover up the horror, isn't it complicit in that horror, isn't it guilty too?

# 14
# Doom and Gloom in a Cloistered Room

LIANE HELLER

Leonard Cohen was born September 21st. Philosopher Arthur Schopenhauer died September 21st. The date coincides with the autumnal equinox, the astronomical event during which daylight and darkness are balanced within a single day. This coincidence serves to illuminate both the similarities and the differences in the two men's explorations of the negative, one tilted away from darkness toward the light of love, the other angled away from love toward the darkness of self-denial, both bent on understanding and expressing the irrational nature of the world. Their chosen enclosure—a room—is also their route to freedom: darkness and (at least some) light counterbalanced within consciousness.

Cohen was twenty-two, a recent graduate of McGill University in his native Montreal, when his first book of poetry, *Let Us Compare Mythologies*, was published in 1956. Already his lifelong quest for love and transcendence is in full flower, shot through with the dark, painful, lonely awareness that neither may be fully attainable in a brutal, broken world. This realization will develop and widen, in later poetry, novels, and songs, into a dystopian view of humanity tempered by his characteristically biting wit and mordant humor, and by an unquenchable tenderness for the warped world he unflinchingly describes. Earth is collapsing under the weight of hatred and greed, he writes; yet there is still a moment for a last kiss.

Schopenhauer was twenty-five when his doctoral dissertation, *On the Fourfold Root of the Principle of Sufficient Reason*, was published in 1813. In it, he already lays out his departures from conventional philosophy's view of the world as comprehensible, of reality as rational, a critique he expands exponentially in his masterwork, the subject-object cataclysm that is *The World as Will and Representation*, published when he was still only thirty. Schopenhauer's Will is a directionless, purposeless, reasonless—and unavoidable—compulsion at the heart of all of us, the heart of every-*thing*, which results in endless conflict and violence as we express, or represent, its force in the world. Daily life, he writes, "is really a constant suffering" (*Will and Representation* II, p. 239).

## On Women

If, for Cohen, "love's the only engine of survival," as he offers stunningly amid his bleakest of apocalyptic visions, "The Future," with its spent landscapes and finality of murderous doom, in the face of which our worst atrocities seem desirable by comparison, then for Schopenhauer it is renunciation of corporeal desire—the ascetic's solution, since the aesthetic one, even music, the most sublime art, can only temporarily free the sufferer from the agonizing pain of living in a world of agonizing pain. (Unlike those who were critical of Cohen for sidelining the "high art" of poetry in favor of the "lowly" pursuit of popular music, Schopenhauer no doubt would have approved, given his high regard for the power of music to soothe the beastly Will. Indeed, Cohen himself, in "A Singer Must Die," unsparingly addresses the question of whether or not he has abandoned his ideals.)

The great American poet Emily Dickinson wrote extensively about the conflict between spirit and flesh, of the renunciation of the immediate for the promise of consummation—poems that Schopenhauer might have appreciated if not for his scathingly dismissive views on the other gender. As he wrote in the denunciatory "On Women," a now notorious essay from the second volume of his 1851 collection, *Parerga and Paralipomena*:

> And you cannot expect anything else of women if you consider that the most distinguished intellects among the whole sex have never managed to produce a single achievement in the fine arts that is really great, genuine, and original; or given to the world any work of permanent value in any sphere. (pp. 619–20)

And yet, as if defying his harsh outlook, Schopenhauer insists that love plays a crucial role in the world—a peculiar kind of love, influenced by his belief that personality and intellect were inherited, and tinged by what in a few decades would be termed eugenics: "The ultimate aim of all love affairs . . . is more important than all other aims in man's life; and therefore it is quite worthy of the profound seriousness with which everyone pursues it. What is decided by it is nothing less than the composition of the next generation . . ." (*Will and Representation* II, p. 566).

As an old man, he also seems to have softened his stance on women's potential. According to Rudiger Safranski, as Schopenhauer posed for the German-American sculptor Elisabet Ney, he told Richard Wagner's friend Malwida von Meysenbug: "I have not yet spoken my last word about women. I believe that if a woman succeeds in withdrawing from the mass, or rather raising herself above the mass, she grows ceaselessly and more than a man" *(Schopenhauer and the Wild Years of Philosophy,* p. 348).

Unlike Cohen, who has flourished in the romantic realm and given to the world an array of beautiful and moving love poems that clearly speak of his rich, complex life of the heart, Schopenhauer experienced few, and dismal, romantic relationships. He had an affair with a servant in Dresden who gave birth to an illegitimate daughter; she was born and died in 1819. Then there was an ill-fated relationship with a nineteen-year-old opera singer. Finally, at the age of forty-three, as described by Alexander Rosenthal, he fell for a girl of seventeen who noted in her diary after he offered her a bunch of grapes at a party: "I didn't want the grapes because old Schopenhauer had touched them, so I let them slide, quite gently, into the water" ("Christmas Celebration Speech," p. 43). Later, bitterly, alone, he wrote: "In our monogamous part of the world, to marry means to halve one's rights and double one's duties" (*Parerga and Paralipomena*, p. 622).

Schopenhauer's dismal history with the opposite sex could not be further from Cohen's experience of and attitude toward women. He has had longtime collaborations with female artists, including musicians Jennifer Warnes, Sharon Robinson, and his current partner, Anjani Thomas. He famously said (to Jack Hafferkamp in *The Rolling Stone* in 1971): "Women are really strong. You notice how strong they are? Well, let them take over. . . . The premise being, there can be no free men unless there are free women" ("Ladies and Gents, Leonard Cohen," par. 7).

Of his reputation as a Lothario, with liaisons ranging from the legendary beauty Marianne Jensen (inspiration for "So Long, Marianne") to singer Janis Joplin to actress Rebecca De Mornay and many others, he told Nick Paton Walsh of the *Observer* in 2001:

> I read with some amusement my reputation as a ladies' man. My friends are amused by that, too, because they know my life. Even when I was younger I was never aware of it, to tell the truth, so I could not take advantage of it. But for someone who has that sort of reputation and has spent so many nights alone, it has a special bitter amusement attached to it. ("I Never Discuss My Mistresses or My Tailors," par. 21)

Indeed, in Cohen's writing about women, as in all of his subject matter, loss and sorrow preside over even the most dazzling passions, as if he knows that ultimately he will be alone with his thoughts and words—as if he knows he must be. "Tower of Song" perfectly conveys the crucially necessary loneliness that artists (or philosophers) must not only face, but also embrace with a devotion that painfully wrenches them away from other affections, over and over, in an endless cycle of intimacy and retreat to the cloistered chamber of creation.

From early songs such as "Hey, That's No Way to Say Goodbye," to middle-period compositions like "Take This Waltz" and "Closing Time," and especially "Love Itself," Cohen discovers the most profound expressions of love in its inevitable passing. The poem, or the song, contains the finest and most beautiful aspects of the physical relationship, given unassailable substance in words found only in the silence of his "little room." And this room in his aesthetic tower also offers him the sanctuary to apprehend and comprehend the sometimes twisted passions, obsessions, complications, and heartbreaks of love.

## Creation

The creative crucible, for Cohen and Schopenhauer, takes precedence over worldly matters. Each, in his way, retreats to advance ideas about the deceptive limitations of the physical sphere. Each recognizes, one as practitioner, the other as practicing observer, the power of art to transcend the anguish of what Schopenhauer calls "the Will" and Cohen, "the World" ("Night Comes On") or "the Big World" (*Flowers for Hitler*). Both Cohen and Schopenhauer commit themselves fully to explorations of the Will, or World, that is each of us in our urges and desires.

But even the transformative power of thinking and writing in the privacy of a room far away from the wants and whims that their willed worlds exact can seem insufficient, and Cohen and Schopenhauer then look to spiritual practice as a possibly greater solution to mundane frustration and suffering.

In 1994, after a tour to promote his recently released album *The Future*, Cohen retreated to the Mount Baldy Zen Buddhist monastery in the San Gabriel Mountains of California, where he had spent much time periodically during the previous decade. He was in poor health, reeling from shattered relationships and intense depression, and he saw the monastic life as a chance to reclaim his life. For five years, that seemed to be the case: Cohen fulfilled the rigorous daily routine, was ordained as a monk and given the monastic name Jikan, which, ironically, means "silent one."

But he could not stay silent; he wrote poem after poem during his time in the monastery, and in the end found it impossible to yield himself to a lifetime of Buddhist practice. Although he did say later that his Judaism was strengthened by his experience as a Zen monk, there was no doubt that he would choose a single path, and no doubt which one it would be. It's difficult to counter many generations of rabbinical practice; it's hard to ignore the fact that one's own name, Cohen, means "priest."

His biblical references are numerous and thrillingly proprietary, and so are his sometimes anguished, sometimes wry allusions to Jewishness in the post-Holocaust world. Buddhist principles do arise in Cohen's work, as in the enjoinder in "Anthem" to forget our "perfect offering," but Cohen's spiritual allegiance and practice now belong to the faith he grew up in, the faith of his ancestors; both his grandfathers were rabbis.

In an extraordinary conversation with American author and editor Arthur Kurzweil, just after his *Stranger Music: Selected Poems and Songs* (1993) came out, Cohen responds to Kurzweil's question about a certain line from "The Future":

> Oh, I *am* the little Jew who wrote the Bible. *I am the little Jew who wrote the Bible.* "You don't know me from the wind. You never will, you never did"—I'm saying this to the nations. I'm the little Jew who wrote the Bible. I'm that *little one*. . . .
>
> A confident people is not exclusive. A great religion affirms other religions. A great culture affirms other cultures. A great nation affirms other nations. A great individual affirms other individuals, validates the being-ness of others and the vitality. That's the way I feel about this thing. (from the Cohen and Kurzweil conversation, titled "I *Am* the Little Jew Who Wrote the Bible," p. 23)

Schopenhauer would have fervently and fiercely disagreed. In a disturbing 1850 essay, "On the Sufferings of the World," he writes: "Judaism is inferior to any other form of religious doctrine professed by a civilized nation; and it is quite in keeping with this that it is the only one which presents no trace whatever of any belief in the immortality of the soul" (p. 14). Within the "despotic theism" of the Old Testament, he contends, humanity is ruled by law alone; the New Testament liberates man from the yoke of law and offers the kingdom of grace, attained by faith, love of neighbor (except, perhaps, adherents of Judaism), and self-sacrifice.

But most practicing Christians don't come off much better under Schopenhauer's cutting gaze; their only mitigation is that they're irretrievably trapped by the base justice and rigid rules of the Old Testament, which, if done away with, might lead to the true "path of redemption from the evil of the world." The path of Christ, he says, "is undoubtedly asceticism, however your protestants and rationalists may twist it to suit their purpose" ("Sufferings of the World," p. 16). Asceticism, to Schopenhauer, is the denial of the will to live—a highly desirable outcome: "To those in whom the will has turned and denied itself, this very real world of ours, with its suns and galaxies, is—nothing." (*Will and Representation* I, p. 412).

Self-abnegation, Schopenhauer's interpretation of the practice of Christ and certain saints, and of the Eastern mystics, offers a means to neutralize the horrendously cruel, violent, ubiquitous effect of the Will he sees as the all-powerful force ruling the physical world. Although this isn't particularly Cohen's view, he'd likely be less resistant to it than to living completely or permanently in the manner prescribed—discipline, he would probably argue, is quite a different process from self-denial.

Even more influential on Schopenhauer than his biblical readings were his explorations of the Upanishads, the founding texts of Hinduism, which he first read in his mid-twenties, pored over all his life, and referred to widely as the summit of wisdom (for example, *Will and Representation* I, p. 355). He was also, like Cohen, drawn to Buddhist teachings, in particular that life entails suffering rooted in desire or ignorance, and that the cessation of suffering is possible. In his major work on ethics, *On the Basis of Morality* (1837), he gives voice to a fundamentally Buddhist principle of liberation from anguish within "the everyday phenomenon of *compassion* . . . the immediate *participation*, independent of all ulterior considerations, primarily in the *suffering* of another, and thus in the prevention or elimination of it" (p. 144).

But what Schopenhauer fails to address is that in religious practice the world over, fulfillment and joy are attainable through the very processes he touts as ideals. Buddha's Third Noble Truth says not only that suffering can be overcome, but also that happiness and liberation can thus be achieved in oneself and in the service of others. Christ is cited in John 16:24 as saying: "Ask, and you will receive, that your joy may be full." Or, from the Vedantic tradition: "Seek happiness not in the objects of sense; realize that happiness is within yourself."

Asceticism, in the great traditions, is not so much the eradication of self—of the Will, as Schopenhauer would have it—as the "extinguishing" (the literal meaning of the Buddhist term "nirvana") of the flames of greed, hatred, and delusion that attack and distort a person's character, that promote misery and disable happiness. Schopenhauer spent a lifetime brilliantly and meticulously mapping the very real misery and suffering of the human condition—of the world as he thought it to be—but it's as if he couldn't bring himself even to recognize, let alone seek, joy in spiritual practice any more than in any other realm. Not for him the open-hearted religious explorations that Cohen has undertaken over the decades—or the celebratory reaffirmation of his ancestral faith in recent years.

Schopenhauer had little to celebrate. He was denied fame until the last decade of his life; he was unrelievedly unhappy in love; and he lived alone from 1833 until his death in Frankfurt in 1860—except for the company of a series of poodles, one of which he named Atman, the Hindu term for the essential self, the eternal spirit.

## An Imagined Dialogue

Suppose Leonard Cohen and Arthur Schopenhauer could meet—in a third room, as it were—and discuss the matters that unite them and set them apart. Since this encounter is imaginary, obstacles such as geography and language wouldn't exist. The two men would have some prior knowledge of each other and could freely discuss will and world and word, art and asceticism, love and, yes, even death, as known to each of them on—at present—either side of the great divide:

**LEONARD:** It's extraordinary, Arthur, that we share, at opposite ends of life, a unique relationship with the date September 21st.

**ARTHUR:** The autumnal equinox, which is supposed to be a day equally divided between light and darkness.

**LEONARD:** Supposed to be? Oh, perhaps you mean that you dwell in a realm where such distinctions no longer signify.

**ARTHUR:** Not at all, for if that were so, this dialogue could not take place.

**LEONARD:** I'd say that I stand corrected, except that I'm seated.

**ARTHUR:** Very well then. I could elucidate—

**LEONARD:** It was meant as a joke.

**ARTHUR:** Oh, I see. I'm afraid humor usually eludes me. I think of such talk as an outgrowth of boredom we're driven to as an anesthetic against the ravages of Time.

**LEONARD:** Yet here we are, outside the grip of Time, at least for a time.

**ARTHUR:** You are a poet.

**LEONARD:** Yes, after a fashion.

**ARTHUR:** A poet who delves into the dark places of life, the suffering that is the nature of everyday existence, the violence of individuation.

**LEONARD:** Yes, and the luminous ones as well.

**ARTHUR:** There's that "darkness and light" again. Good and evil. As if in the everyday physical world such distinctions are possible. Some observable, measurable celestial point—an equinox, during whose perfect balance the warring nations suddenly lay down their swords and shields—

**Leonard:** (*singing*): "Down by the riverside, down by the riverside. I ain't gonna study war no more."

**Arthur:** What is that? It's beautiful.

**Leonard:** It's a traditional gospel song. Inspired by the Bible. Isaiah: "And they shall beat their swords into plowshares, and their spears into pruning hooks: nation shall not lift up sword against nation, neither shall they learn war any more."

**Arthur:** Oh.

**Leonard:** My goodness, Arthur, surely you have something more to say than "Oh," given your extensive commentary on the "Jewish Bible" and the hierarchy of the races.

**Arthur:** Ah, Leonard. A poet, a musician—which I applaud, by the way—*and* a Jew? Of course. Of course I know who you are, in this state of knowing-beyond-knowing I find myself in, suddenly embarrassed, suddenly ashamed—not feelings I was wont to experience in life, yet corporeal sensations all the same.

**Leonard:** Embarrassed? Ashamed? Haven't we all had such feelings? And couldn't they be part of the foundation of the compassion you wrote about so eloquently? Couldn't your state of knowing-beyond-knowing be the fertile ground in which that great tree grows—"And the leaves of the tree are for the healing of the nations"?

**Arthur:** Yes, Socrates. (*Leonard laughs heartily.*) I know that passage; it's from the Book of Revelation.

**Leonard:** New Testament.

**Arthur:** New Testament, Old Testament—they seem interwoven now. I'm not sure why I saw such a rift between them, and between Jew and Gentile, and between the sexes, and the races. . . . Perhaps, in my ceaseless and intense efforts to understand the forces of the Will and the anguish of the individual, I was as much an example of that conflict as the rest of humanity that I was describing.

**Leonard:** That's a good insight.

**Arthur:** And then, I was so unhappy. . . .

**Leonard:** I understand unhappiness very well. I don't know any artists, thinkers, creators who haven't been unhappy. It's a question of having to express the most difficult matters of life.

**Arthur:** But you're not unhappy now.

**Leonard:** No. But it wasn't some great act or event that lifted the sadness of a lifetime. It was more a recognition of and appreciation for the ordinary gifts of daily life—a garden in bloom, my daughter's smile—

**Arthur:** I do regret not having had a family. My relationships were terrible, destructive. It's quite probable that my diatribes against women arose from those experiences, not that it's any excuse.

**Leonard:** Again, as you said, your own philosophy provided exceptional perceptions of the nature of suffering and conflict, and the means, like compassion, to transcend them. But it seems you were not able to partake of them in your own life. Or even now.

**Arthur:** Even now? Even now that I understand?

**Leonard:** But do you extend your understanding of compassion to *yourself*?

**Arthur:** Do you?

**Leonard:** (*laughing*): You must be part Jewish, Arthur, to answer a question with another question like that. But to answer, yes. Not always, maybe not even that often, but I can be kind, compassionate, merciful to myself. Many sages say, and I agree, that otherwise we can't really be good to others.

**Arthur:** "Every man takes the limits of his own field of vision for the limits of the world. This is an error of the intellect as inevitable as that error of the eye, which lets us fancy that on the horizon heaven and earth meet." I'm sorry to quote myself, but it seemed apt.

**LEONARD:** That's wonderful. When did you write that?

**ARTHUR:** Well, in the late 1840s or so; the essay was published in 1851 ("Further Psychological Observations," p. 40). That's when my life was just starting to become successful; I mean, my work was. So when you speak of occasional happiness, I suppose I was at least superficially happy. The kind that comes from approval. It was better than nothing at all. But the kind you describe, that a poet and musician can describe in the minutiae of life, that, no. My own words accuse me of a limited scope.

**LEONARD:** But you've said it yourself, Arthur—the *limited scope*, within which great beauty resides, within each of us. Your powerful words need not accuse you: they can set you free.

**ARTHUR:** Am I not free now?

**LEONARD:** We can't equate freedom and death, although they may sometimes seem alike. Have you not expressed to me remorse, regret, a yearning to experience the liberating compassion and happiness you lacked? Could these not be the great mortal strivings that arose from your monumental philosophical endeavours and endure beyond death?

**ARTHUR:** (*smiling*): Yes, Socrates. That's true.

# V

# Songs from a Mind

# 15
# *Dear Heather* in a Dark Space

CHRISTOPHER KETCHAM

Sable night, mother of dread and fear . . .

—SHAKESPEARE, *The Rape of Lucrece*

It was a particularly nasty night, the kind of wet cold that freezes the skin and forces drafts through the weave of the best wools. I shivered. My mood was no less foul, as I'd spent the better part of the evening at the university library on a thorny research problem which did nothing but stymie me. That and a text message at about eleven that said, "I'm leaving." I did not want to go home to a now empty apartment so I wandered the city for a while until my chin was numb and I was muzzy.

The neon sign glowed CA E; the F was dark. It was warm inside but not all that inviting a place: a few booths and plain round wooden tables with no linens. Dotted around the tables were two, three, or five spindle-backed wooden chairs that I knew would screech when I pulled one out. I chose a booth. There were maybe three people sitting at the tables and the other booths were empty. I was not in the mood to notice much else about the place. I ordered coffee from a waitress with the longest straight black hair I had seen in years. Her long nose and that hair made me think of a raven. But she didn't strut or cackle and just took my order and nodded. The coffee was warm, and bitter. Fitting.

I began to slide down into the booth and pain throbbed in my thawing chin as if to chastise me for taking it outside. I heard Leonard Cohen, coming from somewhere. His was the disembodied voice that speaks to schizophrenics, beckoning me to listen. Not just to listen to his punctuated monotone but to penetrate through the drone to his words and then to their meaning in context where he wanted to take me. It was from his album, his gift on his seventieth birthday, *Dear Heather*. He kept repeating "I was there for you" which, of course, guided me straight back to the subject of the text message. Cohen's line is what I should have texted back to her, but I had done nothing. No, that's not true, I had deleted the message. My coffee had cooled; I didn't want to go back outside; I didn't want more caffeine.

## Come, Civil Night, Thou Sober-Suited Matron, All in Black

The lights flickered; Cohen stuttered and returned to his song. Then the lights dimmed and the demonic voice dropped an octave, then stopped suddenly. Silence and blackness. "Shit," from somewhere—a different voice from Cohen's, higher—maybe the raven. Newspaper, yes it was newspaper rustled—over there, wherever there was. My eyes struggled with a false halo from the sudden shift from light to dark. There should have been emergency lights or at least someone was a smoker. But the darkness remained. For how long had it been dark?

In the light, the space of the café had been before me—it was separate from me. But the dark seemed to cloak me. It touched me. I could feel the air as I reached for my cup to down the last drops of coffee. The cup rang as loud as if I were in a bell tower. I felt unsettled, peculiar, for the darkness was not absence as the light was; darkness enveloped me—no it even penetrated the very core of my being. I felt the back of the booth as if it had grown into me, become me. No, I was not in a Kafka story; I was not Gregor Samsa who awoke one morning as a bug. But this was a kind of metamorphosis, for

I had become part of the dark space of this café—no, the dark space had become part of me. I was for a moment Antoine Roquentin in Café Mably in Sartre's *Nausea*, where his nausea had come out of him—there on the walls of the café, making him one within the nausea (p. 31). But I did not feel the same sickness as Roquentin; I felt only the mysterious but gentle dark space in which I was enveloped.

Actually it wasn't all that unnerving after a time. Rather, it had become exhilarating in a way I had not experienced before. Nor was I panicked to find the light again.

Muted lights passed by the store window and the glow was as from Plato's cave where those inside can only see the shapes and shadows on the other side of a veil and this is their world. My darkness was a different world from Plato's shadowy cave and in the dark the café was somehow clearer than it was in the light.

As the car lights passed, silhouettes of two people appeared, separate from me, but close, so close—and then they reconnected me to the returning blackness. I was part of them and them me, linked by the fabric of space: the café.

The dark space had become personal. It was more mine than the pitiful café of the light. Then as suddenly as the darkness came I wanted to know the raven and the two silhouettes that had appeared briefly. I reached out to them with my thoughts—my space to their space. But there was nothing; no one touched back. I put out my hand, thinking that it could trace the limits of their space, but I touched only the darkness of space. Only the cloak of blackness touched me back.

Strangely I felt free, free from the dilemma of my work and my Dear John text message. It was as if the dark space had flowed into my consciousness, stroking my ego with black salve. I could have panicked, but felt strangely calm. Beyond the expletive, nothing else was spoken. No one else shuffled. No one else seemed to move. Had the dark space enveloped them as well? I wondered.

The lights flickered on after a while, I don't know how long. But the dark space had not withdrawn with the coming of the light. It was as if the dark space had supercharged the light that came back on. Cohen crooned "O love, aren't you tired yet?" But I wasn't.

I thought of Eugene Minkowski's concept of lived space and how the dark in dark space is more personal than the light in light space (p. 405). Dark space envelopes the skin and when you move in dark space, it seems to touch back ever so gently. I wanted to keep the dark space close but already its darkness was fading with every passing moment of light. Then I recalled what Minkowski had also said, that the auditory space, the space where music penetrates, was also a dark space (p. 406). I could close my eyes to listen to Cohen and abstract myself from the light and plunge myself into the world of his sound and his stories. So I did. I closed my eyes and released the light space from its hold on me and let the darkness of Cohen's music cloak me as the dark space had only moments before.

## I Can No Longer Hear You

As I listened to song after song I felt the presence of death. It was as if while listening to *Dear Heather*, I was before death. Martin Heidegger reminds us that death comes only when we are *all in*—when there is no more to experience (p. 280). This *all in*, of course, could come at any time. But it is what we have left to experience which is dear to us, as dear to us as what has been experienced until now. As Cohen reminisced about lost loves, a dead nightingale, and innocence lost on 9/11, he himself was before death, but not in the way Heidegger described as *not yet*. We can't escape death, but we can *be* before it and embrace the possibilities remaining for our being in the world. We are thrown into this world and remain anxious about the possibilities of becoming and this is so also in the face of death. I felt betrayed by Cohen.

His world had contracted, shrunk, and become deformed: a city made smaller by the death of people and its tallest buildings; women who cared for him still even though he had become more of a burden than companion; being there for someone not himself; the stealing of a piece of his world—a lover at a simple dance. Then, there was no more time to roam. On and on, farther and farther inward he penetrated my own waning soul without mercy.

I stopped listening and with eyes still closed I returned to the dark space of the earlier blackout. I felt the presence of Freud. Freud saw pleasure as a kind of release mechanism working against ego instincts that thrust us towards death through repressive forces—a protective mechanism against too much stimulation (p. 96). The ego instincts tend to assist the pleasure instincts in being towards death as a way of releasing tension. I heard and felt Cohen trying to reduce the tensions of bitterness and loss with wry twists to his remembrances—his transcendental moments of morning glory. A perverse release of pleasure? Had Cohen fallen into that Freudian trap, the so-called death wish? I wanted to wring it out of Cohen but that was not possible.

Then I realized that I wanted to wring it out of me, that my own release was the despair, the funk, and the depression that had crept over me and penetrated me as deeply as had the darkness. It had crept into me, the unobtrusive death wish, and I had let it dwell without challenging it, without facing it down. The nausea had crept into me. I was Roquentin again in his café. I was listening, absorbed in the music, and Cohen had become the mellifluous voice of Roquentin's black jazz singer who embraced me with the music . . . and then, like Roquentin, my own nausea disappeared with the end of the song (p. 34).

I realized that Heidegger was right. It wasn't about being towards death, a downward spiral of ever fewer moments towards the inevitable. No, it was being thrown towards my own potentiality for becoming, for being (p. 279). I had been barreling towards demise instead of traveling outward towards the horizon of my own possibilities. But had Cohen let me down or was this his intention in the first place?

I remembered from Cohen's first novel, *The Favourite Game*, that his main character Breavman loved the paintings of Henri Rousseau because they stopped time (p. 39). In Rousseau's paintings the improbable became the probable, with lions not eating shepherds and men riding tigers. But within these works was the hint of darkness in black shapes with minimal relief that played hidden songs or peered through thick undergrowth. The beasts in the heart of darkness stare, stare at you from a dark space as if they know your every move.

Cohen had taken me and I traveled with him into his dark space to feel around in it with him. The smell of death was everywhere and the stench was like smelling salts to snap me out of my funk. My dark space complemented his until I realized that what I had cloaked myself with was the same funk of depression over loss and frustration that Cohen sang about. Sure, my experience had been a kind of Tennessee waltz and precious time had been stolen from me, or I had just let it pass. Cohen had stopped time for me as Rousseau had stopped time for Breavman. And Breavman had stopped time for Heather, his family's maid, when he hypnotized her and in this state took her to his bed. It felt like I too had just woken after being locked in a state of violation (pp. 36–38).

I began to realize that time and possibilities are intertwined, leading to the scarcity of both. Therefore, I needed to absorb Heidegger's argument for pushing, always pushing forward and use mindfulness and reflection to consider and reconsider who I want to become and in the fullest possible measure be that person. No it wasn't self-actualization, because as Cohen had shown me we never complete ourselves as we might want to even in a full life. But conceptually, I saw that a kind of resoluteness would bring meaning back into my own being.

I released myself from the dark space of my thinking and listened to the music once again. Cohen was repeating, over and over, "We rise to play a greater part," and I understood that he first had to lead me down into my own fetid space before he could release me back into a shared space where I could begin again—begin again to rethink my existence as being towards my own future possibilities rather than what had come before. My freedom to do this is temporary because all mortals die; but freedom is the *we're not there yet* which is the only experience humanity can have because death is just the end of experience.

After a time the music ended and Raven made no move to change the state of silence. I heard the whir of a compressor and my own breathing and the occasional whoosh of late-night traffic. A far-off horn. A sigh from Raven as she turned the page of her newspaper. I closed my eyes. I felt comforted again back in this dark space.

My own psychopathology reminded me of the schizophrenic patient Minkowski described who spent more and more time retreating into himself to ward off the possible blows of life (p. 411). He had withdrawn into his past and dwelled there to prevent the same from also becoming his future. His lived space had become smaller and smaller. I thought how too, like this schizophrenic, I had tried to shield myself from the exigencies of being in the world by restricting my lived space. How I had pushed the boundaries between me and others and the things in the world as far away as I could so that I would not have to interact with them. But how could I now back out of this diminished life space and push the envelope of its horizon towards a being towards, not a being away from?

My life space had become irrational not only because of its diminished size but because my lived time had been limited to the past and the past from which I wanted to be protected in the future—and which I kept returning to over and over again in my downward spiral. It had become my own singsong, my own *Dear Heather* of overripe memories representing my self-limiting possibilities for the future. I felt a sense of dread. It was as if a short circuit in the causal chain of my existence had finally been discovered. I had only to reset the circuit breaker. But it wasn't that easy. My ascent from funk would require something and I didn't know quite what. All I did know was that I would need to keep a piece of the dark space at hand to feel it cloak me as I pushed out the boundaries of my lived space and pressed into forward from reverse my lived time. I was not sure how I would be able to accomplish this.

## She Comes Dancing through the Darkness

I opened my eyes. From this dark space I had come into the light again. I realized that light's warmth was a false security, a false security of being in the world without being at all; that one can with eyes open wander through this life blindly when in the dark one can see. I resolved to take this dark space with me and bring it to the fore when I needed it again. And I knew that I would need it again.

I began to see the world and it seemed new and different now in its everydayness. Life was suddenly more precious. I did not want to look back from my seventies with remorse or even longing for what had been. I could no longer afford to waste life chasing after impossibilities and lamenting lost loves. My eyes scanned the café in the light but from the lingering perspective of dark space. The walls bulged with dimension and the floor heaved up towards me in recognition of my new sight. Raven was hunched over behind the counter, staring into a newspaper. She twirled a strand of hair with her finger.

My cup was empty. It was late, probably colder still. My home wasn't. I could walk out of the café and trundle down the path that so many have into an inauthentic being just like I had before, and like others, follow Cohen's lyrics down and into the funk of being, just being in the world with everyone else being in the world. What had been once clear and precise in the light had become obscured in the darkness. But this darkness was not nothing; rather it was a rich space of possibilities as well as dangers and mystery. But the dark space also beckons for close attention and a stepping away from the clarity of the everyday. The night, the darkness reveals mysteries, it doesn't obscure them. In the dark space there are other possibilities for being.

Across from me at a table where little light fell sat a woman. Her dark parka was quilted, and there were many ski tags on the zipper draw. But the parka was stained and filthy and her brown hair was matted and greasy. The parka hung from her, betraying a slight figure underneath. Her face had been comely once but now was tarnished by living in or living too close to the streets. She was still a young woman but the ski tags seemed out of place. She had cupped her hands around a mug and was nodding, the nod of street sleepers who keep one eye open. Her fingernails were black with grime. She was beautiful. She was Suzanne, a long ago song from Cohen, with all her mysteries, sadness, and the freedom of living in the dusk world of the streets, among the castaways from the light world. I returned to the dark space again and reached towards her with my eyes closed. Only silence. But there was hope in the darkness. Hope.

I opened my eyes again and eased myself out of the booth. On the table I lay down cash for the coffee and a dollar as a tip. I thought my leaving might wake Suzanne and if it did I would approach her. I began to walk towards the door. Suzanne's eyes opened. I turned and walked to her.

# 16
# Can You Touch Someone's Body with Your Mind?

RACHEL HALIBURTON

Poets and singers construct worlds for us, and—like philosophers and science-fiction writers—draw our attention to features of the world and elements of our experience that we normally don't even notice. In the process, they take what seems ordinary and make it extraordinary, or transform what seems impossible into the stuff of everyday life. If they are good at performing these transformations, they, too, reveal things that seem true to us that we might never otherwise have noticed. Sometimes the worlds constructed by philosophers and the insights captured by poets come together, so that the latter can explain the former, and the former illuminate the latter.

Such is the case with "Suzanne," a song that asks us to enter into a different world than the one we normally inhabit, and that raises deeply philosophical questions about the validity of subjective experiences, the ways in which we encounter and understand one another, and, ultimately, the nature of reality itself. This world prompts us to see features of ordinary life more clearly: it is a song that simultaneously takes the extraordinary and makes it ordinary, and transforms experiences we seldom notice into things which are transcendent and miraculous. In the process, the song helps us see that the world we actually live in is far more metaphysically interesting and puzzling than we normally think.

When Suzanne invites us to her home near the river, it's a world that's mysterious and fantastical, a place in which mundane experiences like eating oranges and drinking tea encourage us to think about distant lands, a space in which the river is both real (it is a conduit for shipping) and metaphorical (composed of a medium upon which only Jesus could walk, and in which we must risk drowning if we are to be saved), and a place in which castoffs bought from the Salvation Army take on a transcendent aspect as golden sunlight shines down upon them.

Above all, it is a world in which the seemingly impossible becomes possible, a space in which physical bodies can be touched by immaterial minds. What might it mean to touch someone's body with your mind? There are two ways this thought can be understood: first, as a pleasingly poetic but ultimately meaningless turn of phrase; or, second, as an invitation to think about the possibility that thoughts themselves are real, as real as the physical objects our bodies perceive, and among which those bodies can be placed. What kind of metaphysical position underpins Suzanne's world? What metaphysical commitments might we have to make if we want to join her there?

A consideration of how it might be possible for minds to touch bodies will take us to the heart of some of the most difficult metaphysical questions that philosophers can ask—questions about what exists and how we can determine this—and places us at the center of a current philosophical controversy about the nature of reality and the role of consciousness within it. Exploring these issues will require us to consider two very different ways of understanding our experiences, perceptions, and purposes. Indeed, if Suzanne invites us into a distinct world, each side in this debate does so as well. As it turns out, the metaphysics of Suzanne's world are teleological, not materialist, because it is only in a teleological world—a world where not just human activities but everything has built-in purposes, and human beings are not mere physical objects—that we can touch someone's body with our mind. We will also need to think about what kind of world we live in, and whether we can perform this feat here as well.

## The Mechanistic World of Materialism

The first virtual world we will explore, the world of materialism, is tough and bleak. It is a world in which all of our experiences—our emotions, our perceptions, and our thoughts—are ultimately explainable by, and reducible to, underlying physical processes. This virtual world was developed in the seventeenth century, owes many of its features to Descartes (not himself a materialist), and has proven to be enormously useful for the discoveries of modern science. Its structure underpins current science, and is widely accepted by contemporary philosophers. In this world, only the physical is real—or, we might say, only the physical is *really* real. Your perception that you are reading this essay right now, the tart sweetness of the orange you had for breakfast, the pain you felt when you peeled it and the skin squirted acidic liquid into your eye, the smell of orange zest on your hands—all of these things are the result of meaningless physical processes, sensations that arise from the action of purposeless particles in motion. Indeed, in this world, the oranges, the bodies that consume them, and the book that you are reading, are essentially the same things, composed out of the same particles, which are governed by the same scientific laws, and ultimately explainable through them. Our belief that our perceptions are much more than this—that oranges are real, and fundamentally different from books, that feelings are meaningful, that we are more than physical entities and that our lives might have an ultimate purpose—are illusions, a kind of conjuring act performed by our brains which allows us function. They can never give us clear and unfettered access to reality itself.

Notice how different this world is from the world Suzanne shows; it has none of the colors, textures, tastes, and smells—let alone the emotional connections—that permeate the space we share with her. Indeed, in the material world, it is not only perceptions that exist only in our minds, but also the meanings we place on our encounters with one another, and the intentions we place on our own activities. The transcendent image of Jesus as a kind of celestial lifeguard as he stands atop his tower, his loneliness, the audible and visual flow of the river, the color of the sunlight, the beauty of the human body, our concept of perfection, and the trust between us, are all nothing more than perceptions in the mind, things which exist only in our consciousness as representations of reality, but which are never themselves objectively real. What is *really* real are the physical processes which give rise to them, the movements of purposeless particles that can be described in mathematical and mechanical terms. In this world, in short, we are merely physical organisms, and, since our mental lives—our perceptions, emotions, beliefs, experiences—arise from our physical existence, we can ultimately give a physical explanation of these mental events.

Notice, too, that while this is an ordered world, it isn't one that has meanings and purposes built into it. This isn't a world where Jesus can save anyone from drowning. We may believe that our perceptions respond to real things that exist outside of us, that our relationships are meaningful, that there is a reason for our existence, but all we're doing when we make these assumptions is projecting what is going on in our brains onto the natural world, not reflecting in our minds things which really exist out there. In short, in a materialist world, taste, smell, color, meaning, and purpose aren't real—which means, of course, that our thoughts, our subjective experiences, and perhaps even our minds themselves—are ultimately not real either. In this world, while bodies can touch bodies, minds never can.



## The Extraordinary World of Teleology

But there is another possibility we can consider, another virtual world that we can enter. This world provides a teleological explanation of reality, rather than a materialist one. This virtual world of teleology is one that was largely constructed by Aristotle (with help from other ancient Greek philosophers like Socrates and Plato), and it has recently been refurbished and updated by Thomas Nagel.

In Aristotle's teleological world, we begin our explorations of reality through the information provided to us by our senses. When we look around us, we see a world composed of many different sorts of things: houses, cars, moose, people, dogs and cats, smells, sounds, textures, grass, rocks, rivers, the taste of oranges, and the heat of a freshly made cup of tea. Moreover, common sense reveals a world filled with meaning and purpose, not only specifically human purposes but also more generally natural ones. We build cars for transportation and houses for shelter, we domesticated dogs and cats for different purposes; ears and eyes and taste buds perform different functions; different creatures, from mammals to fish to viruses and bacteria, occupy different niches in the ecosystem; and all living creatures need water to live, which demonstrates the existence of an underlying natural order.

In his controversial book *Mind and Cosmos*, Thomas Nagel defends a naturalistic teleological conception of reality, and challenges those who believe that the virtual reality world constructed by the materialists is not itself a representation of reality (as all virtual worlds are) but a true account of reality itself. As he observes, the architects of the materialist virtual world limited its features right from the start by subtracting (from the things they thought it possible to study) anything mental, including intentions, purposes, meanings, subjective experiences, and consciousness itself. They subtracted, in short, everything that makes us human, different sorts of animals from dogs, cats, and moose, different from other kinds of things like rocks, trees, and lakes, leaving us as little more than physical objects—different in appearance, perhaps, from dogs, cats, trees, and stones, but, underneath it all, subject to and defined by the same physical processes they are, and explainable in the same mathematically-based scientific terms.

Nagel believes that this was a fundamental mistake, and argues that it has resulted in a picture of reality that is not only a *false* description of the way things *really* are, but an inadequate account of features of our lives that we already know, namely, the reality of our experiences. While our emotions, perceptions, and experiences are perhaps *explainable* in terms of physical processes, they are not *reducible* to them: the subjective experience of what an orange tastes like, the warmth of hot tea as it moves down your throat, the way the invitation to go home with Suzanne makes you feel, are themselves *real*. Even if it were possible to map out, in some precise way, what's going on in your brain as you sip the tea and chew the oranges, to explain what processes are taking place in your body as you ingest them, and how those processes relate to physical features of the oranges and tea, the subjective experience—the way these things feel to you—is also real, over and above those brain patterns and physical processes. Nagel holds that, "Conscious subjects and their mental lives are inescapable components of reality not describable by the physical sciences," and human beings are nothing less than "large-scale, complex instances of something both objectively physical from outside and subjectively mental from inside" (pp. 41–42).

Further, Nagel argues, in order for consciousness to have arisen at all, evolution itself cannot be a purely physical process, but must include the reality of mental phenomena. Moreover, he believes, our existence as beings capable of reflecting on the world around us, and on the workings of our own minds (among other things) is unlikely to have arisen entirely by chance, but must have been part of nature's "intended" design. As he puts it, "to explain not merely the possibility but the actuality of rational beings, the world must have properties that make their appearance not a complete accident: in some way the likelihood must have been latent in the nature of things" (p. 86). In contrast to the materialist picture in which complex things can be broken down into underlying processes and explained in physical terms, in a teleological world, natural processes give rise to new and unexpected realities. "Teleology means that in addition to the physical laws of the familiar kind, there are other laws of nature that are 'biased towards the marvelous'" (p. 92). One of the marvelous features of a world understood in teleological terms is that thoughts are real, and so are the minds that house them; in such a world, it is entirely possible to touch someone's body with your mind.

## Which Virtual World Is Most Like Our Own?

This exploration of the materialist world and the teleological one allows us to finally answer the questions we began with: what kind of metaphysical picture underlies Suzanne's world? Is her world like the one we live in, or radically different from it? And, finally, if you can touch someone's body with your mind in Suzanne's world, can we do this in ours? I want to suggest three things: first, that Suzanne's world is teleological, and so incomprehensible from a purely materialist perspective. Second, although it is described in poetic terms that make its features appear mysterious and fantastical, Suzanne's world is actually the one we live in. Indeed, the song can open our eyes to features of ordinary life that we often take for granted, but which are actually far more wonderful and extraordinary than we usually notice. And, finally, I will argue that we can touch one another's bodies with our minds; in fact, we do this all the time, because our world is, indeed, "biased towards the marvelous."

A defense of these claims will require us to compare what's going on in the song to something that we're more familiar with. Imagine that you and I are at the food court in the mall (I am a customer, perhaps, and you are an employee at one of the booths, Suzanne to my Cohen on a more mundane level). We are surrounded by other people, some pushing shopping carts loaded with bags, others drinking coffee or lining up to buy subs, pizza, and Chinese food. The servers at the various food outlets (including you, I notice as I place my salad order) look simultaneously bored and stressed out, torn between the necessity of working efficiently and the recognition that the jobs they are doing are repetitive and dull. As we all move through the shared physical space of the food court, we maneuver around one another (shopping carts are seldom crashed into pedestrians, those waiting for seats at the tables move like speed racers when a spot opens up, in order to grab it before anyone else does, you and your fellow employees move around one another in a kind of choreographed dance), and we meet as minds as well: when I place my salad order, we make eye contact, you give me what I ask for, and when I hand you my money in exchange for the salad you just made, we have a shared understanding of what the transaction means.

The commonplace nature of these experiences disguises the fact that what we are engaged in, all of us who are present in the food court at this time, and in all of our encounters with one another as well, is something truly wondrous and philosophically interesting. We find ourselves, in these everyday activities, at the heart of the debate between the materialists and the teleologists about how we ought to understand the nature of reality and the place of human consciousness in a world that we can describe (if we wish) in purely physical terms. Consciousness—our awareness of our own minds, our recognition of the minds of others, and the way in which our experiences feel to us—is simultaneously mysterious and fantastic, the stuff of dreams and nightmares, and banal and ordinary, something we assume, take for granted, and utilize in everything we do.

One of the most striking features of human embodiment—we aren't, after all, *dis*embodied minds either—is that we can never know what it would be like to experience the world as other people do, just as no one else can ever really know what it is like to be us. Nevertheless, each of us knows—and knows that others know—that other minds exist, and that, while particular subjective experiences (what it feels like to be *me*, as I order my salad, or *you*, as you prepare it, what it feels like to be Suzanne making tea and oranges, or Cohen as she serves him) are inaccessible to others, consciousness itself is a shared attribute of human beings. Moreover, one of the reasons why novels, poems, paintings, and songs have the power to move us the way that they do results from their capacity to break down the barriers between us by allowing us, in a very real sense, to imagine what it might be like to be someone else, and to experience the world in the way that they do.

It is consciousness that allows us to function together in the food court (or down by the river at Suzanne's, and elsewhere), because we encounter one another not merely as physical bodies maneuvering through shared physical space, but as *minds* meeting one another as well. We can relate our exchanges in the food court to our visit with Suzanne, to the shared meal of tea and oranges, and the pleasure we take in her company. In this encounter, we are much more than bodies sharing physical space; we are, in addition and most importantly, meeting one another as conscious beings who construct shared understandings together. We know that the oranges and tea come from China, we have all heard the story of Jesus walking on the water (and whether or not we believe it to be true, we recognize that it is a story of some significance), and we experience a shared desire for our interactions with one another to be meaningful.

But how do we do all these things, and how ought we to understand the mental events that make our exchanges with one another intelligible, and our interactions—potentially, at least—meaningful and significant? If we interpret what we experience through the parameters of a materialist conception of reality, it is not only the dimensions of Suzanne's world that become unintelligible (or merely poetic) but also what happens to us when we listen to a song like "Suzanne," and even our mundane interactions with others in places like the food court. Whatever we believe we are doing, whatever meaning we place on our encounters, the moral and social weight we give to them—all of these things are not *really* real for a strict materialist; they are, rather, a kind of coping mechanism which allows us to function in the world, but they are not truly reflective of what is going on beneath the surface. In truth, according to this account, there are no purposes or meanings in the natural world, and we, as physical beings, are just as subject to the underlying physical processes that allow us to exist as are the tables, shopping carts, and foodstuffs that we see when we look around us.

In a teleological world, however, things are simultaneously much more like what we ordinarily take them to be *and* marvelously transformed. In this world, it is clear that consciousness exists as something other than a kind of unintended consequence of unconscious and purposeless physical processes; rather, it is something that is a unique attribute, in its fully developed form, of human beings. As Nagel argues, a materialist conception of reality, despite its widespread acceptance, is ultimately unsustainable, because it is unable to adequately account for the objective fact that consciousness exists (when I order my salad from you, you understand what I'm asking for when I say that I want you to add extra tomatoes and cucumbers; we know that Suzanne's shopping choices demonstrate that she's thrifty), and for the reality of our different subjective experiences (my hunger, your boredom; how tea and oranges taste to Cohen). While we take these things for granted (as the example of what goes on in a mall food court shows), our ability to do the things we do every day is no less strange and miraculous than the images presented in the song: Jesus on his tower, the heroes floating in the seaweed, our desire for love and connection, our fear of loneliness, the trust we place in others. In short, what "Suzanne" helps us see more clearly, what the song brings to our attention, is the way the things we do every day, far from being things we should take for granted, are actually capacities that we should marvel at, as Cohen does and invites us to do too.

Finally, in a teleological world, since thoughts are real, minds can indeed touch bodies. In fact, if we conceive of our world as teleological, we touch bodies with our minds all the time—when we hand over money in exchange for goods, and the person at the checkout hands us what we've bought; when we arrange to meet a friend at a particular time and place; when we listen to a song like "Suzanne" with friends and talk about what it means to us; when my fingers type my thoughts into my computer and you read them in a book. While we can never know what it would be like to be someone else, to experience the world as they do, we all know that others subjectively experience the world, and that their subjective experiences mirror ours in important ways. The shifting perspectives articulated by the narrator (as who is being touched and by whom changes) take us at least partly into one another's experiences and show how we construct shared meanings together, as our minds interact with one another the same way our bodies do. The fact that Suzanne can get us on her wavelength suggests that Cohen's metaphysics are teleological rather than materialist, for it's only when we understand reality in such terms that thoughts are really real and it's possible to touch someone's body with your mind.

# 17
# Is a Tear an Intellectual Thing?

LIAM P. DEMPSEY

> I hate and love. You ask perhaps how can that be.
> I know not; but I feel that it is so, and I am tortured.
>
> —CATULLUS, poem 85

Anyone who watches Leonard Cohen's *I Am a Hotel* cannot help but be struck by the range of emotional expression it presents, from the physical exuberance of the dancers in "Memories" to the melancholy questioning and self-doubt in "The Gypsy's Wife" to the tranquility of emotional reflection in "Suzanne." Indeed, like a hotel's ever-changing denizens, emotions come in many forms and are expressed in many ways.

We can roughly divide theories of emotion into two competing camps: body-based accounts that emphasize bodily reactions, and mind-based accounts that emphasize judgments. The fancy terms for these are "somatic" theories and "cognitive" theories, respectively. Body-based theories capture the *visceral* nature of emotions, connecting them with an organism's survival and situating them within a larger evolutionary story. Mind-based theories work well at explaining socially complex emotions like jealousy and long-term love, those written about by poets as defining that which is quintessentially human.

While it would be misleading to claim that Cohen adopts any specific theory of emotion, his work, like that of all great poets and writers, provides an important window through which to view the nature of one of the most important aspects of human existence. It should be of little surprise that, as a poet and writer, Cohen tends to emphasize the mental elements of emotions. Nevertheless, his work embodies both perspectives. Ultimately, I suggest that even for the poet, it is useful to conceive of emotions as *processes* involving both bodily and mental responses. Understood as a process between complementary but sometimes conflicting systems, a process account is able to capture the rich complexity of emotional phenomena addressed in Cohen's music, including not only love and infatuation but also jealousy and betrayal.

## Bodily Reactions

Famously, the nineteenth-century psychologist and philosopher, William James, and nineteenth-century physician Carl Lange (independently) advanced what is now known as the James-Lange thesis: emotions are constituted by bodily reactions to certain stimuli. Emotional experiences are the perception of these physical disturbances. To see this, James asks the reader to imagine what, if anything, would be left of an emotion if these bodily reactions were absent. Take the case of fear: "what would be left, if the feelings neither of quickened heartbeats nor shallow breathing, neither of trembling lips nor of weakened limbs, neither of goose-flesh nor of visceral stirrings, were present, it is quite impossible to think" (Prinz, p. 46). James's point is clear: the phenomenology of fear is precisely the experience of these telltale physiological reactions to the fearful stimulus. Consider that if a man claimed to be afraid and yet showed none of these bodily reactions, we would likely be very skeptical of his claim.

These bodily expressions are largely automatic and can include not only things like visceral reactions and changes in heart rate, but also facial expressions, a phenomenon Darwin was quite interested in and which has been studied extensively ever since. As we all know from experience, a facial expression is a window into a person's emotional state. When a person adopts the proverbial "poker face," he intends to draw the curtains on this window. More generally, we tend to corroborate what a person says by what her face expresses, which is one reason communication via email can leave the writer's intentions and emotions ambiguous. For law enforcement, face reading has become something of a science and has recently been popularized in pop culture by television shows like *Lie to Me*.

The evidence for the bodily basis of emotions is impressive. Jesse Prinz makes the case in "Embodied Emotions" (pp. 45–47). First, for at least the *basic* emotions, namely anger, fear, sadness, disgust, surprise, and joy, we see tight correlations with specific sorts of bodily changes. Second, likewise, evoking certain bodily changes can induce emotions, from forcing a smile to improve one's mood, to adopting the "power stance" before a job interview to increase confidence. Third, the brain circuits involved in emotions are also involved in bodily regulation and self-maintenance. Fourth, reduced bodily awareness and feedback also results in diminished emotions.

It's not surprising, then, that we characterize so many emotions using embodied metaphors. For instance, it's common to characterize the intense sadness of a lost love in terms of a broken heart, the revelation of betrayal as a kick in the stomach, and the nervousness of a public speaking engagement as butterflies in the stomach. We see many such references to embodied metaphors in Cohen's songs. Cohen frequently invokes the heart metaphor, perhaps the most common embodied metaphor. Expressing the emotional turmoil of love lost in his "In My Secret Life," Cohen describes his heart as feeling like ice, both "crowded and cold." In "The Land of Plenty," Cohen intimates that the heart is a place with space and depth, such that many things may fit in its "caverns." One's heart—or "love"—might be pierced ("Field Commander Cohen") or broken ("The Guests," "The Window," "Teachers," and "Ballad of the Absent Mare") or restless

("The Smokey Life"), or hardened with hatred ("Light as the Breeze"), or layered like an onion ("Wishing Window"). One's heart may stand for the person ("Heart with No Companion" and "Humbled in Love") or it might be something one searches through intimate emotional reflection ("Villanelle for Our Time"). It may even be something about which one can have expertise, about which one can teach ("Teachers"). In "I'm Your Man," Cohen speaks of *clawing* at the heart of the object of his affection, as if he were a dog in heat.

Likewise, Cohen often draws comparisons with the state of the body more generally. In "Wishing Window," we hear that dreams can be so emotionally powerful that stabs of *appetite* can wake one up. And who among us hasn't been woken by the fears, pains, and appetites of our dreams to find ourselves in a cold sweat, hearts racing, and viscera in a knot? In "Bird on the Wire," Cohen expresses regret for the emotional pain he has caused others, likening it to the bodily damage caused by an animal's horns, vividly capturing the visceral nature of feelings of betrayal and regret. Similarly, in "Iodine" and "The Traitor," Cohen draws a comparison between physical pain—of the sort caused by a hornet sting or by applying iodine to a wound—and emotional pain.

More generally, Cohen sometimes characterizes emotions in terms of *trembling* ("Last Year's Man," "Dress Rehearsal Rag," and "Story of Isaac") and describes himself as being *inflamed* ("Last Year's Man") or, alternatively, as having ice upon his soul ("The Butcher"). In like manner, Cohen sometimes describes lust in terms of *hunger* ("Memories," "You Have Loved Enough," and "Closing Time") and *aching* ("Ain't No Cure for Love"). In "Love Calls You by Your Name," loneliness is said to be *shouldered*, emphasizing how loneliness takes a toll on—and is reflected in—the body. Similarly, in "Paper Thin Hotel," the burden of jealousy is *lifted* from him when he recognizes that love is beyond his control. In "Avalanche," Cohen characterizes love in affective terms as being more or less *fierce*. While we rarely if ever describe beliefs and other cognitive states as admitting degrees of intensity or fierceness, we do describe bodily actions and reactions in these terms. As one more example, consider that in "Tonight Will Be Fine" Cohen uses the metaphor of fasting to depict his falling out of love, where he becomes *thin* in comparison to the *vastness* of the woman's love for him. As well, he notes the relation between facial expressions and emotions when reassured of his lover's emotions by her eyes and her smile, in contrast to the sorrow in his lover's "soft" eyes in "Hey, That's No Way to Say Goodbye."

Emotional experience is a thoroughly embodied phenomenon, and this is reflected in the imagery employed by Cohen when expressing the complexities of love, jealousy, and betrayal. We are after all embodied creatures and it is from the perspective of our bodies that we engage the physical and social environments in which we find ourselves. Emotions are intimately connected with our wellbeing as living organisms. It's not surprising, then, that we find the basis of the phenomenology of emotion in the states of our bodies. Again and again, the lyrics of Leonard Cohen reflect this basic fact of human existence.

## Cognitive Theories

In contrast to body-based theories of emotion, cognitive or mind-based accounts view emotions as special sorts of judgment about things one values. Cognitivists will point to the fact that by themselves bodily disturbances don't tell us what emotions are occurring. Take, for example, "Beatlemania." Observed out of context, the tear-filled, twisted faces of these Beatles fans appear to express intense anguish and sadness. Far from this, however, these fans are ecstatic and filled with intense joy—the objects of their greatest affection are before them. These fans are not sad, says the cognitivist, precisely because they *judge* the Beatles to be wonderful and *realize* that finally, they are within their presence. (This example is discussed by John Deigh in "Primitive Emotions," p. 24.) More generally, while certain sorts of facial expressions often track certain sorts of emotions, this connection is not guaranteed. As Cohen says in his "In My Secret Life," he sometimes smiles when he's angry.

Cognitivists also emphasize the fact that with changes in one's judgments come changes in one's emotions (Jenefer Robinson makes this point in "Emotion," p. 28). If the ecstatic Beatles fans were to discover that the men on stage were, in fact, imposters, their overflowing joy would quickly turn, first to surprise, then to anger. Notice as well that emotions like jealousy, envy, guilt, and moral indignation often involve complex evaluations of situations and actions that only make sense in the context of judgment and conscious deliberation. Indeed, the fact that we so often argue about the appropriateness of an emotional response implies, it would seem, that we are evaluating the appropriateness of judgments, which can be, and often are, incorrect. We might argue whether or not my anger over a perceived slight is justified, but we wouldn't argue over whether my back pain is justified. Feelings are feelings, the argument goes, while emotions are judgments, judgments which, given the facts, may be more or less appropriate.

Cognitivists are also usually interested in *different sorts* of emotions from those addressed by body-based theories. As Robert Solomon puts it, "I am interested in the meanings of life, not short-term neurological arousal" ("Emotions, Thoughts, and Feelings," p. 79). What Solomon is interested in are things like "life-long love" and emotions that endure and bring meaning to one's overall existence. He is interested, "not in those brief 'irruptive' reactions or responses but in the long-term narratives of Othello, Iago . . . and those of my less drama-ridden but nevertheless very emotional friends" (pp. 78–79). For Solomon, then, emotions are "intelligent" and involve a person's evaluation of his place in the world. Likewise, Martha Nussbaum, working from the Stoic tradition, conceives of emotions as judgments about things of value over which we lack full control. "The story of emotions," she writes, "is the story of judgments about important things, judgments in which we acknowledge our neediness and incompleteness before elements that we do not fully control" (p. 184).

When considering an emotion like love, bodily reactions can scarcely be the entire story. When, in "Hallelujah," Cohen denies that love is a victory march, he points to the conceptual complexity of love. Even those who consider themselves nonreligious will be familiar with 1 Corinthians 13 and its characterization of love. Love, we're told, "is patient and kind; it is not jealous or conceited or proud." Whether or not one agrees with this biblical characterization of love, there is an important lesson here: the experience of the bodily reactions associated with love cannot be the complete story of love, for there are behavioral, social, and cognitive conditions that must be met in order for it to count as *genuine* love. In a similar vein, love is not just what one feels; it's also something one can *give*—or fail to give—to another, as Cohen notes in "Suzanne." And in "Chelsea Hotel #2" we see the importance of distinguishing infatuation from love, which are sometimes hard to distinguish merely in terms of feeling. Infatuation is of course a powerful and beautiful emotion. But it's also fleeting, limited to a time and a place, to a moment in the narrative of one's life. While Cohen remembers the sweetness of an infatuation, locating in at a specific time and place (the Chelsea Hotel in New York in the late sixties), it isn't love; for one thing, he rarely thinks of her anymore.

In songs like "Why Don't You Try" and "Humbled in Love," we again see the complexities of love, of even the desire for a love that is lacking, and also the strictures of marriage or long-term commitment. Not all loves are lifelong yet the codification of love in a marriage is meant to be. Vows, as Cohen puts it, are difficult. Against the permanency of marriage stands the possibility of many emotionally satisfying infatuations. With the commitment of lifelong love—or at least, lifetime monogamy—a person forecloses on the future possibilities of infatuation. We see a similar tension between monogamy and freedom in "There Is a War," "So Long, Marianne," "Ballad of the Absent Mare," and "I Tried to Leave You." Such tensions are sometimes reflected in the possible asymmetries of love, that is, in cases where the strength of love between two lovers is not equal. In "Iodine," for instance, compassion and pity can sting as much as iodine when one partner needs the other more than she needs him. Asymmetries in love can sometimes result in the loss of one's identity to the other, as reflected in "Fingerprints." Here Cohen seems to intimate that love can lead to emasculation and the loss of one's fingerprints—one's identity—to the other.

Likewise, jealousy appears to have a strong cognitive component. Whether or not a person feels jealousy will depend, at least in part, on how he thinks of himself and his relation to his partner. As Cohen suggests in "Sisters of Mercy," if you don't think of someone as a lover, thoughts about her intimate relations with another are unlikely to produce jealousy. Relatedly, in "Paper Thin Hotel," Cohen expresses relief from the jealousy that might have been aroused by hearing his erstwhile lover making love to another. A burden was lifted from his soul. This relief seemingly resulted from Cohen's—the song's narrator's—realization that love wasn't under his control. In these cases, judgment and conscious reflection play an essential role. Emotions must be analyzed in this sense, and from such analyses, we learn about ourselves and the nature of human existence. In "Villanelle for Our Time" (with lyrics that sound Cohen-like from a poem by Frank Scott), Cohen indicates that we *search* our emotions, emotions that have been informed and influenced by pleasurable and painful experiences from which we may rise again to play some "greater part." And as they can and must be reflected on, so they can be taught to others ("Teachers").

Cognitivists, it should now be clear, emphasize the *social* nature of emotions. So for example, in *The Rationality of Emotion* Ronald de Sousa advances his notion of a "paradigm scenario," a social context in which we each learn culturally appropriate expressions of emotion. But not only are emotions learned and reinforced socially, some only make sense within the context of complex social relationships. Think, for example, of the powerful sense of betrayal you might feel as a relationship unravels due to infidelity, and the sense of regret your partner might feel for causing such emotional pain in a former lover. These socially rich and complex emotions are represented in Cohen's works like "Bird on the Wire," "A Singer Must Die," and "Leaving Green Sleeves." Here we again see the complex interplay of a desire for freedom (from romantic attachment), the emotional pain it has wrought in others, and the regret that he is the cause of such pain. We perhaps see something similar in "Tower of Song" where Cohen expresses surprise and regret for the bridges burnt between himself and a lover and the river that has widened between them. The social and cognitive complexities of love, jealousy, regret, and ultimately forgiveness are also evident in love triangles. Consider Cohen's "Famous Blue Raincoat," where these complexities intertwine, and through which the members of the triangle grow, learning about one another, and themselves. Rather than being brief perturbations, love and the emotional pain of love lost or betrayed may not even diminish over time, as noted in "Ain't No Cure for Love."

## Emotion as a Process

Is a tear an intellectual thing? Yes and no. As is so often the case in philosophical disputes, the truth may lie somewhere in between. Rather than treating body-based and cognitive theories as competing and mutually exclusive theories of emotion, it may be better to approach them as complementary aspects of what is a very complex phenomenon. Jenefer Robinson (pp. 28–43), for example, argues that we should understand emotion as a process between bodily arousal on the one hand, and "cognitive appraisals" on the other. Such appraisals allow for complex emotions like lifelong love, jealousy, and regret, and allow us to interpret our bodily reactions in meaningful ways, ways that relate both to our physical and social environments. They also help make sense of the fact that our emotions track our judgments about people and situations. Bodily arousal, on the other hand, helps explain how we *experience* emotions, the feelings that so color our existence and motivate us to action. Body-based theories also allow us to explain groundless emotions like phobias, which resist rational modification through judgment; someone with a paralyzing fear of flying may accurately judge that flying is one of the safest modes of transportation, though the fear remains. Arguably, there is no simple mapping between emotions and judgments or bodily states; rather, emotions involve a complex exchange between body and mind, and a process account captures this.

Consider again the example of jealousy. Suppose you see your lover in what appears to be an intimate embrace with a stranger. You will likely have a very sudden emotional response. Perhaps you feel as if someone kicked you in the stomach. Your muscles tighten and your heart begins to race. Perhaps you even *flush* with anger or *droop* with sadness. Your attention now focusses on the object of your jealousy—the stranger. Your initial reaction, visceral and largely reflexive, represents the body-based theorist's conception of emotions as pre-cognitive, hardwired bodily reactions. Yet even these initial responses are not free of cognitive content, for you must recognize your lover *as* your lover and *conceive* of her interaction with this stranger as intimate and as a potential threat to your relationship. But now suppose you notice that this stranger bears a likeness to your lover and then recall that her brother, whom you have never met, was to be in town this week. Quickly, your fear turns first to doubt, then to hope. After being introduced to your lover's brother, your jealousy immediately dissipates, quickly giving way, perhaps, to a sense of guilt and embarrassment for having *jumped to conclusions*. I think that in this and similar cases we must recognize the rich and complex interaction between bodily reactions, the reflexes to which none of us are immune, and the more intellectual aspects of our emotional lives: belief, inference, and evaluation.

According to de Sousa ("Emotion," pp. 61–75), such a compromise allows us to explain how language and narrative structure enrich the distinctive emotional lives of human beings. Our sophisticated cognitive architecture enables us to transform the more primitive emotional structures we share with other animals, bringing new depths and new dimensions. Perhaps some of our more complex emotions are quintessentially human. While dogs and horses surely have complex emotional lives, without the cognitive sophistication that perhaps comes only with human-like language, some emotions would seem to be beyond their ken. Take, for example, moral indignation at political injustices and the resulting cynical apathy towards politics and political leaders in the face of such injustice. Songs like Cohen's "Anthem," "On That Day," and "Everybody Knows" capture the existential angst and powerlessness we feel when confronted with the realities of modern human society. Like it or not, the rich (usually) get richer, the poor poorer, our political leaders, our "captains," often lie to us, and there are, indeed, "killers in high places." Such realizations of the inequities and hypocrisies of life leave one feeling *broken*, which I interpret in both bodily and cognitive terms: the recognition of life's unpleasant realities involves complex realizations that may leave us feeling empty *inside*. Cohen's "The Land of Plenty" presents what is arguably a more hopeful or philosophical take on the sorts of problems endemic to modern society.

This sort of compromise between bodily and cognitive approaches to emotion is often well represented in poetry. To take just one example, consider this passage from the Greek poet Aeschylus's *Agamemnon* (specifically, Robert F. Kennedy's famous rendering of the passage, which appears as the epitaph on his tombstone):

> Even in our sleep, pain which cannot forget
> falls drop by drop upon the heart,
> until, in our own despair,
> against our will,
> comes wisdom. . . . .

Note the interplay between physical and cognitive elements. Even when we sleep—even when we're *unconscious*—emotional pain persists, falling like drops of rain upon the *heart*.

Yet from this despair, over *time* and through *reflection*, even against our conscious will, comes *insight* and *wisdom*. Cohen often notes the wisdom that can come from emotional trauma. In "Paper Thin Hotel," for example, he suggests metaphorically that one can only reach heaven after going through hell. Indeed, some of the most profound lessons any of us learn in this life come from situations that evoke powerful emotions, emotions from which we learn and grow.

De Sousa (in his article "Emotions") suggests thinking of emotions in terms of "parallel systems of control" where the older, faster, not fully conscious mechanisms emphasized by body theorists are guided, interpreted, assessed, and *re-assessed* by the newer but slower and more discerning systems of conscious judgment and reflection. Emotions, then, provide information about things we care about, things we value, and this is reflected at the deepest, primordial levels in the states of our bodies. I believe that Leonard Cohen's musical compositions nicely reflect the rich complexity of this interchange between mind and body, for while emotions are indeed evaluated by the mind, they are also *written in the flesh*.

# VI

# Songs of Religion

# 18
# The Prophetic Mr. Cohen

TIMOTHY P. JACKSON

Leonard Cohen is not the New Moses or the Second Coming of Christ or a Reincarnation of the Buddha. Moreover, Marc Chagall can rest easy; Mr. Cohen is an average visual artist. (I, at least, can take or leave his drawings and paintings.) Cohen is, nevertheless, the closest thing we have today to a Biblical prophet. He was born and remains a Jew. He was involved for a time with Scientology. He sustains a long-term love affair with Christian imagery and ethics. He is an ordained Buddhist monk. He has studied with a Hindu mystic in Mumbai. And he is a sincere admirer of Taoism and Sufism.

Shall I call him a chameleon, then? If a chameleon alters its skin color to hide in safety, Cohen wears a coat of many colors and says, "Here I am, send me" (Isaiah 6:8). His combination of sublime lyrics, soulful music, and trenchant social commentary makes him, as I say, prophetic. A prophet embodies revelation and critique rather than concealment and comfort. Cohen has received many prestigious awards—even in his own country—but in the end he's a spiritual witness rather than a popular hero. Is he, then, a second Jeremiah, a fourth Isaiah, or even another John the Baptist?

If the original Baptist lived a simple and disciplined life, full of *askesis* (self-denial) to please God, Cohen was no divine "askeser," at least not early on. He evidently led a rather Bohemian existence: sex, drugs, and rock 'n' roll. If John called for repentance, Leonard suggests that we don't know what the word "repent" means. If John marked the beginning of a rift between Judaism and Christianity, Cohen may yet help heal that old and painful wound. In the end, though, Cohen is not a Zen koan for someone or something else; he's himself. To borrow from Eliot's *Four Quartets*, "there is no competition."

Cohen's maternal grandfather was a rabbi and Talmudic scholar, and he takes seriously the Hebrew meaning of his last name: "priest." I am told that he closes his e-mails with an image of two open hands, palms out, thumb tips touching, fingers opened to a V between middle and ring fingers on both hands.

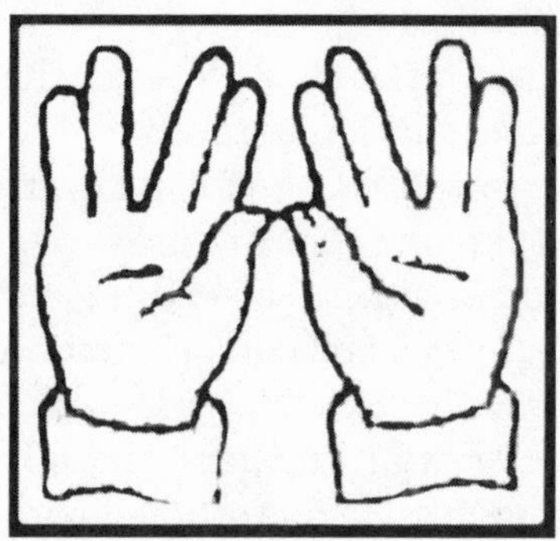

This is the Jewish symbol of priestly blessing. Cohen spent five years (1994–1999) at the Mount Baldy Zen Center in California, studying with Joshu Sasaki Roshi, and was ordained a Buddhist monk in 1996. It's tempting to say that, in spite of these Eastern digressions in the American West, he continues to self-identify as a Jew. This would blur an important point, however. Even though Cohen himself at times dismisses his Buddhist practice as merely a relaxation technique, a means of mastering depression, it's clear that it's also provided him another window on cosmic order (Dharma). I don't doubt that Judaism provides his most formative principles and stories, and so remains the deepest shaper of his spirit, but part of the man's genius is to refuse to allow traditional boundaries to stifle insight. With admirable epistemic humility, he takes wisdom and symbolism where he can get them. A lesser mind might degenerate into a vapid, new-age eclecticism, but Cohen doesn't appropriate a metaphor unless he's lived in it long enough to test its truth and make it his own.

All religion can be seen as the effort to overcome the distance "between the Nameless and the Name," to borrow a phrase from Cohen's "Love Itself." Nevertheless, Cohen leans towards a theism that outstrips most, if not all, forms of Buddhist cosmology. A purely negative or impersonal vision of the universe is usually not enough for him. (In this respect, he's like Thomas Merton, who remained a Roman Catholic while studying with Buddhist sages in Asia.) Cohen longs for a personal Deity with a loving heart and a creative will, so his main preoccupation is with Judaism and Christianity. *He is an observant Jew, but he takes us back to that pregnant moment when Christianity was a form of Judaism.* He wants to be shown "the place / Where the Word became a man . . . the place / Where the suffering began."

For centuries, Christian theologians have appropriated Hebrew texts, awkwardly, as pointing forward to Jesus as the Messiah. At last, with Cohen, we have a Jewish thinker who quotes Christian texts, deftly, as harkening backward to their Hebraic origins. This is enormously courageous and profoundly therapeutic. He helps lead the Biblical tradition toward wholeness and the soul to something higher. Even when he describes, on YouTube, "The Window" as "a prayer to bring the two parts of the soul together," he ends up celebrating something larger than human personality.

## Divine Disconsolation and the Perils of Double-Mindedness

Much of Cohen's most inspired work is either a gesture of gratitude for an unspeakable grace or an act of solidarity with those unjustly afflicted. Although exquisitely sensitive to the pain and suffering of life—he has been labelled "The Prince of Bummers"—he still manages to escape both delusion and despair. His favorite word is "broken," with "cross" and "crack" not far behind, yet recovery and hope typically hover nearby. "Come healing of the spirit / Come healing of the limb." "From this broken hill / All your praises they shall ring." "There is a crack in everything / That's how the light gets in." I would call this the gift of divine disconsolation, the ability to bless without dishonesty—or, perhaps, to bless in confessing dishonesty.

I have called Mr. Cohen a prophet, but at times he is so disconsolate and disconsoling that he sounds more like a seeker, a skeptic, even an atheist. Cohen's public words are frequently addressed to God, but the dialogue sometimes falters. One of the stanzas of "Hallelujah" is a complaint that God (addressed as "you" but pronounced "ya") no longer shows him "what's really going on below," and we are left to speculate on a more mystical or religiously revelatory phase of the author's life. How was he moved, and what made this intimacy with the Deity stop? In "Everybody Knows," Cohen sings to God, or more specifically Jesus, in the second person. These lines, about what Christ has gone through, from Calvary to Malibu, can be read as a continuance of the "God is dead" debate he commented on in his novel, *Beautiful Losers*. "God is alive," he declared there, "God never sickened. . . . God never died" (p. 157). But if so, what does it mean to say that the Christ is in trouble and to suggest that the "sacred heart" is about to "blow"? In "Suzanne," Jesus is described as having sunk "beneath your wisdom like a stone." In "Democracy," Cohen calls the Sermon on the Mount "staggering," but he doesn't "pretend to understand" it. In "Who by Fire?" the counterpoint of religious faith and doubt intensifies. There Cohen asks the haunting question of death or death's god: "And who shall I say is calling?"

This is what I mean by "epistemic humility": the effort to live between dogmatism and doubt, to know one's limits but not be paralyzed or embittered. Perhaps "no one knows where the night is going," but "everybody knows the deal is rotten." Cohen isn't afraid to live on that knife's edge. Even while "waiting for the miracle," he's only "passing through," hoping that the light will "shine on the truth someday." A Biblical expression of this finitude is 1 Corinthians 13:12: "For now we see in a mirror, dimly."

A provocative melding of Biblical languages and liturgies has multiple perils of double-mindedness. Given the troubled relations between Christianity and Judaism—from forced conversions to bloody pogroms to the Nazi Holocaust—the embracing of any New Testament vocabulary by a Jew can seem insensitive, if not murderous. In reference to Cohen's third book of poetry, why pick flowers for Hitler? So many political, economic, and cultural issues are raised even by talking about the "Old" and the "New" Testaments, that it may seem wise to accept the permanent alienation of the two faiths. To our benefit, Cohen is too strong a poet to resign himself to such impoverishment. He typically finds language that reconciles, if not synthesizes, the best of both scriptural perspectives.

In *Book of Mercy*, Cohen refers to "Our Lady of the Torah" and notes that "the Christians are a branch of the tree" (psalm 27). In the song, "The Law," he suggests that Torah and Grace are one. Elsewhere, he sings of the Exodus ("Born in Chains"); he allows that Abraham was "strong and holy" ("Story of Isaac"), even as Jesus was "forsaken, almost human" ("Suzanne"). In Cohen's lyrics, in short, Jew and Christian are again potentially united—*depending on how we as listeners respond.* No prophet, including Cohen, can compel inclusive love of neighbor, but he or she can invite it by beautiful example.

This is what I mean by calling Cohen a strong poet: one who transcends the anxiety of being influenced by others and builds something better out of both old and new bricks (see Harold Bloom's *The Anxiety of Influence*). A strong Rabbinic scholar will learn from Kabbalah; a strong Christian theologian will learn from Gnosticism; a strong empirical scientist may even learn from alchemy. Leonard Cohen learns from all three, and his meditations become prayers. A chameleon uses his ten-inch tongue to capture and kill. When necessary, the prophet skewers others, verbally, and could be a chameleon if he wanted to. But Cohen typically uses his tongue of ten letters to liberate and enliven, with nothing, as he sings, but "Hallelujah" on that tongue.

Cohen's 1992 song, "The Future," is a compelling indictment of mass murder, economic exploitation, torture, abortion, and other social injustices, even some that hadn't yet occurred. It ideologically opposed, before the fact, both the terrorism perpetrated by Islamic fundamentalists on 9/11 and the subsequent torture of Muslims at Guantanamo Bay and Abu Ghraib. Cohen's call for healing (2012's "Come Healing") can teach us, yet again, that if we are to have peace, we must recognize that the eternal Good transcends any temporal liturgy, creed, or nation. To be the bearer of such a message comes with a price. For hearers, as Cohen writes in *Book of Longing*, "the sadness of the zoo will fall upon society" (p. 34).

## Profane and Sacred Love

Another Cohenesque duality, already alluded to, is his need and ability to live a rather worldly life, even as he praises heaven. He is famous for relishing the pleasures and comforts of sex—the Song of Songs meets the Sisters of Mercy—and he has a stunning capacity to weave together sacred and profane desire—as in "Light as the Breeze." Put more bluntly, "naked" is another of his favorite words, and he was apparently "a fearful girler" for much of his youth and middle age. In "Chelsea Hotel #2," he announces, unabashedly, the pursuit of wealth and sex. He makes no secret of his inability fully to commit to any female—he never married, because of "cowardice" and "fear"; the "ladies' man" admits to driving away many beautiful women who cared for him. Whether this was due to a jealous guarding of his personal literary calling or to a more simple narcissism that could not give back, is hard to say.

In "Hey, That's No Way to Say Goodbye," Cohen refers to things that can't be untied. But love's being tantamount to bondage and limitation isn't the whole story for him. In more candid moments, romantic love seems not so much undesirable as too difficult. "I couldn't feel, so I tried to touch," he observes in "Hallelujah." In the end, one would have to ask Marianne Ihlen, Joni Mitchell, Suzanne Elrod, Dominique Issermann, Rebecca de Mornay, and other women in Cohen's life about his capacity to give and receive. Cohen is currently in a stable domestic relationship with his artistic collaborator Anjani Thomas—see "Crazy to Love You"—and, in any case, a prophet isn't the same thing as a saint. Furthermore, roués may grow over time into saints, a theme Cohen has explored variously in fiction and in song.

As articulate as Cohen is about the volatility of romantic love (*eros*), his richest talent is for seeing "with Love's / inhuman eye," as he says in *Book of Longing* (p. 42). Such steadfast love Judaism calls *'hesed* and Christianity *agape*. (Buddhism calls it *karuṇā*, I believe.) If *eros* appraises the value of an object in how it benefits me, *'hesed* and *agape* bestow worth upon an object without insisting on reciprocity. There's great potential for hypocrisy in extoling unconditional love, for who is capable of such virtuous promiscuity? As Cohen concedes, even great masters get beaten up by sacred texts. Nevertheless, both the Hebrew and the Christian Bible see neighbor love as commanded (Leviticus 19:18 and Matthew 22). A self-giving and creative love is at the very heart of God's holiness, and we are to be holy as God is holy (Leviticus 11:45).

## Order of the Unified Heart

In spite of—even because of—the hazards, in praising and enacting divine love the prophet's labors achieve their fullest beauty and goodness. Here he sings both to and for God, and his words become a vehicle of universal charity. Human apprehension and imitation of God will no doubt always be tied up, ambivalently, with sexual desire and fear of death. Venus and self-love have their proper place, and Cohen sometimes pits them against "enlightenment." Nonetheless, not by skirt-chasing, not by navel-gazing, but by being an instrument of God's grace to others, does one enter what Cohen calls "The Order of the Unified Heart." His original emblem of that order is two hearts—one facing up, the other down, but intertwined—symbolizing the unity of opposites:

The image is reminiscent of the Star of David:

Over time, the two-hearts emblem has evolved, by Cohen's hand, into a figure known as The Blessing to End Disunity:

The two hands of priestly blessing hold together, from the heart below, the broken heart above (hear "Come Healing"). At the center of it all is the Jewish term *Shin*, a name for G-d.

## The Question of Islam, Israel, and Terrorism

So far, I've written primarily of Leonard Cohen's affiliation with Judaism, Christianity, and Buddhism. Where does this leave Islam, the third religion of the Book? And where does it leave the questions surrounding Islam's relations with Israel and the West?

Cohen volunteered to serve in the Yom Kippur War of 1973 but ended up in an entertainment unit singing to the troops. Contemporary Israelis love him, and his performances for them often include Hebrew prayers. One might imagine, therefore, that Cohen's Judeo-Christian accents throw down a gauntlet toward Palestine and Muslims in general. This is far from the truth, however. Cohen said some romantic, even downright silly, things after the Yom Kippur War: "War is wonderful. They'll never stamp it out. It's one of the few times people can act their best. It's so economical in terms of gesture and motion, every single gesture is precise, every effort is at its maximum. Nobody goofs off. Everybody is responsible for his brother" (Pike). The camaraderie and self-sacrifice of some soldiers is real and admirable, but this is hardly the whole story of war. Brutality and death of the innocent are at least as common. Cohen knows that if everybody were truly responsible for his brother, this, in itself, would mean the end of lethal combat. For one's brother is the neighbor, anyone and everyone, not just one's friend or co-religionist. The remarks quoted above are balanced by "Lover Lover Lover" and the last lines of "Story of Isaac."

Much more pointedly, in *Book of Mercy* Cohen offers a scathing critique of Israel and all arrogant nationalisms: "Israel, and you who call yourself Israel, the church that calls itself Israel, and the revolt that calls itself Israel, and every nation chosen to be a nation—none of these lands is yours, all of you are thieves of holiness, all of you at war with Mercy" (psalm 27). America, France, Russia, and Poland are also mentioned by name, making it manifest that "these lands" that are not possessed are not merely belated territorial expansions, gained at the expense of local populations (for example, the Gaza Palestinians or the North American Indians). *No nation* deserves *any* land as such; it's given "on condition," based on a divine "Covenant," Cohen reminds us. And because the Covenant has been "broken," "the righteous enemy" "has overturned the vehicle of nationhood." I presume "the righteous enemy" here is God, who punishes "the lawless" of all countries.

Recently, Cohen put his money where his mouth was and billed his 2009 performance in Tel Aviv "A Concert for Reconciliation, Tolerance, and Peace." As reported by Ethan Bronner in the *New York Times*, he gave the profits of $1.5 to 2 million to a charity run by a board of both Israelis and Palestinians, to distribute to groups focused on coexistence in Israel. If Cohen's lyrics suggest how Judaism and Christianity might be healed, after all the hatred and violence that has passed from the latter to the former, then surely it's possible for concerted thought and action to defuse the post-9/11 world. At least one must try to curb the violent fascists of all ethnicities.

Whatever one might think about the acquisition of territory by Israel during the 1967 Six-Day War, whatever one might think about the PLO or Hamas, whatever one might think about a two-state Israel-Palestine solution, it's possible to recall a time when Muslims were the protectors of Jews hounded by Christians—as during the Crusades and, to a lesser extent, the Nazi Holocaust. It's possible to move beyond vendetta at least to acceptance. The internal struggle within both Judaism and Islam for the hearts and minds of believers cannot take as long as the Christian Crusaders took to transcend anti-Semitism and genocide. The weapons of modern terror and anti-terror are too destructive. Cohen may be a voice crying in the wilderness to both Jews and Muslims, but he's not alone.

Cohen's attitude of calm and practical helpfulness in the midst of strife is also evident in his response to 9/11. He counts himself among the "we" who were attacked, but he refuses to indulge in a tirade of offense (or self-recrimination), as theoretically justified as that might be. Instead, he "just holds the fort" and asks simply whether you "went crazy" or "reported." Did you succumb to rancor and the desire for revenge, or did you lend a hand to those saving lives and preserving order? Are you part of the problem, or part of the solution?

## A Personal Trial and Forgiveness

On a more personal level are the financial and emotional tribulations Cohen went through in the 1990s and 2000s. His friend and business manager, Kelley Lynch, embezzled the bulk of his estate while he was on extended retreat at Mount Baldy. The "thirty pieces of silver" in this case amounted to about $5 million, and the betrayal led to bankruptcy rather than the cross, but the hurt must have been acute. The theft was compounded, moreover, by months of harassing emails and threatening voice messages from Lynch. Even so, Cohen maintained remarkable equanimity. At the trial, he announced:

> It gives me no pleasure to see my one-time friend shackled to a chair in a court of law, her considerable gifts bent to the service of darkness, deceit and revenge. . . . I want to thank the defendant Ms. Kelley Lynch for insisting on a jury trial, thus exposing to the light of day her massive depletion of my retirement savings and yearly earnings, and allowing the court to observe her profoundly unwholesome, obscene and relentless strategies to escape the consequences of her wrongdoing.
>
> It is my prayer that Ms. Lynch will take refuge in the wisdom of her religion. That a spirit of understanding will convert her heart from hatred to remorse, from anger to kindness, from the deadly intoxication of revenge to the lowly practices of self-reform. (reported by Sean Michaels in the *Guardian*)

Although pointed, these words carry the very spirit of understanding they invoke. Forgiveness isn't explicitly mentioned, but resentment seems largely overcome with mercy. His response to his "lynching" is a good example of a refusal of animosity that still cares about justice. An oft-remarked irony of the Lynch affair is that Cohen was moved in 2008 to embark on a multi-city tour to recoup his losses, so again the world was treated to his live music and his own heart was "warmed" (Jon Pareles in the *New York Times*). Thus can good come out of evil.

## Being Grateful

A prophet foretells what is yet to be, but she also retells what has already been. Like Dickens's Ghost of Christmas Past, she may even do the former by doing the latter. To read or listen to Leonard Cohen is to see this done in our own day, to be gratified that sacred scripture can still be written. Only chameleons close their cannons and disappear into other people's foliage. We should thank Cohen for keeping the Biblical shop open and serving as a mouthpiece of the divine, even amid his own "convivial disbelief" (*Book of Longing*, p. 24). Now, as "Going Home" makes clear, Cohen is preparing to retire, even to die.

The only question still outstanding is the final form of God's love. Is there personal immortality or nothingness after death? Judaism thrived for centuries without belief in an afterlife, the doctrine first being formulated in the Book of Daniel. Many contemporary Jews and most orthodox Christians affirm resurrection of the dead, but Cohen's position on the matter is unclear. He has narrated *The Tibetan Book of the Dead*, but I know of no place where he directly endorses life after death. In *Book of Longing*, he says "to a young nun": "Your turn to die for love. My turn to resurrect" (p. 14). But the latter seems a this-worldly reanimation. Elsewhere in *Longing*, he says: "I have no interest in the afterlife" (p. 138).

In two places, Cohen appears to deny the eternity of God's own *'hesed*, steadfast love. In the song "Love Itself," Cohen echoes the Buddhist notion that Love eventually reaches "an open door" and is "gone." This idea aligns well with Cohen's Dharma name Jikan, which means "silence" or "the silent one," but it's hard to square with Jewish conceptions of the never-ending grace and creativity of YHWH. If human life and love are finite, does Divine Compassion Itself finally come to no-word and no-thing? In *Book of Mercy*, the prophet speaks of the time when the Lord "suspends his light and withdraws into himself, and there is no world, and there is no soul anywhere" (psalm 29). This too seems to admit a limit to God's love. In the end, does the Lord collapse into narcissism? This is a humbling thought for any creature, but it seems oddly un-Jewish.

Cohen speaks regularly of "heaven" as the abode of God and angels, but it cannot be accidental that he's mostly mum on the question of human immortality. My hunch is that he would be neither Pharisee and insist on life after death, nor Sadducee and disallow it. And "who dares expound the interior life of god?" asks *Book of Mercy* (psalm 10). Mr. Cohen is a prophet for the living and doesn't dwell on such eschatological matters. He has communicated his vision and, to take a phrase from O'Neill's *Beyond the Horizon*, has earned "the right of release," whatever this might mean. "*Nunc dimittis*. . . . Lord, now lettest thou thy servant depart in peace, according to thy word" (Luke 2:29). We can only be grateful. Cohen is.

# 19
# Clouds of Unknowing

BERNARD WILLS

Leonard Cohen has been nothing over the years if not a celebrant of the wonders of the flesh. It may be a cause of wonder then that his later years have been marked by a deep engagement with the concepts of emptiness and detachment explored by Zen Buddhism and (we should remind ourselves) by Christian mystics and Jewish Kabbalists as well. This longing for a kind of nothingness or non-entity has been a persistent undercurrent in Cohen's work for quite some time.

While listening to the 1979 album *Recent Songs* some months back I was struck by a reference in one of Cohen's most gorgeously sensuous songs, "The Window." The reference was to an anonymous medieval work called *The Cloud of Unknowing*. This is a work of "negative" mysticism by which I mean that it demands of us that we seek God in a "cloud of unknowing." By this the author means that in our spiritual quest we should abandon all representations grounded in sensation, imagination, or intellect and seek the divine in a "naked intent of love" that elevates us beyond knowledge and beyond being. Indeed, for the author of the *Cloud* God is a kind of emptiness or non-being that is at the same time total plentitude: the nothing, he says, is the all and it is possessed in a negation or suspension of all our faculties of sensation and mind. What on earth might such an esoteric teaching have to do with a pop record from the late 1970s?

One of the things Cohen's work challenges us to do is to think about such connections. To meet that challenge, we'll explore the undercurrent of negative mysticism that runs through *Recent Songs* and indeed much of Cohen's other work.

## Cohen's Spirituality

It's no secret that Cohen's work has a spiritual dimension. Both Judaism and Catholicism informed his childhood and his novels, and his songs and poems are saturated with Christian iconography to a degree unusual for a Jewish artist. The Christian tradition, I would argue, plays a very specific role in Cohen's symbolic economy. For Cohen, who differs profoundly from thinkers like Nietzsche on this point, Christianity is the religion of the body, of sacralized flesh as the bearer of revelation.

This can be illustrated in a number of ways but for now I'll emphasize one. The person of Jesus in Cohen's songs and poems is heavily eroticized. As the word made flesh he reveals the beauty and vulnerability of the sexualized body. Often, as in the lyric "Suzanne," he's associated with a life-giving female figure who offers wisdom in the form of fulfilled erotic vision. In this perhaps Cohen takes up a tradition in Catholic iconography that "feminizes" the image of Christ to a striking degree. In contrast, the "Jewish side" of Cohen is more detached, ironic, and skeptical. This Cohen is the poet of absence and loss who evokes the smoke that's "beyond all repair" of the holocaust and other disasters of the twentieth century. Jesus himself, despairing on the cross, is "broken / long before the sky would open" as God displayed in the glory of the flesh withdraws into hiddenness and silence, just as woman withdraws inevitably from man or man from woman.

I speak of this as a symbolic shortcut only: I'm not trying to relate these tendencies in any straightforward way to historical Christianity or historical Judaism. Christianity has given rise to powerful iconoclastic tendencies, and as for Judaism one need only read through the interminable genealogies of *Genesis* to realize the degree to which it's grounded in the reality of the body (as an interesting reflection on this one might consider Robert Crumb's earthy and sensuous rendition of *Genesis*). In point of fact, the so-called "affirmative" and "negative" theologies (which I'll discuss below) play their respective roles in both traditions. However, the roles these traditions play in Cohen's personal symbolism (and presumably his psyche) are somewhat more schematic.

Cohen's experience of the immanence of God is focused around Christian images and symbols from his earliest collections of verse. His experience of divine absence, of loss and withdrawal, tends to focus more on the hidden God of which Isaiah speaks, who reveals his name to Moses as "I am who I am": a baffling tautology saturated with indefinable presence yet yielding no clear meaning as to whether God is present in or absent from creation. It's not my concern to say where Cohen comes down on the issue of immanence vs. transcendence (whether God is present in or absent from creation). It's the primary role of an artist to dramatize such conflicts, not resolve them. However, Cohen has come in recent years to focus on the meditative techniques of Zen Buddhism which involve the emptying of the mind of all attachment to self. This movement, I will argue, is already prefigured on *Recent Songs* where the *Cloud* is referenced, a text through which a Western reader might indeed find a path to the wisdom of the east.

## Positive and Negative

First however, we should go over some basic distinctions. The Anglo-Catholic writer Charles Williams has spoken of a fundamental conflict at the heart of the theological tradition between what he calls "the way of affirmation" which embraces images and "the way of rejection" that seeks to transcend them (p. 58). Dante is one writer he considers a master of the former way but we might add such medieval figures as the Abbot Suger (spiritual father and theorist of the gothic movement in architecture) to the list. To be brief, such writers see the glory and power of God directly reflected in the created order from the highest ranks of the angels to the lowest determinations of matter. For this tradition "Being" tends to be the highest *name* of God and "beings" an expression of his power, intelligence, and goodness. In theology, they are engaged in what is called *kataphatic* or positive description of the divine nature—what God is.

Conversely, there is a tradition, founded in Neo-Platonism, according to which God infinitely transcends the created order such that there's no analogical bond between them. For these writers, including the author of the *Cloud*, "Goodness" is a higher name for God than "Being" (referring to Plato's idea of the good). When speaking of God they engage in *apophatic* or negative description of the divine nature. Where the previous tradition affirms positively the other negates such that God is understood not by what he is so much as by what he is not. In Williams's terms, they try not to see God *through* images, which can be dangerously distracting and distorting, but to see God *beyond* images.

One can see this spirit at work in the many outbreaks of iconoclastic fervor that have erupted in the Christian world. In practice, however, these traditions can meld into each other and indeed, both discourses often ground themselves in the same source, the *Mystical Theology* of Dionysius the Areopagite. One of Aquinas's theological projects is to reconcile these two types of theology in his "doctrine of analogy." Jewish authors such as Maimonides and Ibn Gabirol are also strongly wedded to negative descriptions of God. This tendency in Jewish thought is strongly reinforced by the Kabbalah: "He is beyond all measurement, infinite both in his hidden essence and in his ontological and revealed qualities" (Schaya, *The Universal Meaning of the Kabbalah*, p. 22).

As mentioned above, the author of the *Cloud* belongs very much to the latter tradition and indeed, is somewhat rare in being almost a pure example of it. We are told, for instance, "When you first begin, you will find only darkness, and as it were a cloud of unknowing. You don't know what this means except that in your will you feel a simple steadfast intention reaching out towards God" (p. 61). The author claims that the intellect cannot penetrate this cloud: the first step in our ascent to wisdom is, in fact, a meditative suspension of all our faculties of imagination, reason, and intellect. Rather, he says "All rational beings, angels and men, possess two faculties, the power of knowing and the power of loving. To the first, to the intellect, God who made them is forever unknowable" (p. 63). However, he continues, "to the second, to love, he is completely knowable, and that by each separate individual."

This language is startling. The *Cloud* author is asserting a kind of "knowledge beyond knowledge" possessed in the immediacy of love, which sounds more than a little like Leonard Cohen. This is a real contact of the human with the divine that can occur only when "knowledge" of an intellectual kind has been transcended. The soul only "knows" what it loves and it can't love fully until "knowledge" of a propositional kind has been surpassed. We know what God *is* at the very point where we cease trying to think *what* he is and surrender to the bare motion of our will towards its own good. Representational knowledge, as for the Neo-Platonists, is trapped in the duality of thought and its object. It must always "think" of something under the sign of "being." True union can only be the work of love that seeks God beyond being (as a transforming presence rather than an object). Cohen describes this transforming presence in "You Know Who I Am": "I am the one who loves changing from nothing to one." This, as we shall see below, fits well with Cohen's typically Jewish emphasis on the unknowability of God.

## Recent Songs

Now how might we relate these seemingly arcane and paradoxical medieval notions to Cohen's *Recent Songs*? One way into this record may be the strange cover of the Quebec folksong "*Un Canadien Errant*." With its tuneless shouted chorus this song is unlikely to be counted as a Cohen classic. However, it's a peculiarly apt choice for a cover. The song originates from the period of the Lower Canada rebellion and expresses the nostalgia of the exiled rebels. Subsequently, the song has become an anthem among Acadians, recalling as it does the experience of exile and expulsion.

It's not hard to see why this song appeals to a Jewish songwriter like Cohen. Naturally, it may be taken to refer to the historical condition of the diaspora (exile of the Jewish people in the decades following the destruction of Jerusalem by the emperor Titus). More profoundly, though, it may reference Biblical myths (both Hebraic and Christian) of a fall from paradise. Further, it may recall Kabbalistic notions of the creation as an act of divine self-alienation where God surrenders something of his own nature to vacate the pure "space" of creation only to seek himself again through a union with his creation (through which his *shekinah* or "feminine wisdom" is diffused). Indeed, with Kabbalah as its means of transmission, it may recall Neo-Platonic notions of our descent from "the One" and our longing for reintegration with the divine principle within us. (Anyone familiar with the works of the late Pagan Neo-Platonist Proclus will immediately recognize their appropriation by the author or authors of the *Zohar.* This appropriation exactly parallels the Christianizing of Proclus undertaken in the mystical treatises of Dionysius. In the works of Ibn al-Arabi, among others, we find the same phenomenon in the Islamic world.)

This theme of exile suffuses the other songs on the record. "Ballad of the Absent Mare" is one notable example with its seemingly irresolvable cycle of union and separation. Might the line "there is no space but there's left and right" refer to the ten *sephiroth* (or the eternal forms of divine manifestation) which are divided into their "left and right" or "positive and negative" aspects? The subtle play of affirmation and negation in the construction of the *sephirotic* tree is (whatever Cohen's explicit intention) quite apposite to the themes we have broached here. "The Guests," evoking the Sufi poetry of Rumi with its images of drunkenness and passion, creates an atmosphere of intense longing though in the end "the guests are cast beyond the garden wall." *Recent Songs* coincides with Cohen's separation from Suzanne Elrod, so these images of our longing for union and the inevitable tragedy of separation have, for Cohen, a unique force.

Now, however, let's consider "The Window." The speaker of this song explores the implications of regarding the body as a locus of divinity, the "tangle of matter and ghost." Of course, ambiguities abound. The "chosen love" is at the same time "frozen": a telling rhyme, as we shall see. What's more, the word made flesh is "stuttered" rather than proclaimed. Indeed, it is at one point a dead letter. Yet at the heart of the song is an injunction to "come forth from the cloud of unknowing / And kiss the cheek of the moon." These lines suggest, even demand a divine revelation in the fullest sense and evoke an erotic union with nature as the medium and goal of this: "And I saw a new heaven and a new earth; for the first heaven and the first earth had passed away . . . and I John saw the holy city, new Jerusalem, coming down God out of heaven, prepared as a bride adorned for her husband" (Revelation 21:1–2).

The reference to the Book of Revelation in these lines reinforces the suggestion of a sacred union, a marriage even of the creator and his creation. From this perspective the stuttering of the word is blessed and the "broken-hearted host" paradoxically "whole." This suggests that the revelation of God in the flesh is a revelation of compassionate, suffering love: "leave no word of discomfort / And leave no observer to mourn." Indeed, one might take this revelation as a sublime act of condescension by which the creator takes on the limitations of the creature to reveal its hidden nature *as* self-giving love. Viewed from one angle then, "The Window" seems an affirmation of a Christian deity who reveals himself in physical form: "and we beheld his glory, the glory as of the only begotten of the Father" (John 1:14).

Yet this is only one side of the picture. The chosen love is also frozen: the divine must resist the very embodiment that reveals its nature. It can't be frozen in determinate shape or form. What's more the word made flesh stutters: it can't utter the unknowable, unmanifested core of the divine nature. The

Holy One may dream of a letter but it's a dead one: a communication that can't contain the living force and presence of the one communicated. Such a letter can never reach the one to whom it is sent. More tellingly even, the dead letter referred to is in fact "a letter's death." The "letter" here is of course literally a missive or communiqué. Mystically or esoterically, however, a letter is a divine attribute and in Kabbalistic thought Hebrew letters are given deep significance (*The Universal Meaning of the Kabbalah*, p. 40). The one "sent" must die and all forms of it be erased: "he hath no form nor comeliness; and when we shall see him there is no beauty that we should desire him" (Isaiah 53:2).

Clearly this refers to the passion of Christ, which Cohen has evoked in many places in his work. We don't, however, find anything in this song evoking a resurrection: the erasure of the word is final and the tragedy of the incarnation unsurmountable. The flesh betrays the spirit in religion as in *eros*, and love, whether human or divine, is a burden the body cannot sustain. It's perhaps no surprise then that *Recent Songs* ends on a detached, ironic note: "my darling says 'Leonard, just let it go by / That old silhouette on the great western sky.'" The central questions of Western civilization, of matter and spirit, God and humanity, remain suspended beneath the shadow of an absconded deity. We may note in passing that, just as in the *Cloud,* God sheds darkness rather than light. "There is in God, some say, / A deep but dazzling darkness . . ." Henry Vaughan tells us in his wonderful poem "The Night" and this thought seems applicable here. Yet the reference is brief, casual, and even slyly dismissive.

## Self-Overcoming

One might conclude then that Cohen has come to a sort of postmodern, skeptical stance. However, one of the admirable things in Cohen is that he has never stood pat. Since *Recent Songs* Cohen has, as is well known, become increasingly concerned with the meditative traditions of the Far East. Cohen has told us on *Various Positions* that he has longed for "nothing to touch." Taking this cue we might read his later turn to Zen Buddhism as part of his ongoing fascination with negativity and nothingness as *positive* energies.

However, this isn't exactly new territory for Cohen. As Stephen Scobie reminds us, "Cohen's saints must make their wills transparent to Nothing. The self is not sacrificed to some higher cause; the sacrifice of self *is* the higher cause" (p. 10). Scobie speaks of this longstanding tendency in Cohen as part of a "black romanticism" inherited from figures such as Baudelaire and Jean Genet. This black romanticism emphasizes the loss of ego or self through extreme states of consciousness and transgressive and self-destructive behavior. As Scobie puts it, "If the lack of social or political commitment in the fifties threw the artist back onto his naked self, then his exploration of that self might lead to its annihilation" (p. 9).

However, this nihilism of the black romantic isn't all there is to the story. As Scobie tells us, "Cohen always retains a belief in the power and the beauty of love. But love can only enter the world once it has accepted the essential conditions of destruction and loss. Love is only for the broken, the maimed, the outcasts, the beautiful losers" (p. 14). This often lends poignancy and indeed compassion and humanity to some of Cohen's darkest visions. More importantly, it reminds us that at their heart both Buddhism and Christianity are doctrines of compassion: they don't evoke nothingness for the sake of nothingness as in the nihilistic hedonism of the black romantic. The aim of both traditions is the emptying of self for the sake of *salvation*, the liberation of both oneself and of all other beings as well from suffering. Thus, the Buddhist concept of Nirvana is nothingness and emptiness only by excess. As in *The Cloud of Unknowing* the nothing is nothing but the mind's approach to the all.

Indeed, it seems a general fact of experience that things "become themselves" through self-overcoming: "He who would save his life must lose it." So if the artist seeks a kind of selflessness or self-erasure, does this not make his art more comprehensive and objective? If the saint seeks to empty his ego, isn't it to attain a pure, disinterested love of all things? Certainly, in the Buddhist tradition the emptiness of *sunyata* (the void achieved by the cessation of desire) opens us to compassion for all beings and desire for their liberation from suffering. We are reminded by this that the negation or nothingness of which Zen speaks can equally be spoken of as a pure and clarified consciousness that surpasses all limitations of ego or self. If you like, the urge to "nothingness" that has been a longstanding part of Cohen's work can, through Buddhist practice, find an explicitly positive focus.

Cohen hasn't dropped names idly: the reference to *The Cloud of Unknowing* has in fact illuminated *Recent Songs* and indeed the trajectory of his career. It fits neatly in the context of deep spiritual concerns that shape Cohen's earliest work and have persisted even to the present. Indeed, we might say that albums like *Recent Songs* concern themselves with the deepest and most longstanding issues of theology and spirituality. In particular, Cohen has explored the themes of nonbeing and emptiness as "supraconceptual" approaches to the divine. That he has done this in a way which sacrifices nothing of the emotional resonance of his art is a testament to his stature as a poet and musician.

# 20
# The Happy Memes of "Hallelujah"

PETER STONE

Dog eat dog. It's a jungle out there. Survival of the fittest. Eat or be eaten. This is the kind of language people routinely use to describe the music world. It's a rough, tough, take-no-prisoners kind of world. Nobody knows this better than Leonard Cohen. At the beginning of his musical career, for example, Leonard somehow signed away the rights to "Suzanne," one of his best-loved songs, to a producer he worked with. More recently, he decided to begin touring again because his unscrupulous business manager embezzled most of his money, leaving him almost bankrupt. This is the law of the jungle at work here—at its most jungle-like.

In this dog-eat-dog world, it's awfully hard to succeed in the music business. It takes both skill and luck. In *The Prince*, Machiavelli famously said that a leader can only control about half his fate—the rest is up to fortune. That certainly seems to be how the music world operates. Talent helps, but it makes no guarantees. And luck helps a lot, too—indeed, luck can prove essential (Spice Girls, anyone?)—but when the luck runs out, talent can mean the difference between continuing success and disappearance into obscurity (Spice Girls, anyone?).

All of this applies to songs as well as to singers and songwriters. Luck can make a big difference in a song's fate, but at the end of the day, if you want a hit, it helps to have a really great song. Take what is probably now Cohen's most famous song, "Hallelujah." There's an enormous amount of luck in the history of that song. It originally appeared on Cohen's album *Various Positions* (1984). Its American release was very troubled—Walter Yetnikoff, then-president of CBS Records, declined to release it in the U.S. (Yetnikoff supposedly told Cohen, "Leonard, we know you're great, but we don't know if you're any good.") A smaller label released the album in the U.S., and Columbia (parent company to CBS) finally released an American edition in 1990. And yet upon its release "Hallelujah" immediately won some fans, including a number of musicians whose covers kept the song alive and increased its reputation. John Cale recorded it for a Cohen tribute album in 1991. Jeff Buckley, in turn, was much taken by Cale's version of the song, and used it as the basis for his own version, perhaps the most famous one to date. Cale's version could be heard in the movie *Shrek* (2001), and a version by Rufus Wainwright appeared on that movie's soundtrack. From there, the popularity of the song snowballed. The entire process is masterfully chronicled in Alan Light's book *The Holy or the Broken: Leonard Cohen, Jeff Buckley, and the Unlikely Ascent of "Hallelujah."*

It's hard to look at the history of "Hallelujah" and not be struck by how much luck influenced the rise of the song from obscurity to superstardom. And yet it's equally hard not to be struck by the song itself (although apparently Walter Yetnikoff was not). It's a seriously impressive song. But what makes the song so great? What makes the song appeal to so many people? The music matters a lot, to be sure, but what about the lyrics? They are surely a critical part of the story. Why does the song speak to so many people all around the world?

## Genes and Memes

If we want to understand what makes a song succeed, perhaps we should look at how the law of the jungle governs . . . the jungle. The natural world is governed by the laws of evolution, as first described by Charles Darwin in his classic *The*

*Origin of Species* (1859). Can evolutionary theory tell us anything about the appeal of "Hallelujah?" Let's find out.

A good place to start any exploration of evolutionary theory is Richard Dawkins's classic book *The Selfish Gene*, first published in 1976. According to Dawkins, natural selection induces a competition among genes for survival. Some genes, when combined together with other genes, produce an organism that is more likely to survive in its environment than other genes do. More specifically, some genes produce an organism that is more likely to pass on its genes than others. As a result, those genes will be more likely to survive than others. And so the world comes to be filled with genes that are successful at surviving. It looks like the world is filled with selfish genes, genes that are very good at taking care of their own self-interest. (I say "looks like," of course—genes don't think, and Dawkins nowhere says that they do.)

At the end of *The Selfish Gene*, Dawkins concludes that all evolution requires is "the differential survival of replicating entities" (p. 192). But could there be entities other than genes that replicate in an evolutionary process? Dawkins says yes. There is such a thing as *cultural* evolution. Cultural units—including scientific theories, works of art, novels, and yes, Leonard Cohen songs—compete to survive in human societies, just like genes compete to survive in the natural world. Some of them fail to attract human attention, or attract attention but then lose it, and so vanish from human life. Others get our attention and keep it, and so human beings keep talking about them over and over again. Dawkins calls these cultural units *memes*, and argues that evolution works on them much as it works on genes.

If Dawkins is right, then the law of the jungle governs our cultural products—our memes—much as it governs the natural environment. Can this fact help us to understand the success of "Hallelujah?" It might, but before answering this question we must first deal with another. Is "Hallelujah" a meme? This is a tricky question to answer. As Dawkins explains, it's difficult even to decide what a gene is. It's easy to say what genetic material is—it's that stuff that makes up our chromosomes, dictating the construction of the amino acids that control the creation of us. But it can be difficult to say where one gene ends and another begins. Similarly, it's a little hard to say whether we should treat an entire song like "Hallelujah" as a meme, or whether it makes more sense to treat the parts that make up the song as different memes. This is a big problem in theories of cultural evolution. Sometimes an entire work of art, like a song or a movie, attracts and keeps people's attention, and so thrives for a long time. But sometimes a single scene of a movie, or line from a song, has a staying power much greater than the entire work does. This can have strange effects upon our cultural memory. *The Treasure of the Sierra Madre* (1948), for example, is a great Humphrey Bogart movie, a very successful meme. But even more successful is the classic line, "We don't need no stinking badges!" Millions of people who know nothing else about the movie "remember" that line—even though that exact line is never actually uttered in the movie!

So is "Hallelujah" one meme, or a bunch of memes? It's hard to say. The problem is complicated by the fact that there are multiple versions of the song. The version Cohen released on *Various Positions* has four verses, but those four came out of a lengthy, agonizing process lasting years. During this process, Cohen composed and then rejected many verses—perhaps eighty, by his own count. After recording *Various Positions*, Cohen often varied the verses used in live performances of "Hallelujah." John Cale asked Cohen for the complete set of verses for the song before recording his own version. Cohen offered fifteen, and Cale used five—two from Cohen's original version plus three more. Together, these seven verses, plus the famous one-word chorus, seem to make up the song.

"Hallelujah" may contain many memorable lines, but it is the song itself that people continue to play and sing over and over again. And so I'm going to treat the entire song as a meme that has to survive in a world of other songs all competing for our attention. What features do the lyrics of "Hallelujah" have that might help the song outcompete its rivals?

One thing you immediately notice if you look at those lyrics is the abundance of references to religion. The song references biblical stories, such as the story of David and Bathsheba ("You saw her bathing on the roof / Her beauty and the moonlight overthrew you"). It suggests "Maybe there's a God above," and so on. The very title of the song is a religious exclamation, equivalent to "Praise God!" The only other topic that receives anything like the attention given to religion in "Hallelujah" is sex. And even that topic is hard to separate from religion; Jeff Buckley described the song as the "Hallelujah of the orgasm."

Because so much of "Hallelujah" is taken up with religion, it makes sense to ask how and why religious memes survive and thrive, and see if that sheds any light upon the success of "Hallelujah." A good source on this topic is the book *Breaking the Spell: Religion as a Natural Phenomenon* by the philosopher Daniel Dennett. Dennett agrees with Dawkins that culture can be characterized as an evolutionary process in which memes compete for our attention, with the winners surviving and the losers fading away. He believes that this process can be used to understand what causes religious memes to survive. Perhaps *Breaking the Spell* can help us understand the "Hallelujah" phenomenon.

## The Evolution of Religion

Dennett invites us to imagine a world in which our experiences put all kinds of ideas—memes—into our heads. Some of those ideas will survive, and get passed along to other people. Others will get completely forgotten by us. At one time, many of these ideas dealt with supernatural forces—gods, demons, spirits, angels—that allegedly controlled the world. Some of these forces controlled the sun, others the seas, still others the rain, and so on. It's easy to imagine how human beings first came to have ideas about beings like that. Human beings evolved, Dennett says, with "an instinct on hair trigger: the disposition to attribute *agency*—beliefs and desires and other mental states—to anything complicated that moves" (p. 114). If something happens, our first instinct is to ask ourselves, "Who goes there?" An instinct like this makes a lot of sense. If you're not sure whether that long thin thing on the ground is a snake or a stick, assume it's a snake. If you assume it's a snake, and it's really a stick, the false alarm doesn't do you much harm. But if you assume it's a stick, and it's really a snake, the results could be fatal. And so human beings naturally produce a lot of false alarms, as we are readily disposed to imagine everything is caused by some intelligent being or other.

Obviously, this is not the whole story about the origin of religion. It explains a lot about Judaism, the religion into which Cohen was born. It explains less about Buddhism, the religion Cohen practices today. (He's an ordained monk, in fact.) But supernatural beings are incredibly important to religion. This is so true that Dennett defines a religion as a social system "*whose participants avow belief in a supernatural agent or agents whose approval is to be sought*" (p. 9). For this reason, these beings must be front and center in any story told about the way human beings developed religion.

And so people came to believe all kinds of things about the world. Some of them involved supernatural beings, and some did not. But real beliefs have consequences. If you believe that the rain god will deliver rain if you sacrifice a goat to him, then the rain had better follow the sacrifice. Most of the time, we update our beliefs when the real world demonstrates their inadequacies—by giving us a dry goatless day, for example. This makes our beliefs better suited to help us cope with reality. But sometimes we respond to challenges to our beliefs by modifying them so as to render them unfalsifiable. Such beliefs become immune to evidence, impossible to confirm or to refute. This has happened with many of our beliefs, including our beliefs about supernatural beings. (If it failed to happen with a supernatural belief, the belief would get weeded out by our minds as soon as it conflicted with reality.) "The transition from folk religion to organized religion," Dennett remarks, "is marked by a shift in beliefs from those with very clear, concrete consequences to those with systematically elusive consequences" (p. 227). This applies to our surviving religious beliefs. It still happens today, and it works to push religious beliefs into the unfalsifiable category. Dennett gives the example of the athlete who prays to God for a win in a big game, but then invents excuses afterwards if he loses (p. 311).

As a result of all this, it has become very hard to say just what religious beliefs mean nowadays. It was pretty easy to say what Zeus was like; he was a guy with a beard who sat on a cloud and threw lightning bolts when he got mad. But what do people mean today when they claim to believe in "God?" Who knows? Because these beliefs have no observable consequences, different people can mean very different things when they say they believe in "God"—they might not even know what they mean when they say it—and it's virtually impossible to notice the differences. But then do people who all claim to believe in "God" all believe the same thing? As Dennett writes, "If Lucy believes that Rock (Hudson) is to die for, and Desi believes that Rock (music) is to die for, they really don't agree on anything, do they?" (p. 209). Much the same could be said about religious belief in the modern world.

But surely there's *something* religious believers all have in common. What could it be? Dennett believes the answer is *belief in belief*. Religious believers all believe that religious belief is a good thing. People *should* be religious, believe in God, be Christians (or Jews or Muslims or whatever). (Cohen, from a certain perspective, seems to agree.) People believe that religious belief makes life better, that life without religion would somehow be worse, and that therefore it's very important for religious belief to survive and thrive. And so they keep on promoting religious beliefs—by teaching those beliefs to their children, for instance—even if they can't really say just what those beliefs really mean.

To return to the subject of memes, religious memes enjoy two massive advantages that help to ensure their continued reproduction and survival. One is that they've been rendered immune to evidence that might refute them. People can attach almost any meaning they like to these expressions, so long as they take care (most of the time) not to attach a meaning that could be disproved by evidence. And yet despite this immunity from evidence, people continue to believe these memes are immensely important, and need to be spread. Religious people may have many different ideas about just who or what God is—they may not even be sure just what they mean when they say "God"—but they can all agree that everyone should believe in God. The religious therefore have a natural reason to spread these memes, and the memes escape any easy effort to shoot them down. All things considered, it's good to be a religious meme.

Dennett admits that the story he tells about religious memes is tentative and needs further development. But it does account for many features of religious belief. In addition, it sheds a great deal of light on the nature of the appeal of "Hallelujah." Alan Light's book *The Holy or the Broken* analyzes the song in some detail. It also contains many examples of both musicians and nonmusicians explaining why they cherish the song. Dennett's account helps a lot in trying to make sense out of the story Light tells about the song.

## How the Light Gets In

Judging from the history of the song, it's easy to see how the song is seen as expressing religious ideas and themes. But it does so in a highly ambiguous manner—allowing people to draw upon as much of the religiosity as they like, any which way they please. As I mentioned before, religion is the most important, but not the only theme in the song. This is because Cohen himself did not wish the song to be exclusively religious. Light quotes Cohen as saying, "I wanted to push the Hallelujah deep into the secular world, into the ordinary world. . . . The Hallelujah, the David's Hallelujah, was still a religious song. So I wanted to indicate that Hallelujah can come out of things that have nothing to do with religion" (p. 25).

It's quite understandable that Cohen would wish to allow for secular readings of "Hallelujah." After all, people often use religious expressions (such as "God bless you" or "God damn it") without intending to make any religious point. Nevertheless, the religiosity of the lyrics is still there, and so the song allows for many different levels of religiosity. The different verses of the song reinforce this ambiguity. Cohen slaved over the lyrics for the song for a very long time, as he does for virtually all of his songs (unlike Bob Dylan, who supposedly can dash off a song quite quickly). And it appears that he deliberately tried to push the religiosity into the background. Here's Alan Light on the subject:

> It seems that the breakthrough in Cohen's editing—the vision that allowed him to bring the eighty written verses down to the four that he ultimately recorded—was reaching a decision about how much to foreground the religious element of the song. "It had references to the Bible in it, although these references became more and more remote as the song went from the beginning to the end," he once said. "Finally I understood that it was not necessary to refer to the Bible anymore. And I rewrote the song; this is the 'secular' 'Hallelujah.'" (p. 18)

And yet the Biblical references are still there, from David and Bathsheba to Samson and Delilah. And that's just Cohen's original recorded version; Cale used different Cohen lyrics, Cohen and others made use of those changes, and now singers regularly pick and choose which lyrics they want to use. But as a result the religiosity of the song changes depending upon who is singing it. More importantly, the seven verses commonly used today do not fit together perfectly, especially in terms of religiosity. The lyrics, after all, vary from "maybe"—*maybe!*—"there's a God above" to "remember when I moved in you" (Buckley's "hallelujah of the orgasm"). Light explains the result:

> Unlike the breathtaking precision of some of Cohen's songs mentioned above, the lyrics to "Hallelujah" are confusing, slightly out of focus. Perspective shifts between verses. Images from different stories are crosscut, adding up to a mood more than a single coherent

> narrative. The effect is that, whether you hear it on your iPod or in a wedding ceremony, it can be as "religious" a song as you want it to be—a contemporary hymn or just something with a vague aura of holiness. (pp. 217–18)

This fact—that the song is as "religious" as you want it to be—may make it confusing, but it may also help its ability to survive and propagate as a meme.

Of course, there are lots of songs out there with ambiguous lyrics, and that ambiguity does not always help them. But religiously ambiguous songs have an added advantage—belief in belief. People have many different ideas about what religion is or ought to be; some don't really have a clue what it is. But many of them agree that religious beliefs are *important*. And so if you can write good religious lyrics—lyrics that are both well-written and yet sufficiently ambiguous—those lyrics will benefit from this belief in belief. Different people will put their own spin on those lyrics, and even people who have no idea what those lyrics say will still regard them as having special importance. This is a great way for a song to spread.

Something like this certainly seems to have taken place with "Hallelujah." A few examples from Light should suffice to show the gamut of different religious attitudes taken towards the song. Given Cohen's Jewish background, it's not surprising that many Jews appreciate the song's religious attitude; it is apparently even played every Saturday night on the radio network of the Israeli Defense Forces (p. xvii). Rabbi Ruth Gan Kagan, of Jerusalem's Nava Tehila synagogue, has often made use of the song while conducting religious services (including her daughter's bat mitzvah). "'Hallelujah,'" she claims, "is not a hymn of the believer—it's a hymn of the one who is full of doubt, a hymn of the heretic." The idea of heretics and doubters having hymns might seem a bit contradictory, but apparently that doesn't bother Kagan: "Asked how she can reconcile this skeptical sensibility, and the language of Cohen's song, with the more traditional aspects of the High Holidays, Kagan answered immediately. 'I don't want to reconcile!' she said. 'The whole reason of bringing it in was that it *doesn't* reconcile'" (*The Holy or the Broken*, pp. 182–83).

But many Christians also appreciate the religiosity of "Hallelujah." According to Alexandra Burke, who sang the song when she won the UK television show *X Factor* in 2008, "to anyone who's a Christian, that word 'hallelujah'—full stop, that's what you're going to hear" (p. xxiv). Some Christians appreciate the song as is, perhaps for reasons similar to those expressed by Rabbi Kagan. Others, however, appreciate the religious message of "Hallelujah," but feel the need to embellish or add to it. The Holy Trinity Church, in the Channel Islands, has sung the lyrics of "Amazing Grace" to the tune of Cohen's song. The idea for this came from Helen Hamilton, who "presented the salvation offered by Jesus Christ as a counter to the idea that 'it all went wrong.' That, for Hamilton, completed Cohen's narrative—'we will be able to stand there, at the end of time, with nothing on our lips but hallelujah. Not through anything we have done, but through amazing grace'" (*The Holy or the Broken,* p. 184). Needless to say, this "Hallelujah" is rather different from both the "Hallelujah" of traditional Judaism and the "Hallelujah" of the heretic.

"Looking at these different usages of 'Hallelujah,'" Light concludes, "one thing that stands out is not only how the song remains so open to interpretation and flexible in meaning and construction, but also how easily it fits into services and celebrations of multiple faiths" (pp. 184–85). The religious language in the song is compatible with an almost infinite variety of interpretations, and is even capable of appealing to people who are unsure which interpretation they ought to buy. Note that the song's appeal would be much less limited and circumscribed if it made clear claims about the nature of God, religion, or the afterlife, claims that could be evaluated or falsified. But as Dennett points out, religion makes regular use of both the untestable nature of its claims and a generalized belief that religious claims, whatever their nature, deserve respect. "Hallelujah" benefits from this phenomenon, and as a result its continued success as a meme is very likely. Amanda Palmer, a former member of the musical duo the Dresden Dolls, said that the lyrics of "Hallelujah" were "like the *I Ching* of songwriting" (p. xxv). Palmer is quite correct, and both the *I Ching* and Cohen's song benefit from this fact.

## Happy Memes

Dawkins introduced the idea of a "selfish gene" to help us understand the nature of evolution. But people often misunderstand him to mean that people have genes that make them selfish. Dawkins clearly denies this. The forces of evolution, he writes, may favor genes that are good at propagating themselves—genes that are "selfish"—but those same forces have given us genes enabling our altruism, compassion, and fairness. Much the same could be said about memes. They are selfish in the sense that the memes that are good at propagating themselves—at getting us to remember them and repeat them over and over again—are the memes that will survive. But those memes themselves need not make us selfish. Religious memes have a very good survival strategy, for the reasons given by Dennett. But clearly religion does not lead directly to selfish behavior. Indeed, it often promotes self-sacrificing behavior. (This is often a good thing, but not always, as the September 11 attackers demonstrated.)

So perhaps we need a new word to describe memes favored with evolutionary success. Perhaps we could describe such memes as *happy*. After all, successful memes have every reason to be happy—they can expect to live long and healthy (re)productive lives, as people find reason to repeat them and pass them along to others. (Unsuccessful memes have fewer reasons to be cheerful.) In that case, "Hallelujah" contains—perhaps ironically for Cohen—some very happy memes indeed. That song will be sung and cherished for quite some time to come. The analysis of memes offered by Richard Dawkins and Daniel Dennett helps us to understand why.

# References

Adorno, Theodor W. 2003. Cultural Criticism and Society. Translated by Samuel Weber and Shierry Weber Nicholsen. In Theodor W. Adorno, *Can One Live After Auschwitz? A Philosophical Reader*, edited by Rolf Tiedemann, pp. 146–62. Stanford: Stanford University Press,.

Alexander, Jeffrey C. 2002. On the Social Construction of Moral Universals: The Holocaust from War Crime to Trauma Drama. *European Journal of Social Theory* 5, no. 1: 5–85.

Allison, David B. 2001. *Reading the New Nietzsche*. Lanham, MD: Rowman and Littlefield.

Arendt, Hannah. 1994. *Eichmann in Jerusalem: A Report on the Banality of Evil*. London: Penguin.

Babich, Babette. 2013. *The Hallelujah Effect: Philosophical Reflections on Music, Performance Practice, and Technology*. Farnham: Ashgate.

———. 1994. *Nietzsche's Philosophy of Science: Reflecting Science on the Ground of Art and Life*. Albany: SUNY Press.

Badhwar, Neera K. 2003. Love. In *Practical Ethics*, edited by H. LaFollette, pp. 42–69. Oxford: Oxford University Press.

Barbour, Douglas. 1976. Down with History. In *Leonard Cohen: The Artist and His Critics*, edited by Michael Gnarowski, 136–49. Toronto: McGraw-Hill Ryerson.

Beauvoir, Simone de. 2000. *The Ethics of Ambiguity*. New York: Citadel.

Benjamin, Jessica. 1988. *The Bonds of Love*. New York: Pantheon Books.

Bloom, Harold. 1997. *The Anxiety of Influence*. Oxford: Oxford University Press.

Boucher, David. 2004. *Dylan and Cohen: Poets of Rock and Roll*. New York: Continuum.

Brod, Harry. 2004. Jewish Men. In *Men and Masculinities: A Social, Cultural, and Historical Encyclopedia*, Volume I, edited by Michael Kimmel and Amy Aronson, pp. 441–43. Santa Barbara: ABC-CLIO.

Bronner, Ethan. 2009. Leonard Cohen's Legacy for His Concert in Israel. *New York Times*, September 23rd.

Burns, Steven. 2013. Best Readings: Wittgenstein and Grillparzer. In *Wittgenstein Reading*, edited by Sascha Bru, Wolfgang Huemer, and Daniel Steuer, pp. 153–70. Berlin/Boston: Walter de Gruyter.

Butler, Judith. 2008. *Gender Trouble: Feminism and the Subversion of Identity*. New York: Routledge.

Camus, Albert. 1991. *The Myth of Sisyphus and Other Essays*. New York: Vintage.

Cave, Nick. 1999. The Secret Life of the Love Song. Lecture at the Academy of Fine Arts, Vienna, September 25.

*The Cloud of Unknowing*. 2001. Translated by A.C. Spearing. London: Penguin Classics.

Coates, Susan. 1998. Having a Mind of One's Own and Holding the Other in Mind. *Psychoanalytic Dialogues* 8, no. 1: 115–48.

Cohen, Leonard. 1956. *Let Us Compare Mythologies*. Toronto: Contact Press.

———. 1963. *The Favourite Game*. London: Jonathan Cape. Reprint Toronto: McClelland and Stewart.

———. 1964. *Flowers for Hitler*. Toronto: McClelland and Stewart.

———. 1966. *Beautiful Losers*. New York: Vintage. Reprint 1993.

———. 1967. *Songs of Leonard Cohen*. Album. Columbia.

———. 1969. *Songs from a Room*. Album. Columbia.

———. 1971. *Songs of Love and Hate*. Album. Columbia.

———. 1973. *Live Songs*. Album. Columbia.

———. 1974. *New Skin for the Old Ceremony*. Album. Columbia.

———. 1975. *The Best of Leonard Cohen*. Album. Columbia.

———. 1977. *Death of a Ladies' Man*. Album. Columbia.

———. 1979. *Recent Songs*. Album. Columbia.

———. 1984. *Book of Mercy*. Toronto: McClelland and Stewart. Reprint 2010.

———. 1984. *Various Positions*. Album. Columbia.

———. 1988. *I'm Your Man*. Album. Columbia.
———. 1992. *The Future*. Album. Columbia.
———. 1993. *Cohen Live*. Album. Columbia.
———. 1993. Sincerely, L. Cohen. Interview by Brian Cullman. *Details for Men*. January.
———. 1993. *Stranger Music: Selected Poems and Songs*. London: Random House.
———. 2001. *Ten New Songs*. Album. Columbia.
———. 2004. *Dear Heather*. Album. Columbia.
———. 2006. *Book of Longing*. New York: HarperCollins.
———. 2012. *Old Ideas*. Album. Columbia.
Cohen, Leonard, and Arthur Kurzweil. 1993. I *Am* the Little Jew Who Wrote the Bible, November 23, transcript <http://www.leonardcohenfiles.com/arthurkurzweil.pdf>.
Darwin, Charles. 2003. *The Origin of Species*. New York: Signet Classics.
Davidson, Donald. 2004. *Problems of Rationality*. Oxford: Oxford University Press.
Dawkins, Richard. 2006. *The Selfish Gene*. 30th Anniversary Edition. New York: Oxford University Press.
de Sousa, Ronald. 1987. *The Rationality of Emotion*. Cambridge: MIT Press.
———. 2004. Emotions: What I Know, What I'd Like to Think I Know, and What I'd Like to Think. In *Thinking About Feeling*, ed. Robert C. Solomon, pp. 61–75. Oxford: Oxford University Press.
Deigh, John. 2004. Primitive Emotions. In *Thinking About Feeling*, edited by Robert C. Solomon, pp. 9–27. Oxford: Oxford University Press.
Dennett, Daniel. 2006. *Breaking the Spell: Religion as a Natural Phenomenon*. New York: Penguin.
Derrida, Jacques. 1996. The Villanova Roundtable. In *Deconstruction in a Nutshell*, edited by John D. Caputo, pp. 3–28. New York: Fordham University Press.
———. 1997. *The Politics of Friendship*. Translated by George Collins. New York: Verso.
Descartes, René. 1989. *Discourse on Method and the Meditations*. Amherst, NY: Prometheus.
Dickinson, Emily. 1960. *Complete Poems*. Boston: Little, Brown.
Eckermann, Johann Peter. 1925. *Conversations with Goethe*. Vol. IV. Translated by John Oxenford. Leipzig: Brockhaus.

Ekman, Paul. 1972. *Emotions in the Human Face*. New York: Pergamon.
Epictetus. 2004. *Enchiridion*. Translated by E. Carter. Mineola, NY: Dover.
Footman, Tim. 2009. *Leonard Cohen: Hallelujah: A New Biography*. London: Chrome.
Freud, Sigmund. 2010. *Beyond the Pleasure Principle*. Translated by James Strachey. United States: Pacific Publishing.
Gallagher, Shaun, and Dan Zahavi. 2010. Phenomenological Approaches to Self-Consciousness. In *Stanford Encyclopedia of Philosophy,* edited by Edward N. Zalta, <http://plato.stanford.edu/archives/win2010/entries/self-consciousness-phenomeonological>.
Grant, George. 1965. *Lament for a Nation*. Toronto: Anansi Press.
Gregory, Timothy E. 2011. *A History of Byzantium*. Oxford: Wiley-Blackwell.
Grice, Paul. 1989. Logic and Conversation. In *Studies in the Way of Words*, pp. 22–40. Cambridge, Mass: Harvard University Press.
Griffiths, Paul E. 1997. *What Emotions Really Are: The Problem of Psychological Categories*. Chicago: University of Chicago Press.
Hafferkamp, Jack. 1971. Ladies and Gents, Leonard Cohen. *Rolling Stone*, February 4th.
Hegel, Georg W.G. 1977. *The Phenomenology of Spirit*. Translated by Arnold V. Miller. Oxford: Clarendon Press,
Heidegger, Martin. 1962. *Being and Time*. Translated by John Macquarrie and Edward Robinson. New York: HarperCollins.
*The High Holiday Prayer Book: Rosh Hashanah and Yom Kippur*. 1959. Translated and arranged by Ben Zion Bokser. New York: Hebrew Publishing.
Hume, David. 2002. Of the Standard of Taste. In *The Nature of Art: An Anthology*, edited by Thomas E. Wartenberg, pp. 39–47. Orlando: Harcourt.
Kant, Immanuel. 1987. *Critique of Judgment*. Translated by Werner S. Pluhar. Indianapolis: Hackett.
Kierkegaard, Søren. 1983. *The Sickness unto Death*. Translated by Howard V. Hong and Edna H. Hong. Princeton: Princeton University Press.
———. 1986. *Fear and Trembling*. Translated by Alastair Hannay. New York: Penguin Classics,
———. 1989. *The Concept of Irony with Continual Reference to Socrates*. Translated by Howard V. Hong and Edna H. Hong. Princeton: Princeton University Press.

Kimmel, Michael. 2004. *The Gendered Society*. New York: Oxford University Press.

Kirk, G.S., J.E. Raven, and M. Schofield. 1999. *The Presocratic Philosophers*. Cambridge: Cambridge University Press.

*Leonard Cohen: Under Review 1934–1977*. 2007. DVD. New Malden: Chrome Dreams.

Light, Alan. 2012. *The Holy or the Broken: Leonard Cohen, Jeff Buckley, and the Unlikely Ascent of "Hallelujah."* New York: Atria Books.

Lorca, Federico García. 1998. *In Search of Duende*. Translated by Christopher Maurer. New York: New Directions.

Lucretius Carus, Titus. 2004. *On the Nature of Things*. Translated by William Ellery Leonard. Mineola, NY: Dover.

Merleau-Ponty, Maurice. 1962. *Phenomenology of Perception*. Translated by C. Smith. London: Routledge and Kegan Paul.

Michaels, Sean. 2012. Leonard Cohen's Ex-manager Sentenced to 18 Months in Jail. *The Guardian*, April 19.

Minkowski, Eugene. 1970. *Lived Time: Phenomenological and Psychopathological Studies*. Evanston, IL: Northwestern University Press.

Monk, Ray. 1991. *Ludwig Wittgenstein: The Duty of Genius*. London: Vintage.

Nagel, Thomas. 2012. *Mind and Cosmos: Why the Materialist Neo-Darwinian Conception of Nature Is Almost Certainly False*. Oxford: Oxford University Press.

Nietzsche, Friedrich. 1962. *Philosophy in the Tragic Age of the Greeks*. Translated by Marianne Cowan. Baltimore: Regnery.

———. 1967. *Birth of Tragedy*. Translated by Walter Kaufmann. New York: Vintage.

———. 1974. *The Gay Science*. Translated by Walter Kaufmann. New York: Random House.

———. 1981. *Twilight of the Idols and The Antichrist*. Translated by R. J. Hollingdale. Harmondsworth: Penguin.

———. 1983. *Beyond Good and Evil*. Translated by R. J. Hollingdale. Harmondsworth: Penguin.

———. 1989. *On the Genealogy of Morals*. Translated by Walter Kaufmann. New York: Random House.

———. 2002. *Beyond Good and Evil*. Translated by Judith Norman. Cambridge: Cambridge University Press.

Novick, Peter. 1999. *The Holocaust in American Life*. New York: Houghton-Mifflin.

Nussbaum, Martha. 2004. Emotions as Judgments of Value and Importance. In *Thinking About Feeling*, edited by Robert C. Solomon, pp. 183–99. Oxford: Oxford University Press.

Ogden, Thomas H. 1994. *Subjects of Analysis*. Northvale, NJ: Aronson.

Ondaatje, Michael. 1970. *Leonard Cohen*. Toronto: McClelland and Stewart.

Pareles, Jon. 2012. Final Reckonings, a Tuneful Fedora and Forgiveness. *New York Times*, January 27.

Pike, Robin. 1974. September 15th 1974. *ZigZag* magazine, October.

Plato. 1997. *Apology*. Translated by G.M.A. Grube. In *Plato: Complete Works*, edited by John M. Cooper, pp. 17–36. Indianapolis: Hackett.

———. 1998. *Phaedo.* Translated by Eva Brann, Peter Kalkavage, and Eric Salem. Newburyport, Mass: Focus Classical Library.

———. 2003. *Phaedrus.* Translated by Stephen Scully. Newburyport, MA: Focus Classical Library.

Prinz, Jesse. 2004. Embodied Emotions. In *Thinking About Feeling*, edited by Robert C. Solomon, pp. 44–60. Oxford: Oxford University Press.

Robinson, Jenefer. 2004. Emotion: Biological Fact or Social Construction? In *Thinking About Feeling*, edited by Robert C. Solomon, pp. 28–43. Oxford: Oxford University Press.

Rodriguez, Juan. 1976. Poet's Progress—To Sainthood and Back. In *Leonard Cohen: The Artist and His Critics*, edited by Michael Gnarowski, pp. 63–68. Toronto: McGraw-Hill Ryerson.

Rorty, Amelie O. 1993. The Historicity of Psychological Attitudes: Love is Not Love Which Alters Not When It Alteration Finds. In *Friendship: A Philosophical Reader*, edited by Neera Badhwar, pp. 73–88. Ithaca: Cornell University Press.

Rorty, Richard. 1989. *Contingency, Irony, and Solidarity*. Cambridge: Cambridge University Press.

Rosenthal, Alexander S. 2002. Christmas Celebration Speech. *Leuven Philosophy Newsletter* 11: 42–44.

Safranski, Rudiger. 1990. *Schopenhauer and the Wild Years of Philosophy*. Cambridge, MA: Harvard University Press.

Sartre, Jean-Paul. 1949. *Nausea*. Translated by Lloyd Alexander. London: Purnell and Sons.

———. 1975. Existentialism Is a Humanism. In *Existentialism from Dostoyevsky to Sartre,* edited by Walter Kaufmann, pp. 345–68. New York: New American Library.

———. 1992. *Being and Nothingness.* Translated by Hazel E. Barnes. New York: First Washington Square Press.

Savile, Anthony. 1972. The Place of Intention in the Concept of Art. In *Aesthetics*, edited by Harold Osborne, pp. 158–76. Oxford: Oxford University Press.

Schaya, Leo. 1973. *The Universal Meaning of the Kabbalah*. Translated by N. Pearson. London: Penguin Books.

Schneider, Pat. 2013. *How the Light Gets In: Writing as a Spiritual Practice*. Oxford: Oxford University Press.

Schopenhauer, Arthur. 1969. *The World as Will and Representation*. Vols. I–II. Translated by E.F.J. Payne. New York: Dover.

———. 1974. *On the Fourfold Root of the Principle of Sufficient Reason*. Translated by E.F.J. Payne. La Salle, IL: Open Court.

———. 1995. *On the Basis of Morality*. Translated by E.F.J. Payne. Cambridge, MA: Hackett.

———. 2007. Further Psychological Observations. In *Studies in Pessimism*, translated by T. Bailey Saunders, pp. 34–53. New York: Cosimo.

———. 2007. On the Sufferings of the World. In *Studies in Pessimism*, translated by T. Bailey Saunders, pp. 5–18. New York: Cosimo.

———. 2007. On Women. In *Parerga and Paralipomena*, vol. II, translated by T. Bailey Saunders, pp. 614–26. New York: Cosimo.

Scobie, Stephen. 1978. *Leonard Cohen*. Vancouver: Douglas and MacIntyre.

Sextus Empiricus. 1996. *Outlines of Pyrrhonism*. Translated by Benson Mates. New York: Oxford University Press.

Simmons, Sylvie. 2012. *I'm Your Man: The Life of Leonard Cohen*. New York: HarperCollins,

Solomon, Robert C. 2004. Emotions, Thoughts, and Feelings: Emotions as Engagements with the World. In *Thinking About Feeling*, edited by Robert C. Solomon, pp. 76–90. Oxford: Oxford University Press.

Sternberg, Robert. 1994. *Love Is a Story*. Oxford: Oxford University Press.

Walsh, Nick Paton. 2001. I Never Discuss My Mistresses or My Tailors. *The Observer* (London), October 14th.

Webster, Jason. 2004. *Duende*. London: Black Swan.

Williams, Charles. 1979. *The Descent of the Dove*. Grand Rapids: Eerdmans.

Winnicott, Donald W. 2005. Mirror-Role of Mother and Family in Child Development. In *Playing and Reality*, pp. 149–59. New York: Routledge.

Wittgenstein, Ludwig. 1998. *Philosophical Investigations*. Oxford: Blackwell.

Wynands, Sandra. 2000. The Representation of the Holocaust in *Flowers for Hitler*. In *Intricate Preparations: Writing Leonard Cohen*, edited by Stephen Scobie, pp. 198–209. Toronto: ECW Press.

Zahavi, Dan. 2003. *Husserl's Phenomenology*. Stanford: Stanford University Press.

# Our Hands Bloody with Commas

**Adam Auch** was born and raised in Windsor, Ontario. He currently works as a part-time instructor and writing tutor at Dalhousie University in Halifax, Nova Scotia, where he recently completed a PhD in philosophy. He credits his brother, Nathan, for sparking his interest in Cohen's music. In his research, he wrestles with philosophical issues related to language, knowledge, and communication. When he's not doing that, he spends far too much time drinking tea, solving crossword puzzles, and indulging in analog photography. Otherwise, he has been known to wander through train stations humming "Lili Marlene" while he waits for Hank Williams to finally get back to him.

**Babette Babich** is Professor of Philosophy at Fordham University in New York City. Her most recent book, *The Hallelujah Effect: Philosophical Reflections on Music, Performance Practice, and Technology* (2013), discusses k.d. lang's cover of Leonard Cohen's "Hallelujah" and desire (male and female) in the context of phenomenological sociology and classical critical theory (Adorno), technological culture, and music from the ancient Greek lyric to Beethoven's dissonance (Nietzsche). In 1996, she founded *New Nietzsche Studies*, the journal she continues to edit. She specializes in continental philosophy of science and technology and has published on the politics of academic philosophy including women in philosophy in addition to a wide range of secret chords.

**Steven Burns** studied philosophy at Acadia University in Nova Scotia, before doing graduate studies at the Universities of Alberta,

Western Australia, and London (PhD, 1970). He is now retired after teaching for forty-four years at Dalhousie University and the University of King's College in Halifax. His Cohen chapter began as a one of a series of lectures on Philosophical Themes in Canadian Literature, which he gave at the University of Vienna in 2006. Ludwig Wittgenstein has been one of his main research interests, and in 2001 he published a translation of *On Last Things,* a book by the 23-year-old Otto Weininger which Wittgenstein much admired. He first encountered Leonard Cohen's poetry while studying in Edmonton, and sometimes believes that the sisters of mercy shared a room downstairs in the house he lived in.

**Liam P. Dempsey** teaches philosophy at Kwantlen Polytechnic University in Greater Vancouver. He received his PhD in philosophy from Western University in 2003. His research and teaching interests include philosophy of mind, emotion theory, and early modern philosophy. He has recent publications in *Southern Journal of Philosophy*, *Philosophy and Phenomenological Research*, and *Journal of Consciousness Studies*. Like a bird on a wire, he strives always to balance philosophical analysis with cutting-edge empirical research.

**Paweł Dobrosielski** was born in 1984, and is a philosopher and culture analyst who works at the University of Warsaw, Poland. His main academic interests concern social memory and public discourse. He is constantly beating the odds and cherishing his little winning streak as long as it lasts.

**Rachel Haliburton** is Associate Professor of Philosophy at the University of Sudbury–Laurentian University. She firmly believes that popular culture is a source of fascinating philosophical insights, and that she is doing research when she listens to music, watches *Doctor Who*, and reads murder mysteries. She would like to teach at least one class wearing the famous blue raincoat, as she thinks that it would spruce up her dowdy professorial wardrobe.

**Liane Heller** is an editor at the *Halifax Chronicle Herald*, where she also writes a bi-monthly column, "On the Bus." A former feature writer at the *Toronto Star*, she won the Media Club of Canada award for her coverage of the Vietnamese invasion of Cambodia in 1978 and has received several other awards for news reporting.

Heller is the author of six books, including four poetry collections, most recently *Code of Silence* (2009). She has also contributed poetry, essays, and reviews to magazines and periodicals. Despite her very public profession, Heller favors the solitude of her secret life.

**Jason Holt** is Associate Professor at Acadia University, where he teaches courses in philosophy and communication for the School of Kinesiology. His research focuses on aesthetics, philosophy of mind, as well as popular culture and philosophy. His books include *Blindsight and the Nature of Consciousness*, which was shortlisted for the 2005 CPA book prize, various edited volumes, and literary books, most recently a book of poetry, *Inversed*. He doesn't mind being small between the stars but large against the sky.

**Timothy P. Jackson** is Professor of Christian Ethics at The Candler School of Theology at Emory University in Atlanta, Georgia. He is also a Senior Fellow at The Center for the Study of Law and Religion at Emory. Professor Jackson has previously held teaching posts at Rhodes College, Yale University, Stanford University, and the University of Notre Dame. He has been a Visiting Fellow at The Center of Theological Inquiry, The Whitney Humanities Center at Yale, The Center for the Study of Religion at Princeton, and The Program for Evolutionary Dynamics at Harvard. A native of Louisville, Kentucky, Jackson received his BA in Philosophy from Princeton and his PhD in Philosophy and Religious Studies from Yale. He is the author of *Love Disconsoled: Meditations on Christian Charity* (Cambridge, 1999) and *The Priority of Love: Christian Charity and Social Justice* (Princeton, 2003). His current book project is entitled *Political Agape*, and he hopes it will help democracy come to the USA.

**Christopher Ketcham** is a recovering academic living above a network of tapped out garnet mines now turned mushroom farms in eastern Pennsylvania. In the cool damp of the dark space of the mines *Dear Heather* isn't auditory cheesecake; it is the spore of the fungi, full of promised nourishment, but which has not yet seen the light.

**Christopher Lauer** is Assistant Professor of Philosophy at the University of Hawaii-Hilo. He specializes in German idealism and the ethics of recognition and is the author of *The Suspension* *of Reason in Hegel and Schelling* (Continuum, 2010) and *Intimacy: A Dialectical Study* (Bloomsbury, 2015). A father of a three-year-old and a one-year-old, he increasingly finds that he aches in the places he used to play, but thus far he has resisted the urge to hit the open road—though, just in case, he's got this rig that runs on memories.

**AGUST MAGNUSSON** originally hails from the gallery of frost that is Reykjavik, Iceland. He can currently be found bringing enlightenment to the huddled masses of Milwaukee, Wisconsin where he works as an underpaid philosophy professor. Mr. Magnusson is currently working on a dissertation on Kierkegaard and finds himself constantly thwarted in his efforts to immerse himself in existential despair by the cheerfulness that keeps breaking through in his life. He is a longtime devotee of the works of Leonard Cohen and an avid collector of orange crates. Mr. Magnusson, a onetime political candidate for the office of mayor of Boogie Street, can usually be found doing the dishes or playing Thomas the Tank Engine with his son Joakim.

**MARCIN NAPIÓRKOWSKI** is Assistant Professor in the Faculty of Polish Studies, University of Warsaw, and from 2013 to 2014 was a visiting researcher at the University of Virginia. He is author of two books on contemporary culture and collective imagination: *Mitologia współczesna* (*The Contemporary Mythology*) (2013) and *Władza wyobraźni* (*The Power of Imagination*) (2014), and over thirty research papers published in various academic journals. He is also an occasional columnist and commentator for Polish newspapers and magazines. As a philosopher he has spent a long time reading Heidegger and watching from his lonely wooden tower, but because of vertigo he switched to popular culture and now writes mainly about urban legends, conspiracy theories, and celebrated songwriters.

**SIMON RICHES** is a researcher and trainee clinical psychologist at the Institute of Psychiatry, King's College London. He previously taught philosophy at University College London and Heythrop College, University of London. He holds a PhD in philosophy from University College London and has also studied philosophy at the University of Southampton and psychology at the University of East London. His research interests lie in epistemology and the intersection between philosophy and psychology. He is editor of *The*

*Philosophy of David Cronenberg*, and contributor to *The Philosophy of David Lynch*, *Dune and Philosophy*, *Dexter: Investigating Cutting Edge Television*, *101 War Movies You Must See Before You Die*, and *101 Gangster Movies You Must See Before You Die*, as well as other volumes on popular culture. He has tried, in his way, to be free.

**WIELAND SCHWANEBECK** earned his PhD in 2013 from Dresden University of Technology with a study of the impostor motif in American literature and film. He gave up a career in music, for though he's been practicing his burning violin for ages, his Mozart continues to sound like bubble-gum. As long as they keep ejecting him from the Tower of Song, he will focus his energies on teaching and researching topics in Gender and Masculinity Studies, Adaptation Studies, and British film history, stopping occasionally to ask himself why he doesn't look good in a hat.

**GARY SHAPIRO** is a philosopher who has been lecturing both in the US and in Stockholm, Ireland, Athens, and Turkey since his recent retirement as Tucker-Boatwright Professor in the Humanities and Philosophy at the University of Richmond. His books include: *Nietzschean Narratives; Alcyone: Nietzsche on Gifts, Noise, and Women; Earthwards: Robert Smithson and Art After Babel*; and *Archeaologies of Vision: Foucault and Nietzsche on Seeing and Saying*. Shapiro is currently completing a book on *Nietzsche's Metapolitics of the Earth*, after which he will turn to thinking about the meaning of land and earthwork art as ways of making sense of the relations of humans with the earth. In the spirit of Cohen's naming the place of thinking and philosophy as the space between the nameless and the named, he plays with questionable and questioning expressions like "geoaesthetics of the anthropocene" and "post-periodization."

**BRENDAN SHEA**, PhD, teaches philosophy at Rochester Community and Technical College. He has published articles on the history and philosophy of science, ethics, and the philosophy of popular culture. Somewhat embarrassingly, he first learned who Leonard Cohen was when watching the 1990 Christian Slater film, *Pump Up the Volume.*

**PETER STONE** is Ussher Assistant Professor of Political Science at Trinity College Dublin. He received his PhD from the University of Rochester in 2000. He has previously taught at Stanford University and held a Faculty Fellowship at Tulane University's Center for Ethics and Public Affairs. Much of his research concerns the contributions that random selection can make to democracy and justice. He is the author of *The Luck of the Draw: The Role of Lotteries in Decision Making* (Oxford University Press, 2011) and the editor of *Lotteries in Public Life: A Reader* (Imprint Academic, 2011). He has also published articles in such journals as the *Journal of Political Philosophy*, the *Journal of Theoretical Politics*, *Political Theory*, *Rationality and Society*, and *Social Theory and Practice*. Last time he checked, his friends were not gone, and his hair wasn't grey.

**Lisa Warenski**, PhD, is a philosopher who works primarily in epistemology, metaphysics, and the general philosophy of science. She teaches at City College and The Graduate Center of the City University of New York. Lisa is a former dancer and choreographer. Lisa first heard the song "Suzanne" one night at the age of thirteen when she was drifting off to sleep. She didn't hear it again, but never forgot it, until some years later after the performance of a duet that she choreographed. One of her dancers then played *Songs of Leonard Cohen* for her for the first time, and she has been gripped by "Suzanne" ever since. She knows that she's half crazy. (But that's why you want to be there.)

**Bernard Wills** is Professor of Humanities at Grenfell Campus Memorial University in Corner Brook, Newfoundland. He has a doctorate in Religious Studies from McMaster University and a Master's in Classics from Dalhousie University. He hails from Cape Breton Island, Canada though he has spent well over a decade in Newfoundland. He is of such an age as to recall enjoying Leonard Cohen on his mother's eight-track cassette player. In spite of this he continues to root among the garbage and the flowers of contemporary culture turning up scholarly papers, essays, and poems as he goes.

**Edward Winters** studied painting at The Slade School of Fine Art before reading philosophy, taking his doctorate in philosophy at University College London. He has published widely in aesthetics and art criticism. He was co-director of History and Theory in the School of Architecture at University of Westminster and was head of fine art graduate programs at West Dean College. He has also taught history and philosophy of art at University of Kent. His latest book, *Aesthetics and Architecture*, is published by Continuum. As a result of a residency in southern Spain, he is currently working on a philosophical travelogue in conjunction with a series of fine art prints, entitled, *Málaga Suite*. He regrets having played the favorite game so carelessly, but is grateful for a life in bars, where he fought against the bottle in the graceful company of beautiful losers.

# Index